Japanese food and cooking

Japanese
food and cooking

A timeless cuisine: its traditions, techniques,
ingredients and recipes

Emi Kazuko
with recipes by Yasuko Fukuoka

LORENZ BOOKS

This edition is published by Lorenz Books

Lorenz Books is an imprint of Anness Publishing Ltd
Hermes House, 88–89 Blackfriars Road, London SE1 8HA
tel. 020 7401 2077; fax 020 7633 9499
www.lorenzbooks.com; info@anness.com

© Anness Publishing Ltd 2001, 2002, 2003 2004

UK agent: The Manning Partnership Ltd;
tel. 01225 478444; fax 01225 478440; sales@manning-partnership.co.uk
UK distributor: Grantham Book Services Ltd;
tel. 01476 541080; fax 01476 541061; orders@gbs.tbs-ltd.co.uk
North American agent/distributor: National Book Network;
tel. 301 459 3366; fax 301 429 5746; www.nbnbooks.com
Australian agent/distributor: Pan Macmillan Australia;
tel. 1300 135 113; fax 1300 135 103; customer.service@macmillan.com.au
New Zealand agent/distributor: David Bateman Ltd; tel. (09) 415 7664; fax (09) 415 8892

A CIP catalogue record for this book is available from the British Library.

Publisher: Joanna Lorenz
Managing Editor: Linda Fraser
Senior Editor: Margaret Malone
Copy Editors: Susan Fleming, Jan Cutler and Gwen Rigby
Editorial readers: Hayley Kerr, Diane Ashmore
Indexer: Hilary Bird
Designer: Nigel Partridge
Photographers: Craig Robertson (recipe section) and Janine Hosegood
Stylist: Helen Trent
Food for Photography: Julie Beresford, assisted by Atsuko Console (recipe section); and Annabel
Ford (reference section)

1 3 5 7 9 10 8 6 4 2

NOTES

Bracketed terms are for American readers. For all recipes, quantities are given in both metric and
imperial measures and, where appropriate, measures are also given in standard cups and spoons.
Follow one set, but not a mixture because they are not interchangeable. Standard spoon and cup
measures are level.
1 tsp = 5ml, 1 tbsp = 15ml, 1 cup = 250ml/8fl oz
Australian standard tablespoons are 20ml. Australian readers should use 3 tsp in place of 1 tbsp
for measuring small quantities of gelatine, flour, salt etc.
Medium (US large) eggs are used unless otherwise stated.
To avoid repetition, the instructions for cooking rice and the method for making
su-meshi are provided in full only the first time they appear in the recipe section; on pages 136
and 128, respectively. For all later uses, refer to these pages or refer to the section on rice and
rice products on pages 44–45 in the reference section, which also provides full instructions. The
glossary at the back of the book provides a quick guide to unusual and new Japanese ingredients.

CONTENTS

INTRODUCTION

To many people, Japan is an exciting and exotic country, mixing tradition and modernity to striking effect. Its food culture is certainly no exception, and in many ways reflects Japanese culture. For example, the minimalism that exists in Japanese aesthetics, such as poetry and music, art and architecture, is also evident in the culinary culture, whether it be in the taste, flavour, presentation or in the cooking itself. Similarly, the meticulous attention to detail that the Japanese display in many areas, from painting to microchip production, is equally evident in their approach to food and drink.

FRESHNESS AND SIMPLICITY

Perhaps one of the defining features of the Japanese cuisine is the relationship that exists between how food is used and nature. Where possible, food is eaten in as natural a state as possible, as this is considered the best, if not the only, way to experience the true taste of food. This is at the heart of the Japanese philosophy of eating. So the fish and shellfish caught in the seas of Japan are often eaten raw, or only very lightly cured with vinegar or salt.

Above: The simplicity and minimalism that underlie Japanese architecture and art are also reflected in their approach to food and drink.

Likewise, fresh, seasonal agricultural products are only lightly cooked to preserve their bite and flavour, or they may be slightly salted. How and what people cook is also highly influenced by the season and by local produce. As a result, Japan is home to many delicious regional dishes.

To further maintain the purity of food, Japanese cooking rarely mixes different food types, and sauces are normally served in separate dishes as dipping condiments. This is in contrast to the practices of many other cuisines which use long, slow cooking techniques, often with the addition of sauces and spices, so that the food becomes something very different from the raw ingredients.

The Japanese aesthetic regarding food and drink may be described in artistic terms, and Japanese cooking can be compared to the famous *ukiyo-e* woodblock prints. The striking beauty of *ukiyo-e* lies in its economy of line and simplicity, and it is this same elegant

minimalism that is found in all good Japanese cooking. The unique approach of Japanese chefs to their food inspired French chefs in the 1970s to develop nouvelle cuisine, where food was artistically arranged on the plate. However, nouvelle cuisine became notorious for its overemphasis on presentation rather than the size of the serving, forgetting that Japanese meals consist of several, not just a few, small dishes.

CULTURAL INFLUENCES

It is interesting to observe how Japan's food culture has developed differently to those of its neighbours, particularly China's. For instance, while many of the same herbs, spices and sauces are used in both Chinese and Japanese cooking, the Japanese results are quite different. Buddhism is also present in both countries, but in Japan it has led to the development of the tea ceremony and *cha-kaiseki*, the formal meal served with it. These two elements are unique to the Japanese cuisine.

Below: This ukiyo-e woodblock print is of Irises at Horikiri, part of "100 Views of Edo", by Hiroshige (1797–1858), a garden still popular with visitors today. The elegance for which these prints are renowned is also a key element of good Japanese cooking.

USING THIS BOOK

As dishes are often served raw or only lightly cooked, careful selection and preparation of fresh ingredients is one of the most important aspects of Japanese cooking, and is also where a real part of the pleasure resides. The following pages introduce key ingredients and equipment and explains all the essential techniques and practices. No special knowledge is needed, and, apart from a few absolute essentials, such as a pair of chopsticks, most kitchens will easily be able to accommodate Japanese recipes with minimal fuss.

The recipes offer the best of local and national Japanese cuisine, from simple sushi appetizers to hotpots for all to share. As they say in Japan, just heed what nature is offering and enjoy.

Below: Japan stretches through 16 degrees of latitude, starting in the north alongside Russia to the warmth of the Pacific in the south, and local produce varies accordingly. Japan's extensive mountain ranges further add to the variety of produce found in any one area. The surrounding seas are also among the most fertile of the world, where cold and warm currents merge.

THE DEVELOPMENT OF JAPANESE CUISINE

The first traces of food to be found in Japan were in the remains of prehistoric settlements scattered across southern Japan. An amazing variety of nutritious foods was discovered ranging from wild animals, such as boars and deer, and all sorts of fish and shellfish to plants, nuts and berries. The various cooking techniques, cutting, crushing, grinding, grilling and boiling, were well advanced and the excavated remains from before 200BC suggest that the Japanese had a varied and balanced diet ideal for their needs. This early culinary sophistication in ancient Japan reveals one of the defining features of Japanese cuisine: an ability to use and develop nature's bounty for the community.

Below: This colour woodblock print by Hiroshige (1797–1858) shows the communal nature of rice cultivation.

Above: A 19th-century portrait of Izumi Tadahira (d.1189) with a poem, from "Famous Generals of Japan". By the 12th century, feudal warlords had taken over the running of regions, greatly improving rice cultivation.

RICE: A STAPLE FOOD FOR ALL

In Japan, rice is so important that the word for cooked rice, *gohan* or *meshi*, also means meal. It not only plays a major part in Japanese cooking, but, since its introduction in the 2nd century BC., rice and its cultivation have been the very foundation of the nation itself.

Rice was probably introduced to Japan from South-east Asia, and the earliest evidence of crop production was found in village settlements dating from around the 2nd century BC to the 2nd century AD. Rice cultivation revolutionized life in the western region of Japan, and from there soon spread further east. The first nation, Yamato, was formed in the west in the 4th century; the first known historical record book mentions "brewed sake" (an alcoholic drink made from fermented rice) being presented to the *Tenno* (emperor) and a definition of "refining rice".

From the 8th to the 12th centuries, when aristocratic culture blossomed, rice became firmly established as a staple food, cooked in various ways for

Above: Coloured woodblock illustration by Hiroshige (1797–1858), showing workers transporting rice.

the upper classes, although the majority of the population was dependent on other lesser-quality grains such as millet. It was the popularity of rice that led to the development of other basic accompaniments, such as seasonings and sauces, and of various cooking techniques. The aristocratic class also contributed to the establishment of eating etiquette, which subsequently influenced *cha-kaiseki*, the meal served at the tea ceremony, and later Japanese cuisine as a whole.

At the royal court, an increasing number of annual ceremonies and rituals were performed, including Shinto ceremonies (the indigenous religion), and these would be accompanied by food and sake. Sake was, and still is,

regarded as a sacred liquid, cleansing evil spirits. Eating and drinking became an important part of the procedures and cooking itself became a ritual: traces of this can still be seen today in the way top Japanese chefs handle and care for their knives.

By the end of the 12th century the aristocratic society had been replaced by feudal warlords. Techniques of rice production rapidly improved under the feudal system and rice became fully available to the general public on a daily basis during the 13th century.

COMMUNITIES FOUNDED ON RICE

Rice production is a communal process and villages became large "rice production lines", cultivating the same land, generation after generation, for hundreds of years. The nation was founded on the basis of this village society and even in modern, highly

industrialized Japan, this social cohesion is still evident today. Rice production is very labour-intensive and time-consuming work, and contributed to the Japanese work ethic of industriousness and endurance. Rice also yields more per unit of land than any other crop, which enabled Japan to be among the most densely populated countries for many centuries.

Basic methods of cooking rice, such as boiling, steaming, grilling (broiling) and roasting, as well as early steaming utensils, have long been in evidence in Japan, dating as far back as 200BC. Furthermore, because rice stores well, it was possible for the people to use it for their basic daily food source rather than depend on other, less predictable, crops, animal meats or catches of fish and shellfish. Rice became the staple food and Japanese cuisine developed around it.

THE IMPORTANCE OF SALT

With the development of rice cultivation, salt started to appear and play a great part in the culinary scene. It was extracted from the sea and replaced the former source of salt: animals' intestines. However, due to scarcity and its poor storage qualities, salt was mixed with animal or plant fibres and proteins. The mixture, called hishio, was in effect a nutritious, fermented food as well as a seasoning, and transpired to be one of the most important developments in Japanese culinary history.

The three basic kinds were grain hishio (salt-fermented rice, barley or beans), meat hishio (seafood or animal meat) and grass hishio (plant, berries or seaweed). Hishio later developed into some of the most well-known and important Japanese foods, such as miso and shoyu (grain hishio), shiokara and sushi (meat hishio), and tsukemono pickles (grass hishio).

The idea of fermentation was further developed to produce alcohol using barley, yam and glutinous rice. Although at first this was an alcoholic food, rather than a liquid, it was the origin of Japan's most celebrated drink, sake.

A SACRED LIQUID

During the aristocratic period (the 8th–12th centuries) sake grew in popularity with the upper classes as an important element in ceremonies, rituals and drinks parties and was considered a sacred liquid. There were two kinds: white sake, which was an opaque liquid, and black, which had the added flavour of burnt leaves. The black sake was for presentation to the shrine.

With the influx of Koreans into Japan in the 16th century, new techniques arrived to develop sake further, now using ordinary rice, and over the next few centuries sake improved into the fine, clear drink of today.

SAKE ETIQUETTE

Emerging from the customs of feudal society, Japanese drinking etiquette was established during the 15th–17th centuries. Principal guests initiated the party by drinking three cups of sake each. (This ritual is still seen today at Shinto weddings where the bride and groom drink from three cups in turn, taking three sips from each.) After this initiation ritual, guests moved to a party room and a banquet commenced. Sake played the primary role in the Japanese banquet and indeed dishes of food were mere accompaniments to the appreciation of the drink, the opposite to the development of wine in the West.

Below: Sake is still considered a sacred liquid. The first sake barrels of the year are traditionally dedicated to the parish shrines such as this Tenmangu in Kyoto where the sake barrels are displayed at the entrance to the shrine.

FOREIGN INFLUENCES

From the earliest times, neighbouring China and Korea have exerted great influence over Japan. From AD630 to AD894 more than ten trade missions as well as 500–600 students were sent to the T'ang dynasty of China bringing back cultural influences with them. For example, *Kana*, the Japanese phonetic alphabet, was developed from Chinese characters and the popularity of all things *Chinoiserie* among the upper classes involved all aspects of life, including art, architecture and food. In AD647, a Chinese monk presented milk – sheep's as well as cow's – to the *Tenno* (emperor) and was rewarded with the milking job in the royal household. However, milk never became established as a daily part of the Japanese diet and disappeared completely, as in China, around the 13th century following the arrival of Zen Buddhism.

Right and below: Both Japan's native religion, Shintoism, and Buddhism, introduced from China, have had a large impact on Japanese's culinary culture. Shijyoryu Hochoshiki, *the symbolic cutting of the tofu, is held at Nagano Shinto shrine, right, and the ceremonial dedication to god of the first vegetables from the year's crop is held at a Buddhist temple, below. Some Buddhist temples have restaurants on the premises, serving vegetarian food.*

THE IMPACT OF BUDDHISM

Japanese cooking is largely fish- and vegetable-based and if meat is included it is used very sparingly and often cooked with vegetables. This can be traced back to as early as the 6th century when Buddhism first arrived via China, proclaiming animal slaughter and meat eating to be a sinful act. An Imperial ordinance issued in AD675 banned the eating of beef, horse, dog and chicken. However, the ban seems not to have been fully effective since another official ban had to be issued in AD752 to commemorate the opening of the eyes of the Great Buddha at Todaiji Temple in Nara. As part of that decree, it was forbidden to kill any creature for the whole year, and records show that fishermen were compensated for their loss of earnings with rice. Even with the bans it was not until the period of the 9th–12th centuries that this non-killing philosophy fully spread from Buddhist monks to the upper classes and then to the wider public. Through all, the samurai class continued to enjoy shooting and eating wild boar, deer and birds, in keeping with their lifestyle.

Zen Buddhism and food rituals

At the end of the 12th century, Zen Buddhism, a strict sect of Buddhism, arrived from China and, with it, *shojin ryori*. This was originally simple vegan cooking performed by the monks as

part of their severe training. It usually consisted of a bowl of rice, soup and one or two other dishes, but it now refers to a formal vegetarian meal. Many Japanese dishes may appear to be vegetarian but, in fact, vegetables are often cooked in dashi soup: a fish stock. Authentic *shojin ryori* should be purely vegan cooking.

Accompanying the Zen philosophical movement, Chinese foods and cooking techniques (particularly frying) were introduced to Japan. One important arrival was tea, which, although it had been brought back by earlier missions to China, did not become established as a drink among Buddhists and the upper classes

until a Zen Buddhist brought back seeds at the end of the 12th century. This led eventually to the development of *cha-kaiseki* (the formal meal served before the tea ceremony), which established the form of Japanese cuisine.

INFLUENCES THROUGH TRADE

Other foreigners, including the Spanish, Portuguese, Dutch and English also greatly influenced Japan as trading with them progressed from the mid 16th century to the closure of the country in the early 17th century. These early foreigners, especially the Portuguese and Spanish, were disparagingly called *Nanban* (southern barbarians), because they arrived in Japan from the south through South-east Asia, and, to Japanese eyes, lacked sensitivity and bodily cleanliness.

The influence their food and cooking methods had upon the Japanese is still evident today. Any dish or sauce with the name *Nanban* derives from this period; *nanban-zuke* (fried fish or vegetables marinated in a piquant, vinegary sauce) is one such dish. (The name was also used for many other things such as paintings and furniture design.)

With trade, many new vegetables and fruits also arrived: watermelons, sugar cane, chillies, figs, potatoes and the kabocha squash, which derives its name from its parent country, Cambodia. The Portuguese also brought the tomato to Japan although initially only as a decorative plant.

The most famous foreign import of this period, tempura, was introduced by the Portuguese Jesuits and is now one of the most popular Japanese dishes among Westerners as well as the Japanese themselves. There are several theories as to the root of the word tempura, but one possible explanation is that it derives from the Latin word *tempora*, meaning the Ember Days,

Left: Black lacquer Japanese lunch box with Nanban *figures, from the 17th century. The Japanese called early Europeans, the Spanish and Portuguese in particular,* Nanban, *meaning southern barbarians.*

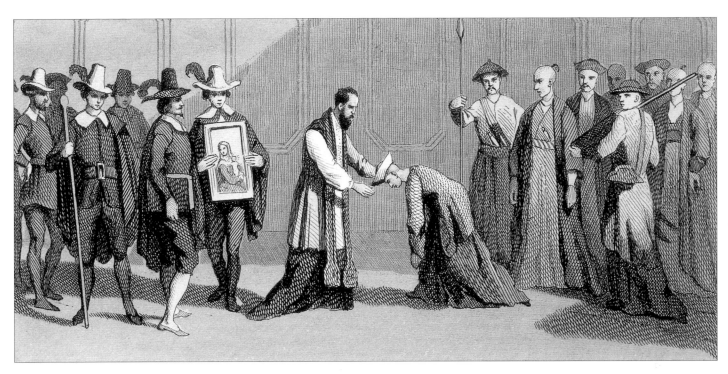

Above: Black and white illustration of the Jesuit Francisco Xavier meeting with Japanese representatives, c. 1551. The Franciscan Xavier first introduced Christianity to Japan in 1549. The Jesuits also engaged in trade with the Japanese, an activity that aroused controversy in Europe and in Japan.

or *Quattuor Tempora*, relating to when Roman Catholics were forbidden to eat meat and ate fish instead. Another theory suggests that it is derived from the Portuguese word *tempero*, meaning seasoning, but no one really knows. One thing is certain however: the first Tokugawa shogun, *Ieyasu*, liked sea-bream tempura so much that he died from overeating it.

Meat-eating was reintroduced by the *Nanban* and became popular among Catholic feudal lords. (There is still a large Catholic community in Nagasaki on the southern island of Kyushu.)

Sweets (candy) and cakes also joined the league of foreign imports and many still bear the names of their foreign

Right: Japanese pottery is renowned for its fine craftsmanship, such as is evident here in this 19th-century Satsuma porcelain vase.

origin: *konpeito* and *aruheito*, both little spiky sugar balls, derive from the Portuguese words *confeitos* and *alfeloa*; *karumera*, a fluffy sugar cake, from *calamela*; and *kasutera*, wet sponge cake, a speciality of Nagasaki, from *castella*. Drinks such as shochu and red wine also arrived at this time and were regarded as *Nanban* drinks.

CHINAWARE

Another significant influence foreigners had on Japanese culinary history is the substantial development of chinawares produced by the Korean potters brought back to Japan after Japan's assault on Korea in 1592. The Korean potters were extremely ahead of their time in pottery technology and helped to found the basis of Japan's pottery industry. It was the Koreans who first succeeded in making the Japanese porcelain at Arita, now a world-famous name for pottery.

China instead of metal soon became fashionable for serving food and Japan subsequently became one of the greatest china-manufacturing countries in the world, producing such exquisite and diverse chinas as Bizen, Hagi, Imari, Karatsu, Kutani, Mashiko, Mino and Seto, to name but a few. Glassware also made its way to Japan at around the same time.

The variety of good quality chinaware complemented the food that was served on it. This attention to presentation helped to further refine the Japanese food culture and is still an essential part of Japanese cuisine today. Present day Japanese tableware is a very colourful affair, and designs from other countries, such as Wedgwood, are starting to appear.

THE IMPACT OF ISOLATION

The closure of the country to outside contact for 260 years from the early 17th century gave *washoku* (Japanese food) an opportunity to establish its own unique identity. Tokyo became the capital due to the presence of the shogun, but Kyoto remained the cultural centre, where aristocratic and temple *kaiseki* cooking further developed with the introduction of new seasonings such as shoyu (soy sauce) and sugar.

All regions, which were ruled by lords, started to industrialize, and became fiercely competitive, producing and trading their own local specialities. Tokyo, as well as Osaka, near Kyoto, became a centre where all foods and different cooking techniques converged. The regional lords were required to visit Tokyo in turn, bringing their local produce with them. This constant arrival of new ingredients and various cooking methods from all regions contributed to the rich character of Japanese cuisine we see today.

The establishment of restaurants also had an important impact on *washoku*. The first known restaurant in Tokyo opened in the late 17th century, and many more rapidly followed. The restaurants each specialized more or less in a single dish or ingredient such as sushi, soba, *kabayaki* (grilled eel) or tempura, and this unique feature of the Japanese restaurant scene is still strong to the present day.

Below: Typical street scene in Japan just before the opening of the country to the outside world, c. 1850.

Above: Traditional ways meet modern technology in this illustration of early Japanese train travellers.

RE-OPENING JAPAN

After the country was opened up in the mid 19th century, meat eating was reintroduced. The emperor Meiji Tenno himself ate beef in 1872 and this opened the floodgates to the public's conception that meat-eating was something new and fashionable. Beef-based dishes, such as *sukiyaki* and *shabu shabu*, are inventions of this period. French and English breads also flooded in but they were regarded as snacks and cakes.

Integrating newly arrived European cooking methods and ingredients into Japanese cooking, many eclectic dishes, called *yōshoku* (Western food) as opposed to *washoku*, were created. *Tonkatsu*, pork cutlet, is the most noteworthy, and numerous *tonkatsu* restaurants opened up all over Japan.

Thus, while the closure of the country may have delayed Japan's modernization for 200 years, it is this period of isolation from the outside world that allowed Japanese cuisine to become established. As a result, instead of being overwhelmed by the introduction of these foreign culinary influences, Japanese food and cooking techniques influenced Western cuisine, and vice versa, in a positive way.

SUSHI: A NATIONAL FAVOURITE

The most famous sushi, called *nigiri*, are hand-moulded fingers of vinegared rice with slices of raw fish on top. They are only one form of many types of sushi and are a relatively new invention from Tokyo. No one really knows when the word was first used; strictly, the word sushi means to vinegar (originally the rice was thrown away), but as the vinegared rice became the essential ingredient, sushi developed into a term signifying vinegared rice dishes.

LONG-PRESSED SUSHI

The oldest sushi still found in Japan is the *funa-zushi* of Shiga. This type is a *nare-zushi*, or long-pressed sushi, made using freshwater fish such as funa, a type of carp, dojo (loach) or namazu (sheatfish). The fish is first salt-cured and then marinated in cooked rice and salt. This is a way to preserve fish; the rice and salt are discarded. The origin of this oldest-surviving sushi can be traced back to hishio, a mixture of raw fish and salt, although some say it goes right back to various other similar fish-preserving methods that existed in China as early as 300BC. Although at one stage the Chinese also developed this method of using rice mixed with salt, the technique had disappeared completely from the Chinese culinary scene by the 17th century.

Above: Chefs working behind the counter in a local sushi restaurant in Miyako, northern Japan.

Below: The outside of a small sushi restaurant in Beppu, Kyushu, Japan. Delivery boys on motorcycles transport freshly made sushi to homes.

MODERN-DAY SUSHI

The process the *nare-zushi* then took to develop into the present-day sushi is well recorded. First it was simplified; the *nare-zushi*'s long-term pressing, for almost a year, was greatly shortened to about ten days so that the rice could also be eaten before it fully fermented. To hasten the fermentation process and prevent the raw fish from rotting, vinegar was added to the rice. The result is a simple *oshi-zushi*, meaning pressed sushi, a speciality of Kansai, the region around Osaka. But it was in Tokyo in the 19th century that the process was sped up even more, with the development of *nigiri*, instant sushi.

Sold from street stalls and stores as a snack, *nigiri*, also known as *edomae*, was the fast food of its time. It was and still is the most famous sushi of all.

Today, sushi restaurants abound and sushi chefs are regarded as highly skilled craftsmen who train for a number of years at their craft. Indeed, top sushi restaurants are becoming very expensive places to eat. So, even though sushi remains a snack food, it is undoubtedly a high-quality one.

THE TEA CEREMONY

If it was the English who transformed tea drinking into a lifestyle, it was the Japanese who perfected it as an art form. The tea ceremony is the generally accepted translation for *chadō* or *sadō*, literally meaning "way of tea". Also known as *chanoyu,* the ceremonial aspects are just one part of what is a deeply philosophical and profound occasion. It is not exaggerating to say that the tea ceremony is the essence of Japanese culture itself, embracing all divisions of visual art such as scrolled

Right: A 19th-century woodcut showing tea being served at the shogun's palace.

Below: A roadside tea shop on Tokaido, an ancient street running from Tokyo to Osaka. Woodblock print, 1833.

Right: The tea ceremony embodies, for both preparer and receiver, simplicity, mutual respect, harmony and stillness. Tea pavilions and houses surrounded by gardens of natural beauty provide a physical and spiritual haven.

paintings and calligraphy, pottery, flower arranging and even architecture. The tea ceremony expresses the Japanese philosophy for life and etiquette, not just for drinking tea but for entertaining guests and being entertained. It teaches a person where they stand in society and how to behave.

The tea ceremony has now lost much of its connection with Zen Buddhism, but is still very popular among women, particularly young women as part of their bridal training. Learning the way of tea usually takes over ten years, and the learning process can continue throughout a person's life.

EARLY TEA-DRINKING

Tea was first introduced to Japan from China in the 8th century but it was not until the Zen monk, Eisai (1141–1215), brought back tea seeds from China in 1191 that the habit of tea drinking and tea parties began to spread among Buddhists, aristocrats and samurai classes. Early tea drinking consisted of a tea tasting party where the guests bet money on naming the variety of tea they were drinking. This was often followed by a sake drinks party. During the turbulent civil wars of the 15th–16th centuries, the tea party evolved into appreciating tea in tranquillity away from the upheavals of war.

It was another monk, Murata Jukoh (1423–1502), who refined the tea party by placing more emphasis on the Zen philosophy of *wabi* and *sabi* (serenity and simplicity) and establishing *wabi-cha*. He applied to the tea ceremony the famous Zen teaching, *ichigo ichié*, literally meaning "one life, one meeting", whereby participants should conduct the meeting as if it were a once in a lifetime event, never to be repeated, and thus significantly broadening the meaning and understanding of the way of tea.

THE PRACTICE OF CHANOYU

The present day *chanoyu* owes most to Sen-no Rikyu (1522–1591) who put the philosophy of the tea ceremony into practice by laying out every aspect of *chanoyu* in detail. *Chanoyu* became so highly regarded as a social as well as a philosophical activity during his lifetime that he was appointed tea master by two consecutive great shoguns, Nobunaga and Hideyoshi. Sadly, he became too powerful for Hideyoshi to bear and he was eventually forced to commit suicide by the shogun.

Rikyu's teachings of the heart of *chanoyu* can be condensed into four principal characters: *wa* (harmony); *kei* (respect); *sei* (cleanliness); and *jaku* (serenity). In practice, however, he set out seven rules for *chanoyu*: arrange flowers as they appear in nature; burn charcoal only to just simmer the water

in the pot; serve the right amount of tea; make the surroundings cool in summer and warm in winter; prepare for *chanoyu* in good time; be ready for rain, even in fine weather; and respect fellow guests.

Today, three schools of *chanoyu*, *Ura-senké*, *Omote-senké* and *Mushanokoji-senké*, established by Rikyu's three grandsons, follow his teachings. These teachings have spread not only all over Japan but also abroad.

Together with the Zen teaching of *mu* (nothingness), the heart of *chanoyu* was essentially a belief in how one should treat other people in a closely knit society, without thinking of yourself. Sadly, this philosophy seems difficult to apply in the modernized, self-centred era that today at time typifies Japan since its economic expansion and rapid industrialization after World War II.

The rituals of the tea ceremony

Though this cannot describe the sense of the occasion, the following is a brief explanation of the most formal noon *chaji*: first guests enter the room in which the ceremony is to be held via a very small sliding door (often no bigger than the size of an average dog flap), scrolls and flowers are appreciated by the guests before seating, with the main guest at the top, and then descending in order of importance. *Kaiseki* is served on individual trays, and may last up to two hours, followed by the "first charcoal", involving viewing the incense case. Occasionally incense sniffing is also conducted. Then wagashi (Japanese rice cakes) are served, after which everyone retires to the waiting room.

Upon return, again via the small door, the *koicha* (thick tea) ceremony follows. The host prepares, in front of the guests, matcha (powdered tea) using hot water from the pot. The tea is made into a thick batter-like consistency, hence the name. The bowl is passed around, and everyone sips from the one bowl. The second charcoal is then viewed (to admire how well its burning), followed by the *usucha* (light tea). The tea maker again prepares the tea in front of the guests, this time of a thin consistency, with a bowl for each person. Finally, guests appreciate tea bowls, scrolls and flowers before retiring. Throughout, the conversation is conducted between the main guest and the tea maker (host); the other guests should not speak much.

The above programme differs slightly for the winter half of the year when kaiseki is served after the first charcoal.

Different tools, equipment, scrolls, flowers and sweets (candy) are used according to the season and guests wear a kimono of the season as well. The event often lasts for several hours and can be very tiring for young girls who are not used to wearing the kimono and sitting on the floor with legs tightly folded for long periods. However, the ceremony produces a feeling of elation accompanied by an awareness of your whole being and a sense of immersion in an increasingly long-forgotten culture.

CHAJI AND CHA-KAISEKI

At about the same time as the tea ceremony was being developed, a form of *shojin ryori* (the Zen Buddhist monk's vegetarian cooking) was also brought back from China. The meal eaten by monks during training is not only vegetarian but modest. *Cha-kaiseki* was developed in line with *shojin ryori*, and early *cha-kaiseki* consisted of bowls of rice and soup and two or, at most, three dishes only.

The tea ceremony accompanied by *cha-kaiseki* is known as *chaji*. The tea ceremony is the main focus, rather than the meal, so *cha-kaiseki* is served first, in order that it does not compete with the appreciation of the tea. Over time, this meal has developed into *kaiseki ryori* (the formal multi-course meal).

The word *kaiseki* comes from "embraced stone", a warmed stone monks held against their body to help them endure hunger and cold. Present-day *cha-kaiseki* normally consists of rice, soup, an hors d'oeuvre, a grilled dish, a simmered dish, a small serving of clear soup, a main dish, a salted vegetable and hot water. Sake is also served. Depending on the occasion, a fish dish, another simmered dish,

Above: The tea ceremony traditionally played a big part in a young girl's bridal training in Japan and training can continue over a lifetime.

a dressed vegetable and a vinegared vegetable will also be added. The dishes and presentation should all reflect the season in which the *chaji* is held.

Formal tea ceremonies

The seven main *chaji* occasions are:
Noon *chaji* The most formal, starting between 11 am and 12 noon
Morning *chaji* Held only in summer, commencing from 6 am
Evening *chaji* Held only in winter, commencing from dusk
Dawn *chaji* Held in midwinter, commencing from 4 am
See-after *chaji* Held for absentees who could not attend the *chaji*
After-meal *chaji* Tea only held after breakfast, lunch or dinner
Ad-lib *chaji* For unexpected guests

The programme for a *chaji* depends on the occasion and will contain various stages. It is a long, formal and very complicated ritualized affair, which for most Westerners will be something both daunting and intriguing.

TRADITIONS AND FESTIVALS

Japan still maintains many of its old traditions and festivals, from family celebrations on children's days to grand national festivals with processions and people wearing full samurai costumes. These are nearly always accompanied by special celebration food. Today people no longer prepare elaborate food for each festival, as in the past, but nevertheless they still make or buy some special food and drink for each occasion. The following are some of the Japanese annual festivals and the particular foods associated with them.

NEW YEAR'S DAY

January 1st is the most important day in the Japanese calendar and people go to Shinto shrines to pray for happiness and prosperity during the coming year. The celebration food, called *o'sechi ryori*, consists of various cooked foods such as konbu (kelp seaweed), beans, herring eggs and gomame (dried small fish), and is normally served in square, lacquered containers with tiers, called *jubako*. Dishes vary but they were traditionally chosen for their particular significance regarding people's hopes

Below: New Year's Festival, by Kunisada (1786–1864), woodcut. Kite flying is traditional on New Year's day.

for happiness and prosperity. *O'sechi* is eaten for brunch, perhaps after coming back from the shrine, followed by *o'zoni* (glutinous rice cake in chicken soup). The celebration lasts for three or seven days, depending on the region, and during this period people visit their friends, families and colleagues. *O'sechi* and *o'zoni* are served throughout this time.

SEVEN HERBS RICE GRUEL DAY

Each year on 7 January, *nanakusa gayu* (rice gruel with seven herbs) is eaten. It is comprised of seri (Japanese parsley), nazuna (shepherd's purse), gogyo (catweed), hakobera (chickweed), hotokenoza (henbit), suzuna (turnip leaf) and suzushiro (radish leaf). These traditional Japanese herbal medicines are eaten in the hope of ensuring good health throughout the year. Nowadays, however, it is not always easy to find these wild herbs, so other herbs are often substituted.

THE COMING-OF-SPRING DAY

Japan has a very hot, humid summer, and a dry, often very cold winter, with a beautifully warm spring and autumn in-between. Each season lasts almost equally for three months. The coming of spring, celebrated on 4 February, is particularly welcomed with a ritual of

throwing beans on the previous night. This ritual, normally using grilled soya beans, is to scare devils out of the house, and is accompanied by shouts of "devils out, happiness in". Afterwards, everyone eats the same number of beans as their age, and this is said to protect them from any suffering. Holly branches and sardine heads used to be placed at the gate and door of the house to scare away devils, but this is not often practised, particularly in big cities.

THE GIRLS' FESTIVAL

Also known as the Dolls' Festival or the Feast of Peach Blossoms, families with young daughters celebrate their healthy growth on 3 March by displaying an elaborate set of dolls on a red-carpeted tiered altar. The dolls portray the appearance of the aristocracy in the Heian Period (AD794–1185), with the prince and princess on the top tier and their subjects, together with decorations, on the lower tiers (a full set has a total of seven tiers). Tiny rice crackers and small diamond-shape rice cakes in assorted pretty colours are among the decorations displayed, together with a cup of white sake, which is now made from sake pulp diluted with hot water. The families usually have a party for the girls on the day.

Above: An illustration of a regional lantern festival, held at cherry blossom time, c. 1912. Cherry blossom viewing is popular throughout Japan.

THE EQUINOX DAYS

For seven days around the spring equinox (on or around 21 March) and the autumn equinox (on or around 21 September), there are the traditional Buddhist celebrations, when people visit family cemeteries to appease the spirits of their ancestors. The speciality food is *o'hagi*, which is a rice ball covered with sweet azuki bean paste. Azuki is often used for celebrations, possibly because of its joyous red colour, although the reason for eating *o'hagi* on this day is not known.

FLOWER VIEWING AND FLOWER FESTIVAL

The Japanese peoples love of flowers is renowned and many people make every effort to go to those gardens featuring the flowers of the season. In early April, when cherry blossoms are blooming, there is a slot on all television channels for the nationwide "cherry blossom forecast" as well as for the weather. Using cherry blossoms as an excuse, families, friends and colleagues get together and have parties under the full bloom, late into the night. No particular food is eaten but many take *bento* (lunch) boxes, along with sake, beer

and whisky. The flower festival is held at temples on 8 April, the birthday of Shakyamuni Buddha, the founder of Buddhism. Sweet sake is poured over statues of the Buddha and is also drunk.

THE CHILDREN'S DAY

Also known as the Boys' Day, the Japanese celebrate small boys' healthy growth on 5 May just as they do girls on 3 March. Decorations of paper or fabric carp streamers are attached to a tall pole in the garden or rooftop so that they trail in the wind. The sight of these "live" carps bravely meeting the

Below: The carp has long been a symbol of bravery representing families' wishes for young boys to grow up as brave and strong as the carp.

challenge of swimming up a tumbling waterfall symbolizes the families' wish for their boys to grow up to be as brave as the carps. *Kashiwa-mochi* (oak-leaf-wrapped glutinous rice cakes stuffed with sweet azuki bean paste) are eaten on this day.

SUMMER FESTIVALS

The Japanese love festivals and many traditional events are held during the summer, starting with the Festival of the Weaver Star on 7 July. The *Gion* Festival of Kyoto, one of the three greatest festivals of Japan, held during 17–24 July, leads various Shinto festivals all over Japan. Sake is always associated with these festivals as it is the sacred liquid dedicated to the gods and goddesses.

Fireworks are enjoyed in summer and the most famous of all displays is held on the Sumida River in Tokyo towards the end of July. Parties on river banks or on boats are very popular at this time of the year.

O'bon, a Buddhist ritual to welcome ancestral spirits to the home shrines on 16 August, brings Japan to a standstill for the whole week as people working away from home travel back to visit the family cemeteries. The *Daimonji-yaki* Festival of Kyoto on 16 August, where a spectacular fire on the mountain in the shape of the Chinese character *dai*, meaning big, can be seen from far away, is said to be related to the tradition of *o'bon*. Regional summer festivals are held around this time with dancing in *yukata* (summer kimono) and evening fairs featuring an array of stalls selling street foods.

THE HARVEST FULL-MOON VIEWING

On the night of the full moon, around 17 September, a tray with dumplings and another food typical of the autumn harvest, such as potatoes, together with some pampas grasses in a vase, is displayed by the window used by the family to view the moon. The next full moon, a month later, is marked with chestnuts in the same way.

CELEBRATIONS FOR CHILDREN

On 15 November the Japanese celebrate children reaching the ages of three, five and seven, and families with children of that age go to the shrine. Red and white sweets (candy), called *chitose-amé*, symbolize the families' wishes for the children's health and longevity, and are carried and eaten by the children. At home *o'sekihan* (rice cooked with azuki beans) is usually served.

WINTER SOLSTICE

The winter solstice normally occurs on 23 December and there is an ancient custom of taking a hot bath with yuzu juice (a Japanese citrus fruit), which is believed to help the bather stay healthy throughout the cold winter. It is also traditional to eat kabocha squash on

this day, usually cooked in a thin rice porridge. Yuzu and kabocha squash are also offered to the gods, expressing the anticipation of spring.

NEW YEAR'S EVE

People traditionally eat soba noodles on New Year's eve while listening to bells ringing 108 times – representing the elimination of 108 sins – starting from midnight at temples throughout Japan.

Above: Decorated boats at the Sanno festival at Tsushima, Owari Province. Woodblock print, 1853 by Hiroshige.

New Year's eve is a busy day given over to New Year preparations. This was particularly so for merchants in the Edo Period (1603–1867) who had to complete their financial accounts for the year. Soba was an ideal quick meal and it became a nationwide tradition.

SEASONAL AND REGIONAL FOODS

The seasons in Japan last for about three months each, with each new season bringing different produce and a changing catch of fish from the surrounding seas. Geographically, Japan stretches through 16 degrees of latitude, starting in the north alongside Russia to South Korea and the Pacific Ocean at the other extreme, with local produce varying from region to region. Japan is also a country with huge mountain ranges running through the centre from north to south, covering some 75–80 per cent of the land. The produce, as a result, varies not only by season and region but also by altitude.

The clash of warm and cold currents makes the seas around Japan among the world's richest fisheries, with an enormously varied range of fish and shellfish. Japan consumes some three thousand different kinds daily, and that does not include regional varieties.

In Japanese cooking the idea of season persists strongly. There is even a word for seasonal food, *shun*, and this concept is always in the Japanese mind: whenever they cook or eat they look out for something that is in *shun*.

Below: Rows of mezashi *(eye-skewered half-dried sardines), a popular daily snack throughout Japan.*

SEASONAL FOODS AND DISHES

There is no doubt that the wealth of the seas as well as the variety of fresh local produce contributed to the development of a cuisine rich in regional specialities. The following represent a sample of Japan's fish and vegetables, together with dishes typical of the season.

Spring

Vegetables such as peas, broad (fava) beans and mangetouts (snow peas) are crisp and tender in early spring. One speciality of the season is fresh young bamboo shoots cooked with rice. New ginger shoots are used for making vinegared ginger sticks for grilled fish and ginger slices to accompany sushi. It is also clam-picking time on beaches, and along the rivers anglers are blessed with masu trout. Japanese strawberries are also available in early spring.

Summer

Early in May the season's new katsuo (bonito or skipjack tuna) arrives, and *katsuo no tataki* (seared and sliced katsuo *sashimi* with herbs and spices) is cherished at this time of the year. Other fish such as aji (scad or horse mackerel), kajiki (swordfish), suzuki (sea bass) and maguro (big-eye tuna) are all in *shun*, and best eaten as *sashimi* (raw fish thinly sliced).

Above: Fresh produce and dried goods at a local market in Tokyo.

New eda-mame (green beans in the pod) are just lightly boiled and served as an accompaniment to chilled beer during the hot summer. Ume (Japanese green apricots) become available from early June, which is the traditional month for *tsukemono* (pickling) in the cook's calendar. Rakkyo (Japanese bulb vegetable), umeboshi (dried and salted ume) and umeshu (ume liqueur) are all prepared for the coming year, or in the case of umeshu for consumption the following summer.

Autumn

In Japan, autumn never passes without either eating grilled samma (saury) or at least smelling the aroma released as it is grilled by a neighbour. Salmon, mackerel and sea bream are also all in season; salmon is salted while the others are good for *sashimi*.

Aubergine (eggplant) is renowned as being so good that mothers-in-law hide it from their daughters-in-law. The king of mushrooms, matsutake, dominates during this season and is either cooked with rice or steamed in clear soup. Autumn is also a fruit season and in particular the beautiful Japanese persimmon, kaki, arrives in abundance.

Winter

The most famous winter fish of all must be fugu. So notoriously poisonous is this fish (just a hint of its liver can prove fatal), that a special license is required to handle it. *Fugu-chiri* (fugu hotpot) is the dish of the season along with *anko-nabe* (monkfish hotpot).

Shungiku (garland chrysanthemum), which is in *shun* at this time of the year, is a good accompaniment to hotpot dishes. The two popular Japanese vegetables, hakusai and daikon, are at their best in winter and are pickled in bulk for the coming months. Japanese citrus fruits, such as mikan (satsuma) and yuzu, are abundant and yuzu is even used in baths (chopped in half and added to the hot water – though quite a few are needed). Fishing for wakasagi (Japanese smelt) on ice-covered lakes is a favourite pastime among winter anglers.

REGIONAL FOODS AND DISHES

The regional foods and dishes vary greatly from Hokkaido, the northern island, to Kyushu, the southern island, so "what's in season?" and "what's the

Below: The Tokyo fish market deals with the largest volume of fish in the world. The Japanese consume 3,000 kinds of fish and shellfish every day.

speciality here?" are inevitable questions every Japanese foodie asks wherever he or she goes. Local restaurants are the best places to taste regional variations though all local cuisines are represented in Tokyo and Osaka. The regions are so proud and eager to promote their speciality foods that they even produce their own versions of *bento* (packed lunch) using local produce, which are sold on the platforms of their mainline stations. These are called *ekiben* (station *bento*) and some of the famous *ekiben* are introduced below as a quick reference to the regional foods.

Hokkaido

Most of the seafood (crabs, oysters, squid, salmon, trout, herring, cod and konbu) come from here. Hokkaido is also the only place in Japan where sheep are reared, so *ghengis khan-nabe* (lamb barbecue) is a local speciality. Ramen, miso-ramen (ramen noodles in miso soup) in particular, was first developed in Sapporo, the capital of Hokkaido. Regional *bento* includes *kani-meshi* (crab rice) at Oshamanbe station, *ezo-wappa* (assorted Hokkaido specialities with rice) at Asahikawa, and *ika-meshi* (squid rice) at Mori.

Right: A fruit stall in a Tokyo market.

The north of Honshu

From Akita and Niigata through to Toyama facing the Sea of Japan is Japan's treasured rice belt, which consequently produces some of the finest sake. The regional produce also includes various sansai (mountain vegetables) and the maitake mushroom of Akita. A hotpot dish called *shottsuru* using local fish called hata hata (sailfin sandfish) is Akita's winter speciality while *wanko-soba* (buckwheat soba served in mouthfuls) is a Morioka speciality. In Sendai there are fish products such as *sasa kamaboko* (ground fishcake wrapped in bamboo leaves) and nearby Mito is famous for its natto (fermented soya beans) production.

Regional *ekiben* examples include *maitake-wappa* (maitake mushroom on Akita komachi rice) at Akita station, *sansai-kurimeshi* (mountain vegetables and chestnuts with rice) at Morioka, *gyu-meshi* (beef rice) at Niigata and *sake harako-meshi* (salmon caviar on rice) at Sendai.

Tokyo and the central region

Japan's capital and the surrounding areas, known as Kanto, may no longer produce much agricultural produce but it is a culinary centre for regional foods and dishes. It has the finest restaurants,

not only of Japanese cuisine but also of other cooking traditions. Tokyo-style cooking tends to use more seasoning and shoyu than Osaka cuisine. *Nigiri-zushi* (finger sushi with a slice of raw fish on top) is a Tokyo speciality.

Shinshu, the central mountain region, is well known for its soba, wasabi, grapes and wine as well as eels from Lake Suwa, while Shizuoka, the coastal county facing the Pacific Ocean, produces tea and mikan (satsuma). *Kama-meshi* (nine local ingredients on top of tea rice in a pot) at Yokokawa is the most famous of all *ekiben* since it started the *ekiben* phenomenon in Japan some 50 years ago.

Kansai and the west

An area of great importance in culinary matters, Kansai includes both Osaka and Kyoto. The old capital, Kyoto, is considered the birthplace of Japanese cuisine and Osaka is now the culinary heart of Japan. The down-to-earth approach of the Osakans is most evident in their food.

Specialities include udon and *udon-suki* (*shabu shabu*, meaning beef and vegetable hotpot, with udon). In Kyoto there are many *ryotei* (old inn-style restaurants) in the most beautiful, tranquil surroundings, and yuba (dried tofu milk skin) is still produced by hand

Above: Mushrooms grow in abundance across Japan, and are an essential part of everyday cooking.

there. Kansai produces the best *wa-gyu* (beer-massaged Japanese beef), also known as Kobe or Matsuzaka beef, and other beef dishes such as *sukiyaki* (beef and vegetables cooked in sweet shoyu), *shabu shabu* and steak are specialities. In Kansai is a *sukiyaki ekiben* that has a unique device attached to the box to

automatically warm up the Kobe beef inside. Nagoya, the third largest city after Tokyo and Osaka, produces hatcho-miso (black miso), and kishimen (ribbon noodles) is a famous speciality.

The Kii peninsula, south of Osaka, produces tea and mikan. There are a few good somen eating places around there, while *masu-zushi* (trout sushi) at Toyama station and *mehari-sushi* (sushi wrapped in pickled mustard leaf) at Shingu are two of the oldest established *ekiben* in this region.

Shikoku and Kyushu

Fresh fish and shellfish are abundant all the year round in these two southern islands and *Tosa-no tataki*, lightly seared katsuo (skipjack tuna) sashimi, is a famous speciality of Shikoku. Various citrus fruits are also produced on these islands, while Kyushu is the largest shiitake producer in Japan. *Kashiwa-meshi* (chicken rice) at Hakata station, *ko-dai* sushi (small sea bream sushi) at Tokushima, anago-meshi (conger rice) at Takamatsu and *tonkotsu bento* (simmered black pork with rice) at Nishi Kagoshima are some of the best *ekiben*.

Below: A typical bustling, fruit and vegetable market in Ameyokocho Street, in the Ueno district of Tokyo.

COOKING AND EATING

The philosophy of Japanese cooking is to serve food that has retained as much of its natural flavour as possible. It is therefore essential to choose ingredients at their best – they should be very fresh and in their season. If the food needs to be cooked at all this is done for the minimum time possible. The Japanese cook belives that vegetables are best eaten raw or only very lightly cooked, to retain their crunchiness. Otherwise, they may be salted a little to draw out the cold water of the raw ingredient.

PREPARATION AND COOKING METHODS

The most important aspect of Japanese cooking lies in the preparation. As the food is eaten with hashi (chopsticks), it needs to be cut into bitesize pieces. Vegetables of various shapes and textures are cooked to the correct crunchy softness so that they will be appetizing as well as attractive. Fresh fish is almost always filleted and often thinly sliced to eat raw as *sashimi*. Meats are also thinly sliced most of the time or else minced (ground) meat is used.

If the food, especially vegetables, is to be cooked, it is always very lightly done to retain crispness. Cooking

Below: A diner in Tokyo's Ginza district with decorations of red lanterns.

methods include simmering, grilling (broiling), steaming and frying; roasting is not really part of the Japanese cuisine. Many fish and vegetable dishes involve griddling over a direct heat, but in modern houses this is not done due to the smoke produced, in which case pan-frying may be substituted. Japanese cooking also uses various pickling and marinating methods.

Above: A sumo wrestlers' hotpot restaurant in Tokyo, near the Sumo stadium and wrestlers' accommodation.

TYPICAL MEALS

The traditional Japanese breakfast is a substantial meal. It consists of a bowl of hot, freshly boiled rice, miso soup, thick omelette roll, pickled vegetables and grilled (broiled) small salted fish such as horse mackerel. Today, however, busy people, particularly the young, prefer Western-style ready-made foods such as bread, ham and cheese plus salad and fruits with tea or coffee.

For lunch, Japanese soba (buckwheat noodles), udon (flour noodles) and Chinese-style ramen (egg noodles) are very popular at home as well as in restaurants, while single-dish meals include a tonkatsu rice bowl, a *bento* (lunch) box or curry. Half the population of Japan is said to eat out every single day and lunch is the meal most people eat in restaurants rather than taking a lunch box, which are nowadays mostly made by the mother for her children.

Dinner at home in Japan is a rather casual affair, with each member of the family having a bowl of rice and miso soup probably with an individual main dish of either fish or meat. Two or three

other dishes such as simmered vegetables, marinated fish and pickles will be placed in the centre of the table for everyone to help themselves. Second servings of rice and soup are available, and fruit and green tea are always served to finish the meal.

MENU PLANNING

A formal Japanese banquet will start with hors d'oeuvres, clear soup and *sashimi* (thinly sliced raw fish) followed in turn by a grilled dish, a steamed dish, a simmered dish and finally a deep-fried dish, accompanied by vinegared or dressed salads. The meal finishes with boiled rice, miso soup and pickles. All dishes are served individually on a tray. There are not many desserts in Japanese cuisine possibly because sugar is used in much of the savoury cooking. Also the vast amount of food

Left: Families often eat gathered round the kotatsu *(heated table).*

Below: Meal time at ryokan, *a Japanese old style inn. Each diner's food is served on an individual legged tray.*

Etiquette

It is a Japanese custom to hold your cup or glass when someone pours you a drink, and you are expected to return the courtesy.

The same pair of hashi (chopsticks) is used throughout the meal. When not in use, the hashi are left on a hashi rest if there is one. They should be laid close to you, neatly parallel to the edge of the table. Never stick them upright into the rice: the Japanese are rather superstitious and hashi standing vertically in rice reminds them of the incense sticks that stand in ashes at funerals. Never transfer food from one pair of hashi to another; at Japanese funerals, relatives of the deceased pick the human bones from the ashes and transfer them between themselves in this way.

eaten, over a number of courses, leaves little room for more by the end of the meal. Wagashi (Japanese cakes), which are eaten at tea time with green tea, are too sweet and heavy to eat after a meal, so fresh fruit and green tea usually end the lengthy banquet. Warmed sake is drunk throughout the meal until the rice is served.

At home a simpler traditional dinner will be served consisting of individual bowls of soup and boiled rice with at least three main dishes, each one cooked differently: for example, *sashimi*, a grilled dish and a simmered dish. They are placed in the centre of the table for all the family to serve themselves on to individual plates.

For dinner parties at home, a standard menu consists of a plate of hors d'oeuvres to accompany drinks (when a toast may be made) followed by a first course, the main dish and then bowls of rice and soup with some pickles. Sake or ordinary grape wine is not served after the rice has arrived. Fruit and green tea ends the meal.

DRINK

There have been many attempts in the West to find out which wine goes best with Japanese food, and some food and wine experts even claim Champagne best suits the cuisine. However, nothing really matches the mellow, delicate flavour of sake because it does not override the subtle nature of Japanese cuisine. Moreover, while wine may have been developed to complement the food, it was the other way round with sake. It is no exaggeration to claim that Japanese cuisine was developed together with, perhaps even for tasting with, sake.

The Japanese drink lager beer more than any other drink and often start a meal with a glass of ice-cold lager. The lager is usually followed by sake, which is drunk cold in summer and warm in winter, or by shochu (rough sake). A very alcoholic beverage, one of the more popular ways of drinking shochu is to dilute it with hot water and add an umeboshi (dried salted Japanese apricot) to it.

MENU IDEAS

The following are some traditional seasonal menu ideas.

Spring

Oshi-zushi (smoked-salmon pressed sushi
Wakatake-ni (simmered young bamboo shoots in dashi (fish stock)
Beef *teriyaki* with broccoli
Iridori (simmered assorted vegetables with chicken)
Rice cooked with peas and miso soup with clam and spring onions (scallions)
Assorted fresh fruit and green tea

Summer

Boiled eda-mame (green beans in their pods) with salt
Katsuo no tataki (seared and sliced katsuo *sashimi* with herbs and spices)
Yuan chicken with fine green beans
Plain boiled rice and miso soup with wakame (seaweed) and tofu
Fruit salad with kanten cubes and chilled mugicha tea

Autumn

Yakitori (grilled chicken)
Grilled aubergine (eggplant) with miso
Tempura
Plain boiled rice and clear soup with matsutake (or cep) mushrooms and somen noodles
Kaki (persimmon) and green tea

Right: Yakitori *(grilled chicken)*

Left: Saba-zushi *(mackerel pressed sushi)*

Winter

Shungiku goma-aé (edible chrysanthemum leaves with sesame dressing)
Saba no Tatsuta-agé (fried marinated mackerel fillets)
Sukiyaki (wafer-thin beef slices and assorted vegetables)
Plain boiled rice
Yokan (sweet azuki paste cake) and green tea

SUSHI PARTIES

The following are two typical menus for a sushi party, which would be easy and fun to try at home.

Sushi Party 1

Yakitori (grilled chicken)
Salad with Japanese-style dressing
Assorted sushi, such as *saba-zushi* (mackerel-pressed sushi) and three-colour *nori-maki* (nori seaweed sushi)
Fruit and green tea

Sushi Party 2

Tsukune (skewered minced (ground) chicken balls)
Salt-steamed kabocha squash
Temaki-zushi (hand-rolled sushi)
Assorted pickles
Fruit and green tea

EQUIPMENT AND UTENSILS

The most important aspect of Japanese cooking is preparation, cutting in particular, so Japanese kitchens are equipped with a battery of delicate utensils to ensure fresh ingredients will not be spoilt or damaged. Natural materials such as wood, bamboo or earthenware and stoneware are preferred for Japanese cooking to modern stainless steel or plastic versions since they provide a gentle touch on fresh ingredients and absorb extra moisture.

If your kitchen is well equipped with a few basic essential tools, such as a variety of sharp knives and a cutting board, along with a good selection of Western utensils, you really do not need to add anything special to cook Japanese food. Nevertheless, some traditional Japanese utensils, such as the grater, would be useful additions. Many of the utensils shown here are now available at high-quality kitchenware shops, as well as at specialist Japanese shops.

KNIVES

For the Japanese, knives are the cook's heart and soul; professional chefs must have their own and they move with them from job to job. There are well over 20 types of knives used in a professional kitchen, but an ordinary household set is not too different from that of a very good Western one, with the exception of a special *sashimi* knife, which is about 30cm/12in long with a 2.5cm/1in wide sharp blade.

Many Japanese knives have a single sharp edge on one side of the blade only so they are thinner than most Western equivalents, which makes them better for doing delicate cutting jobs. Top quality knives made in Japan are produced from one piece of carbonized steel in the same way as Japanese swords, with the names of famous blade makers normally inscribed on the shoulder of the blade.

Lesser-quality knives are made from two pieces of steel with only the lower blade made of carbonized steel and the rest of soft steel. Steel is prone to rust, so requires constant care. Stainless steel, ground mixed steel and ceramic knives are also available and are a popular choice for use in ordinary household kitchens.

A standard set of knives consists of a thin blade for vegetables; a cleaver for large fish, meat and poultry; a *sashimi* knife for slicing fish; and a small knife for peeling and chopping. Look for the maker's name on the blade shoulder as a sign of quality before buying.

Japanese cutting styles
Ingredients need to be cut into sizes and shapes suitable for eating with hashi (chopsticks). There are a number of cutting shapes that can be used, and each has its own specific name. Some examples are: sengiri (shreds); wagiri (rounds); arare (dice); hangetsu (half-moons); tanzaku (oblong and thin); sainome (cubes); sasagaki (shavings); and hanagiri (flowers).

The hyoshigi (clapper shape) cut is rectangular and thick, suitable for fairly dense vegetables.

Below: Japanese knives, from front, vegetable knife, sashimi *knife, cleaver and all-purpose knife. These knives are all made from one piece of carbonized steel with the maker's name engraved on the blade shoulder.*

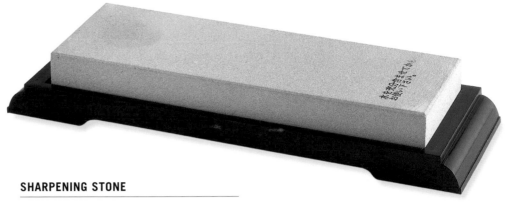

Shaping vegetables by hand
Practise your decorative cutting techniques with affordable everyday ingredients, such as carrots, where it won't matter too much if you need to start again.

Slice a medium-size carrot into thick chunks then, with a very sharp knife, slice each piece into simple shapes, such as flowers.

SHARPENING STONE

Maintaining well-sharpened knives is an important role of the cook, and Japanese chefs take as great care in selecting grinding stones as in choosing good knives. Natural stone is the best quality and professionals sharpen knives using three stones with varying degrees of density: coarse, medium and dense. However, if you do not carry out the sharpening process properly, you can easily spoil knives, so many people in Japan use professional sharpeners.

CUTTING BOARD

If you cut ingredients properly you are assured of success in Japanese cooking, and the cutting board becomes your stage. The Japanese word for chef, *itamae*, means literally "before the board", and no Japanese cooking is done without a board. Because of hygiene considerations plastic boards are more popular among housewives, but professionals still prefer wooden

Below: More hygenic than wooden chopping boards, plastic ones are increasingly being used in Japanese homes.

Above: Japanese sharpening stone

boards, since they are gentler to knives, as well as to ingredients.

Boards should be washed thoroughly after use and different ingredients, particularly raw fish and meat, should never be placed on a board at the same time.

SHAPING CUTTERS

Westerners are often amazed how, in Japanese restaurants, everyday vegetables are transformed into beautiful and delicate flowers, leaves or birds. Simple shapes are easily achieved by the use of shaping cutters but many chefs prefer cutting by hand; this forms an important part of their training. Hard and long vegetables, such as carrot and daikon, are first cut into thick pieces with a sharp knife and then sliced. To do properly by hand takes much practice and so shaping cutters may be a more achievable way to add interest and fun to cooking and eating. Simply slice your vegetable and stamp out shapes with the cutters.

Above: Quick and easy to use, shaping cutters come in various sizes.

Left: Porcelain and aluminium graters

KATSUO-BUSHI SHAVER

A block of dried skipjack tuna is one of the very basic foodstuffs found in Japanese cooking, since its flakes are the main ingredients for making dashi stock, and the sound made by housewives shaving katsuo-bushi traditionally greeted families most mornings. Today, however, flakes in packets are popularly used. The older generation still use freshly shaved katsuo-bushi and it is far superior to ready-made, whether for dashi or for use as a simple garnish on top of vegetables.

The shaver comprises a plane on top of a box and the shaved flakes drop through into a drawer underneath.

GRATER

If you are going to choose just one Japanese utensil, the oroshi-gane or daikon-oroshi (fine-toothed daikon grater) is definitely the one. There are various types and materials vary, including aluminium and porcelain, but they are all basically a flat surface with numerous fine spikes on it.

The most convenient and cheapest grater is made of aluminium and has a small curved base at the end of the spikes to catch the juice that is exuded during grating. Japanese cooking uses a lot of grated daikon and fresh root ginger, and both the grated flesh and the juice are used in the recipes. With ginger, sometimes only the juice is used, making this feature very useful.

Most graters usually have a small area with finer spikes for grating dense spices such as garlic and fresh wasabi. There is even a grater made of shark's skin, designed especially for grating wasabi, but this is confined to the professional kitchen.

Above: A bamboo whisk is used to prepare the tea during the traditional tea ceremony.

BAMBOO WHISK

When preparing tea for the Japanese tea ceremony, matcha, a high-grade, bright light green powdered tea, is whisked with this special bamboo utensil, rather than brewed in a pot.

A traditional ceremonial ritual, the tea is prepared in front of guests in individual warmed cups. The tips of the whisk need to be soaked in hot water beforehand so that they aren't stained by the vibrant green tea. A little water is added to a small quantity of tea in a bowl, then vigorously whisked, until frothy. Do not let the tea stand; rather serve immediately. Eat wagashi (Japanese cakes) before drinking the tea.

Above: Shaver and block of katsuo-bushi (dried skipjack tuna)

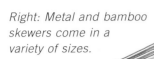

Right: Metal and bamboo skewers come in a variety of sizes.

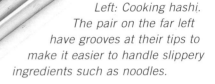

Left: Cooking hashi. The pair on the far left have grooves at their tips to make it easier to handle slippery ingredients such as noodles.

GRINDER AND PESTLE

The Japanese suribachi and surikogi (grinder and wooden pestle) grind to finer granules or paste than their Western counterparts, the mortar and pestle. The suribachi is made of clay in the shape of a large pudding bowl, with numerous sharp ridges on the inside surface so that ingredients as diverse as sesame seeds and minced (ground) meat or prawns can be ground into a paste. It then becomes a mixing bowl. A food processor may be easier for grinding larger ingredients, but small items, such as sesame seeds, are best prepared by hand using a suribachi and surikogi.

COOKING HASHI

Once mastered, hashi (chopsticks) will become an indispensable tool in the kitchen as well as on the table. From beating eggs to turning over smaller items of food in a frying pan, a pair of hashi is a much more convenient tool than a fork. Cooking hashi range in lengths, usually ranging from 25cm/10in to over 35cm/14in, and often a pair is tied with a string so that one won't become separated and lost. The longest one for deep-frying keeps your hand away from splashing hot oil. Hashi are also very elegant eating utensils. There are many different kinds, including the husband-and-wife pair, children's hashi and even hashi for a packed lunch. They are often visually attractive too.

WIRE-MESH GRILL

Japanese cooking was developed using wood and charcoal as fuel, so grilling over a fire – wood, charcoal or now, commonly, gas – is the usual cooking method. This simple, round wire mesh, called yakiami, is placed over the fire on which fish, meat or vegetables, or even tofu, are cooked. It is a very useful piece of everyday equipment, but the standard metal oven shelf will also serve the purpose.

SKEWERS

Metal and bamboo skewers make grilling easier and prevent food from breaking into bits while cooking. They are also useful for checking how food is cooking without making obvious holes in it. Skewers come in various sizes and the largest metal skewer can be used to pierce a whole fish to create a wavy shape so that it looks alive on the plate once it has been grilled.

When food is served on the skewer, such as *yakitori* (grilled chicken) or *dengaku* (grilled tofu), bamboo is used, since it not only looks better but is also easier to handle than hot metal. Small flat bamboo skewers are useful for soft ingredients such as tofu, preventing them from slipping during cooking.

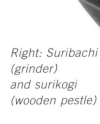

Right: Suribachi (grinder) and surikogi (wooden pestle)

Grilling with bamboo skewers

Soak bamboo skewers in water for at least 30 minutes before use to prevent the wood from burning while grilling.

STEAMER

The Japanese use a steamer as often as Westerners use an oven. It is an ideal utensil for gently cooking fresh ingredients in a way that will not diminish their nutritional content or damage their shape. For this reason the steamer is perfect for Japanese cooking.

The traditional Japanese steamer does not look any different from the ones now commonly available in the West except that it comes with a removable base pierced with holes, which is perched in the pan. Choose the widest type that you can find.

Although the microwave oven has replaced many utensils, the steamer still rules supreme in Japanese cooking. The microwave oven, however, is extremely handy for heating cooked food, particularly leftover rice.

If you do not have a steamer, it is possible to improvise with a wok and trivet. Place the trivet in the wok, fill the wok one-third full of water and bring to the boil. Place the food in a heatproof bowl on the trivet, cover the wok with the dome-shaped lid and steam the food until it is cooked.

Above: Steamers with pierced base. Japanese steamers usually feature a removable base.

STRAINER

The Japanese mesh strainer, or zaru, which is made of bamboo or stainless steel, is another item increasingly making its way into Western kitchens. Extremely effective, it can be used to strain even tiny grains of rice and very fine noodles. Japanese zaru come in a number of sizes and shapes, with different uses. Flat zaru, for example, are used to cool or air-dry ingredients, in particular vegetables, that are left on them after cooking. Needless to say, all zaru must be washed carefully after use and dried out completely before storing.

Right: Bamboo strainers, or zaru, can be used to strain a whole range of ingredients such as noodles and vegetables, but these large bamboo ones are not really suitable for straining rice as the grains are likely to get caught in the mesh.

PAN AND DROP-IN LID

The traditional Japanese pan, made of aluminium or copper, often has a finely indented surface so that it does not become too hot too quickly and so that the heat spreads evenly over the pan. A one-handled pan, called yukihira, will be useful for Japanese as well as other styles of cooking. Drop-in lids are very handy when you are cooking delicate ingredients, such as vegetables or tofu, which you do not want to move about in the pan. The light touch of the wooden lid, placed directly on the food in the pan, keeps it still on the base.

Left: Traditional Japanese pan with a wooden drop-in lid used when cooking delicate ingredients, such as tofu.

Below: The Japanese wooden sieve with its unique mesh will produce a much finer texture than is attainable using a food processor.

SIEVE

Uragoshi, the Japanese sieve, consists of a wooden round frame 20cm/8in in diameter and 7.5cm/3in deep, with very fine horsehair, stainless steel or nylon mesh. It is used to sift flours and to strain wet food, by placing it upside down on a plate and pushing the food through the mesh with a wooden spatula. Horsehair is prone to splitting when too dry, so soak the sieve in water before use except when sifting. After use wash carefully, clearing the bits stuck in the mesh, and remove the mesh from the frame and store separately. For stainless steel and nylon mesh, dry thoroughly.

OMELETTE PAN

Tamago-yaki-nabe (the Japanese omelette pan) is reserved for making *tamagoyaki* (rolled omelette) only. There are many sizes, shapes (rectangular or square) and makes, but the best Japanese one is made of copper, plated inside with tin. Though handy, the straight-sided pan can be replaced by an ordinary frying pan or a small ordinary omelette pan. Trim the edges of the cooked egg to make a rectangular shape.

Above: A Japanese omelette pan used to make rolled omelettes

34

UTENSILS FOR COOKING WITH RICE

Rice is the staple grain of the whole of Asia, which is well over half the world's population. In Japan, evidence of its production dates as far back as the 2nd century BC. It is not exaggerating to say that rice is at the heart of all Japanese cuisine. Not surprisingly, there are a number of utensils specifically designed for the cooking and use of rice.

RICE COOKER

Traditionally in Japan rice was cooked over a real fire, usually wood, in an o'kama, a cast-iron pot with a round base and a tutu-like skirt around the pot that kept the heat to the lower part of the pan. Once cooked, the rice was transferred to an o'hitsu, a deep wooden container with a lid, from which the rice was served. This process has now been replaced by the electric cooker, which can keep the rice warm all day. The older generation, however, still yearns for rice cooked over a wood fire, and the ultimate aim of electric rice cooker manufacturers is to re-create the taste of wood-fire cooked rice as closely as possible.

Above: Wooden sushi tub

Right: Lacquered and wooden spatulas

RICE KEEPER

The wooden o'hitsu used to be an object every household possessed, but since the introduction of electric rice cookers, which cook and keep rice warm in the one unit, it is more often simply a fashionable addition to modern kitchens or dining rooms. After cooking, rice is transferred to it and, after serving, the remaining rice is kept in it. The wood may not keep the rice warm all day as the electric cooker does, but it does absorb extra moisture and keeps the rice pleasantly moist.

SPATULA

Héra or shamoji (the wooden spatula) is probably the most indispensable utensil in a Japanese household. It is often used as a symbol representing the entire household (at such occasions as housewives' protests against rising household costs). There are now many types of Japanese rice spatulas, including bare wood or lacquered ones. The spatula is used for aerating cooked rice and also for pressing wet food through a sieve on to a plate.

Left: Electric rice cooker

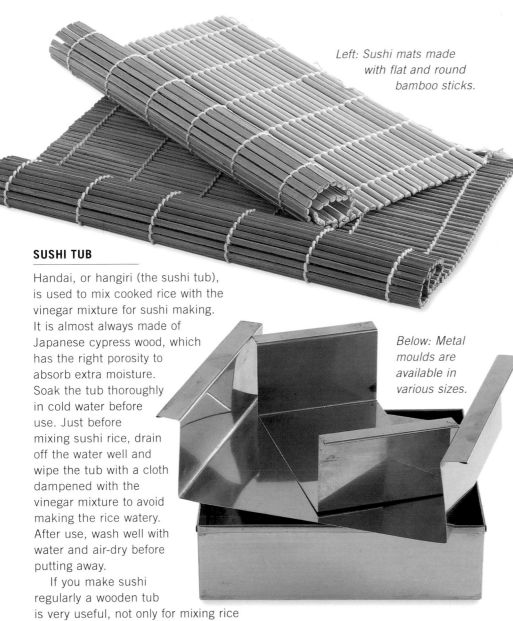

Left: Sushi mats made with flat and round bamboo sticks.

SUSHI MAT

Makisu (a bamboo stick mat) is increasingly found in many Western households due to the popularity of sushi. It is a necessary item for making *nori-maki* (nori-rolled sushi), but is also used for other purposes, such as squeezing water out of cooked salad vegetables before they are dressed. There are basically two types of makisu: one, measuring about 22 × 20cm/9 × 8in, and made of bamboo sticks with a pale green, shiny, flat side, is for sushi rolling; the other, a little larger in size, which has triangular or round bamboo sticks threaded together, is for making a pattern of lines on the roll, as when preparing *tamagoyaki* (thick egg omelette). After use, carefully wash away any food stuck between the sticks, wipe and leave to dry completely before storing.

WOODEN MOULD

The rectangular wooden mould is for making *oshi-zushi*, pressed sushi. This, like the sushi tub, should be soaked well in water before use. Wet the mould before packing with fish and su-meshi. Cover with the lid and press tightly or place a weight such as a book on it. Other moulds are also used to shape cooked rice for party canapés or children's lunch boxes.

METAL MOULD

This double-layered mould is a very useful tool for setting mousse or tofu as well as liquids such as kanten.

SUSHI TUB

Handai, or hangiri (the sushi tub), is used to mix cooked rice with the vinegar mixture for sushi making. It is almost always made of Japanese cypress wood, which has the right porosity to absorb extra moisture. Soak the tub thoroughly in cold water before use. Just before mixing sushi rice, drain off the water well and wipe the tub with a cloth dampened with the vinegar mixture to avoid making the rice watery. After use, wash well with water and air-dry before putting away.

    If you make sushi regularly a wooden tub is very useful, not only for mixing rice but also for serving. An ordinary large mixing bowl may not absorb moisture as a Japanese sushi tub does but it is certainly an acceptable substitute if you make sushi rice only occasionally.

Below: Metal moulds are available in various sizes.

Below: Wooden sushi mould for shaping rice into individual canapés, left, and a rectangular wooden sushi mould for making pressed sushi.

COOKING AT THE TABLE

Always great fun, cooking at the table is very easy to do well and it also enables diners to appreciate fresh food immediately after it's cooked. There is a Japanese utensil designed for every one of the numerous dishes that are cooked at the table, but a portable gas burner and a flameproof earthenware pot are suitable for most dishes. Below are some of the special Japanese pots and pans.

EARTHENWARE POT

Hotpot dishes are Japanese winter favourites; they are used to cook *sukiyaki*, *shabu shabu*, *oden*, *yudofu* (pot-boiled tofu) and griddles at the table. The Japanese household normally has a table with a gas or electric burner fitted in the centre, the lid to which is removed when they cook at the table. An earthenware pot is ideal for cooking soups, such as *shabu shabu*, *oden* and *yudofu*, as it heats up slowly and retains the heat for some time. It can also be used to cook udon noodles. The pot also looks good on the table. After use, leave it to cool down, then wash it carefully with a sponge and leave to air-dry. Never heat an earthenware pot without water in it.

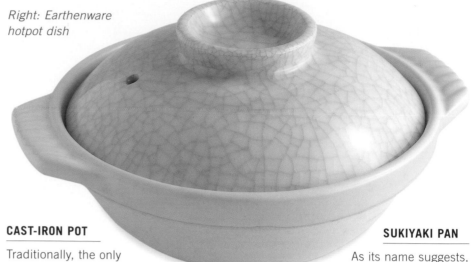

Right: Earthenware hotpot dish

CAST-IRON POT

Traditionally, the only heating in the house was a hibachi (fire urn), or irori (floor hearth) for a farmhouse, placed in the centre of the living room. A cast-iron pot was placed on it, or hung from the ceiling, so boiling water was available all day for tea or so that slow-cooking foods could be simmered gently. While the hibachi and irori are now, unfortunately, rarely used, the cast-iron pot is, not only for its handsome appearance but also for the practicality of cooking and serving hotpot dishes either at home or in restaurants. It is normally black with a wooden lid and a removable handle, which rests on the pot's rim when not in use.

Below: Sukiyaki pan

SUKIYAKI PAN

As its name suggests, this pan is used only for cooking *sukiyaki* at the table and an ordinary frying pan can be used instead. It is a heavy iron pan with a deep rim, since *sukiyaki* beef is first pan-fried, then shoyu sauce and other ingredients are added. Diners serve themselves from the pan and add more ingredients as they eat.

YUDOFU POT

Pot-boiled tofu, *yudofu*, is a favourite Japanese winter dish, traditionally prepared in a yudofu pot, though an ordinary large pan or earthenware pot can be used. The yudofu set usually consists of a pot, a tall metal shoyu dish with flat feet to stand in the pot, a small perforated metal spoon and individual serving bowls. The shoyu dish filled with shoyu is placed in the centre of the pot, which is filled with hot water (so the shoyu also gets warm) surrounded by cubed tofu on a bed of a piece of konbu (dried kelp). Diners mix the sauce with some shoyu from the pot, along with grated fresh root ginger and a herb for flavouring, and serve themselves.

SHABU SHABU POT

This Mongolian-style pot is a popular way of cooking *shabu shabu* (pot-cooked beef) though an earthenware pot is also suitable. It has a central funnel surrounded by a moat into which hot stock is poured. The pot is placed on a portable gas ring or electric ring on the table and diners cook small pieces of meat and vegetables in the hot stock.

Below: Tray for serving tempura.

Above: Tempura fryer

Above: Shabu shabu pot

The word *shabu shabu* is onomatopoeic, suggesting something splashing around in water, such as when hand-washing clothes; using hashi (chopsticks), diners move thinly sliced beef in a similar motion in the stock to prevent it over-cooking. Once all the meat and vegetables are eaten, rice or noodles are added to the stock and served to finish off the meal. There are a few makes available but the best, and most expensive, ones are made of brass.

TEMPURA FRYER

Normally made of heavy iron, the tempura deep-frying pan is two-handled, with a half-circle metal rack perched on the edge for draining. There are several sizes, ranging from those for two people to family-size fryers. A large wok or any deep frying pan can do the job just as well.

Tempura is mostly served on bamboo trays though there are also metal ones, made to the same shape. While not necessary, these trays do make lovely serving tools. When arranging the tempura, first place a piece of washi (Japanese paper) on the tray.

ELECTRIC GRIDDLE

This is an essential piece of equipment for the Japanese household and has already started appearing in Western kitchens. It is a round or square non-stick metal griddle with a rim about 5cm/2in deep and an electric heating device underneath. There are many types and makes, but the most popular is the round one, about 40cm/16in in diameter, with a see-through glass lid. The griddle is placed in the centre of the table surrounded by prepared fresh vegetables, meat or fish and shellfish, and diners help themselves. It's an easy family meal, suitable for busy people. Some deeper griddles can be used to roast a whole chicken or other meat.

After all the ingredients have been cooked and eaten, add a little hot water while the griddle is still hot and wipe it clean with kitchen paper. Leave to dry completely before putting away.

PORTABLE GAS STOVE

A very practical piece of equipment, the portable gas stove can be used not only at the table to cook all kinds of hotpot dishes but also outside for mini-barbecues. It has a gas ring and a compartment for the gas cylinder at the side. One cylinder lasts for about two hours, and these are sold either individually or in packets of three. Remove the cylinder after use and store separately.

CROCKERY AND CUTLERY

The appearance and presentation of food is very important to the Japanese, so serving dishes play an important part in Japanese cooking. Japan has been renowned as producers of fine china and porcelain for many centuries and great works of art have been developed around the *kaiseki* tea ceremony and formal banquets.

Japanese tableware is probably the most varied in the world. Even a simple family supper requires individual rice bowls, soup bowls, plates and sauce dishes, as well as serving plates and bowls, and of course sake cups. Lacquer is widely used not only for trays but also for bowls intended for soup or simmered dishes, and for sake vessels. Wooden dishes, as well as utensils, are also popular not only because they are pleasing to look at but also because the natural material complements so well the country's food philosophy.

CHINA DISHES

Japan produces some of the finest china in the world, with such well-known names and styles as Arita, Bizen, Hagi, Imari, Karatsu, Kutani, Mashiko, Mino and Seto.

A household normally possesses sets of rice bowls and soup bowls, various different-size plates, noodle bowls, serving plates and bowls, small dishes for dipping sauces and probably a set of lacquered trays. However, apart from rice bowls and soup bowls, ordinary Western plates can be used for other dishes quite easily.

Below: Hors d'oeuvres tray with sashimi china dish left, bowl for simmered food, at back, and soup bowl, right.

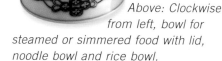

Above: Clockwise from left, bowl for steamed or simmered food with lid, noodle bowl and rice bowl.

Right: China soba set: sauce jug (pitcher), condiment dishes and sauce cups.

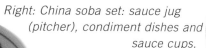

China used for a banquet:

The *kaiseki* (Japanese formal banquet) consists of more than a dozen courses, each served separately in plates, bowls or cups of different shapes, sizes and patterns; the materials are chosen with an artist's eye to suit the season and the food being served.

In order of serving, plates, bowls and trays can include an hors d'oeuvres tray, a small sashimi dish, a clear soup bowl and

a bowl for a simmered dish. Separate plates are then used for a grilled dish, a plate or bamboo basket for a fried dish, and a plate for a steamed dish. Finally, the rice, soup and noodles are served in their own bowls, accompanied by a sauce dish.

Left: Sauce dishes in two sizes, and a rectangular hors d'oeuvres plate.

BENTO BOXES

In the West, *bento* is known as a dish, as in *makunouchi bento*, but it really means easy meal or take out meal, usually for lunch or a picnic. There are many types of *bento* box, from lacquer to plastic, and sizes vary from the *makunouchi bento* box, a size similar to a laptop computer, to pretty children's lunch boxes. Elaborate boxes such as *makunouchi* are hardly designed for an "easy meal", and they are normally made of lacquer with five or six compartments and a sauce corner inside. Some ordinary lunch boxes consist of two boxes, one for fish, meat and vegetables, which is positioned on top of another box for rice.

Below: Trays for serving soba noodles can be round with a lid or square.

SERVING TRAYS

At Japanese banquets trays are used in place of table mats. This is because foods for the tea ceremony were traditionally served separately on lacquer trays with legs, which acted as individual tables. Smaller trays, either lacquer, wooden or bamboo, are often used as dishes on which foods are arranged directly or with decoratively folded Japanese paper between the food and the tray.

Above: Square jubako (lacquered food boxes) with matching hashi (chopsticks) and set of bento boxes.

SOBA TRAYS

Japanese soba noodles, which are dipped in sauce before being eaten, are normally served on a soba tray, which is a bamboo mat perched on a bamboo or wooden frame. There are many shapes (square, rectangular or round) and sizes vary greatly. A soba china set normally includes a sauce jug (pitcher) and five sauce cups and condiment dishes.

Below: Flat bamboo tray for serving food.

HASHI

In contrast to the numerous items of crockery, the only Japanese cutlery is hashi. Hashi, or more politely ohashi, are shorter and more delicate than Chinese chopsticks and the lower ends are pointed. Traditionally they were made of ivory, but today various woods, lacquer or plastic are popular. They vary in size, and sometimes colour too, depending on who they are meant for. Men's hashi are thicker and usually 2.5–4cm/1–1½in longer than women's, and there are various children's hashi as well. In a Japanese household each family member usually has his or her own daily pair and another pair kept in a hashi case for use with a lunch box.

Hashi are growing in popularity the world over, and many modern Western-style designs, even using silver, have been introduced to the market. However, Japanese people never use metal hashi when they eat, since metal ones are used to pick the bones from the ashes of the dead at the crematorium and are therefore not considered a good omen. The Japanese also traditionally serve a bowl of rice with a pair of very thin metal hashi every morning to their house temple, which is dedicated to their relatives' and ancestors' souls; metal ones are for the Buddha, as they say.

Below: Condiment jar for shoyu with a matching saucer.

Above: Simple wooden hashi in decorative pouches.

Above: Hashi come in various sizes, colours and materials. Rests are used to avoid placing hashi on the table.

WARIBASHI

For guests, simple wooden hashi, called waribashi, can be used. This is a long piece of wood divided in the centre up to the top end where it is broken off for use. Some plain wooden hashi are already made into pairs. There are numerous types and shapes, neatly encased in their own paper pouches with various colours, illustrations and inscriptions. Some waribashi pouches are designed to use only for celebration meals, so be careful not to use them at a funeral. You would know by the colour of the pouch; if red or similarly bright colour is used, it's for a celebration or a special occasion. If there is a knotted string, or illustration on the pouch, with no loops on the knot, it's particularly used for weddings.

HASHI REST

During the meal, Japanese place hashi crossways on a hashi rest or on a dish, and never directly on the table. The hashi rest is a boat-shaped piece of porcelain, metal or wood (which may be lacquered), about 5cm/2in long.

CONDIMENT DISH

On the Japanese table a condiment jar for shoyu takes the place of a salt and pepper set on the Western table. The size of a short, narrow tumbler, it has a spout and a lid, and matching saucer.

Shichimi (powdered seven-chilli pepper) and sansho (green pepper) are also placed on the table either in the manufacturer's jars or in small, lidded dishes with a tiny spoon in each.

DRINKING VESSELS

Just as the presentation of food is important in Japanese cuisine, attention is also given to how drink is served.

SAKE JUGS

Never serve sake from the bottle; instead a tokkuri (sake jug/pitcher) should always be used. It is normally made of china and is heat-resistant so that sake can be warmed in it before serving. The normal tokkuri holds 180ml/6fl oz/¾ cup, which relates to the old Japanese measurement of one "go".

SAKE CUPS

There are numerous types and makes of sake cup, but basically there are two categories: choko, or more politely ochoko, and guinomi. The ochoko are smaller cups, the size of half a golf ball, and the rim is open like a flower; some are so open that the cup itself is almost flat. The guinomi are slightly larger cups with a straight rim and are for more casual drinking. There are also larger, flat cups, the size of a small tea saucer. These are more formally called sakazuki and are used for occasions such as toasting someone

Right: Sake jugs (pitchers) and cups

or drinking to their future. Traditional Shinto wedding vows are also made by the couple toasting each other in sake, and the wedding sakazuki are made of ceremonial red lacquer.

Shochu, distilled alcohol made from various grains and even potato, is drunk in a glass, either straight or diluted.

TEAPOTS

The Japanese teapot looks similar to Western models except for the handle. No Japanese teapot has a fixed hollow handle attached to the side as do Western ones, instead it has either a pan handle or a detachable basket-like looped handle. The smaller pots, called kyusu, tend to have a straight pan handle and are used to make better quality teas. These pots have the capacity of only two to three cups. The terracotta kyusu is regarded as particularly good for top quality teas because of its natural feel. The ones for more casual use, dobin, are larger and normally have a looped handle. All Japanese teapots strain tea leaves at the bottom of the spout; a strainer is not needed when you pour the tea out.

Left: Japanese teapots

Above: Japanese teacups come in various types and sizes, ranging from tiny ones, little larger than eggcups, to larger ones with lids, and his and hers sets.

TEACUPS

Japanese teacups and mugs range in size from eggcup to the gigantic mug served at sushi shops, and have no handle as the tea is normally drunk lukewarm. The tall cups usually have a lid and a husband and wife set are also available consisting of a pair of cups, one slightly larger than the other, with lids and saucers. Saucers are wooden, either plain or lacquered.

The tea ceremony is a totally different affair from daily tea drinking. Bowls rather than cups are used and the powdered tea is whisked, using a bamboo brush, in front of the guests.

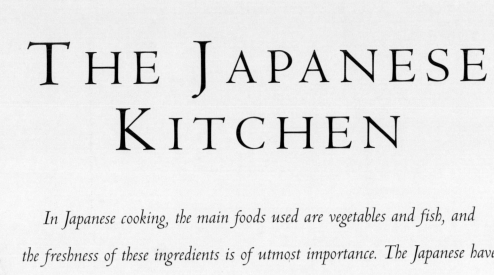

THE JAPANESE KITCHEN

In Japanese cooking, the main foods used are vegetables and fish, and the freshness of these ingredients is of utmost importance. The Japanese have also developed, with characteristic meticulous and delicate care, numerous processed foods. The following pages introduces both fresh ingredients and processed foods, discussing their aroma, taste, texture and appearance, and includes essential preparation and cooking techniques.

RICE AND RICE PRODUCTS

Since prehistoric times rice has been grown and eaten in Japan, and because of its rich content of vegetable protein, carbohydrate, vitamins and minerals, it quickly became popular all over the country. By the 7th century it was firmly established as the staple food and has remained so ever since.

Japanese cooking really developed around rice. The plain, yet delicate and subtle flavour of rice made it possible for the Japanese people to develop an appreciation of the exquisite flavours and textures of other natural produce available to them.

As well as a number of types and forms of rice, numerous by-products such as sake, mirin, vinegar and miso have also been derived from rice. Following is a look at the most essential and useful types of rice used in Japanese cooking.

URUCHIMAI

The short grain Japanese variety, *Oryza sativa japonica*, as opposed to the neighbouring South-east Asian countries' long grain, *jawa* and *indica*, was developed over the centuries to suit the climate as well as the taste of the Japanese people. Once cooked, it becomes quite tender and moist but firm enough to retain a little crunchiness. Unlike long grain rice, it becomes slightly sticky, enabling it to be picked up in mouthfuls with a pair of hashi (chopsticks). It has a rich, slightly sweet flavour.

There are over 300 different types of short grain rice grown all over Japan in water-filled paddy fields; brand names such as Koshihikari and Sasanisiki are among the most popular. However, most of the Japanese rice sold in the West is produced in California on dry land and some varieties come from Spain. They vary slightly in hardness, but Kahomai (the hardest), Nishiki, Maruyu and Kokuho (all Californian) and Minori (Spanish, the softest) are some of the popular brand names available.

Below: Some popular examples of Japanese short grain rice, clockwise from left, Kahomai, Maruyu, Minori, Kokuho and Nishiki

Cooking Japanese rice

1 Wash the rice thoroughly in cold water changing the water several times until the water runs clear, then drain the rice in a fine mesh strainer and set aside for 1 hour.

2 Put the rice in a deep pan and add 15 per cent more cold water than rice (for 200g/7oz/1 cup rice you will need about 250ml/8fl oz/ 1 cup water). The water level should not be more than a third from the base of the pan.

3 Cover the pan, place over a high heat and bring to the boil; this may take 5 minutes. Turn the heat to the lowest setting and simmer for 10–13 minutes, or until all the water has been absorbed.

4 Remove the pan from the heat and set aside, still covered, for 10–15 minutes before serving.

COOK'S TIP

To cook genmai (brown rice), wash and drain the rice, then put 2 parts water to 1 part rice into a pan. Bring to the boil, cover, then simmer for 40 minutes.

GENMAI

There are degrees of polishing in rice production, and genmai, brown rice, is the least polished type. It retains its bran and germ and only the husk is removed. It is the most nutritious rice, and is high in fibre, but it takes a lot longer to cook than white rice and is very chewy. Genmai is widely available at health food stores and Asian stores.

MOCHIGOME

This short, opaque grain, also known as glutinous rice, makes a very sticky, dense rice when cooked. It has a high sugar content and is often steamed rather than boiled, then pounded to make mochi (rice cakes) and senbei (rice biscuits). Mochigome is also an important ingredient for making mirin (sweet rice wine).

Culinary uses of rice

As the staple food of Japan, rice is served in one form or another at every meal, including breakfast. It is almost always consumed boiled and served in a bowl together with a bowl of miso

Above: Genmai, brown rice

soup. Other foods are often just mere accompaniments to the rice. Plain boiled rice is also served with other cooked food such as *tonkatsu* (pork cutlet) and tempura (fried fish and/or fried vegetables) arranged on top as a one-dish meal, usually for lunch. Sometimes seasonal produce, such as young bamboo shoots in spring, green peas in summer and chestnuts or matsutake (wild mushrooms) in autumn, is added while the rice is boiling so an additional typical flavour of the season can be appreciated.

Boiled rice, mixed with vinegar, sugar and salt, also forms the base of all sushi, and top sushi chefs spend at least the first three years of their training perfecting the techniques for cooking rice. For babies and the elderly as well as the sick, *kayu* or more politely *okayu* (rice gruel) can be cooked with three to four times as much water as that used for plain boiled rice. Boiled rice, either hot or cold, can be added to soup to make *zosui* but it is not suitable for frying.

Mochigome is often used to make celebratory dishes such as *sekihan* (rice cooked with red beans) for birthdays and other family celebrations and *ohagi* (steamed mochigome rolled in sweet red bean paste), for the equinox days.

Above: Mochigome

Making sushi rice

Su-meshi (vinegared rice) is the base for all kinds of sushi and it is essential to correctly cook the rice. As a guide, to make *hoso-maki* (thin nori-rolled sushi), 350g/12oz/1¾ cups short grain rice should make six rolls (about 36 pieces), sufficient to serve four to six people.

1 Cook the rice following the method, opposite. For extra flavour, add a 5cm/2in square of konbu (dried kelp) to the pan of rice and water, removing before the water reaches boiling point.

2 In a measuring cup, mix 45ml/ 3 tbsp Japanese rice vinegar (or white wine vinegar), 37.5ml/ 7½ tsp sugar and 10ml/2 tsp sea salt to the above amount of rice and stir well until dissolved.

3 Transfer the cooked rice to a wet wooden sushi tub or a large mixing bowl, and sprinkle the vinegar mixture evenly over the rice. Using a wooden spatula, fold the vinegar mixture into the rice; do not stir. Leave to cool before using to make sushi.

Preparation and cooking

When cooking Japanese rice it is imperative that it is washed thoroughly first in cold water and then left to drain, ideally for an hour but at least for 30 minutes. This ensures that the rice slowly absorbs the right amount of water left on the surface of the grains without turning it soggy. If time is limited, soak the rice for 10–15 minutes in plenty of water, then drain well. When the rice is well moistened it will turn a soft opaque colour. As a general rule, about 200g/7oz/1 cup rice is needed for two people. It is not advisable to cook less than this

Shaping Japanese rice

When making individual *su-meshi* blocks don't worry if the blocks don't look very neat. To make them perfectly requires at least two years' practice in a sushi restaurant kitchen.

To shape Japanese rice, wet everything – from your hands to the mould, if using – and keep the work surface tidy at all times. Use both hands to squeeze the rice into a densely packed shape.

Using moulds

When making moulded sushi, one option is to use small plastic moulds, which are easily available. Otherwise you can line an eggcup with clear film (plastic wrap), push a topping in, add a dab of wasabi paste, then fill with *su-meshi*. Seal the end with the clear film and press with your fingers. When ready, remove from the eggcup and unwrap from the clear film.

quantity of rice since the moisture isn't retained satisfactorily in a small amount.

The width, depth and material of the pan used will also make a difference to the end result. One of the best ways to get consistently good results is to use an electric rice-cooker. The microwave oven is not generally used for cooking Japanese rice, but for just one person it may produce a better result than cooking on a stove.

Mochigome (glutinous rice), on the other hand, should be soaked overnight and then steamed, rather than boiled, for 35–40 minutes. A large bamboo steamer is best so that the grains can be spread thinly. If boiling rice, use up to 20 per cent of mochigome in a mixture with ordinary rice.

Genmai should also be soaked for a few hours, ideally overnight; it should then be boiled with twice as much water and cooked for three times as long as ordinary rice.

Storage

Rice tastes best when newly harvested, and then it gradually deteriorates. Although it keeps for a long time, it is best eaten as soon as possible. Transfer raw rice to an earthenware, ceramic or plastic container with a lid and keep it in an airy, cool place away from direct sunlight. Keep rice perfectly dry; if the moisture content creeps up, the rice will soon turn mouldy. Rice available in the West is normally powdered with preservatives, hence its longevity.

Right: Mochi (rice cakes), made from mochigome rice, are traditional fare for New Year's Day.

RICE PRODUCTS

It is no surprise that the Japanese have developed various products out of rice and that these, in turn, have found a secure place in Japanese cooking.

Mochi

The main product of mochigome (glutinous rice) is mochi (rice cakes), hence the name.

Mochi cakes were traditionally made by hand, an arduous task involving pounding steamed mochigome rice to a very smooth, pliable consistency, then shaping and drying the mass to make a mochi block. The block is normally made into small circular shapes or cut into rectangular pieces, which are eaten, either fried, grilled (broiled) or very lightly boiled, with other accompaniments. Mochi hardens very quickly and is a good preserved food. It is eaten in soup as part of the New Year's celebration meal as mochi is believed to bring long life and wealth. It is also eaten with soy sauce or wasabi.

Mochi can be made at home with an electric mochi-maker, a brilliant recent Japanese invention, but excellent ready-made mochi cakes in packets are easily available at Japanese supermarkets and an unopened packet lasts for months.

Mochi with cheese and nori seaweed

This quick and easy snack is a tasty introduction to mochi.

1 Slice some Cheddar cheese a little smaller than the mochi cakes and about 5mm/¼in thick.

2 Grill (broil) the mochi cakes on each side under a medium heat for 2–3 minutes, turning them frequently to prevent burning. While the grilled mochi are still hot, make a horizontal slit at the side and insert a cheese slice.

3 If you wish, cut an 18 × 20cm/ 7 × 8in nori sheet into four to eight pieces and wrap one piece around each of the cheese stuffed mochi cakes before serving with a little shoyu (Japanese soy sauce).

Right: Nuka (rice bran), is most valued for its strong flavour and is a good base for pickling vegetables.

Shiratama

This flour is comprised mostly of starch taken from mochigome (glutinous rice), which is first soaked in water, then sieved and dried. It has a subtle flavour and is mostly used in wagashi (Japanese cakes) and sweet dumplings.

Domyoji

Mochigome rice is finely crushed to produce this flour, which is generally used for making wagashi (Japanese traditional cakes) and sometimes for cooking, usually in steamed dishes.

Nuka

This rice bran is traditionally used for pickling vegetables. The rice bran is first lightly roasted to bring out its flavour, then mixed with brine to make a mash, which ferments and makes a unique pickling base. The strong flavour seeps through to the fresh vegetables, making them not only soft with some crunchiness but also adding a very characteristic taste. The smell of rice bran is quite strong; it may not be to everyone's taste but once used to it you will be surprised at how delicious rice bran is. Nuka is now readily available at larger Japanese supermarkets.

Right: Shiratama flour, front, and Domyoji flour

MUGI

Once a substitute for rice whenever production was low, mugi, or barley, is now regarded as a health food by the Japanese; it contains more protein and ten times more fibre than rice. However, it is very difficult to cook and the husk is too deeply ingrained to remove. The Japanese solution to this is to squash or halve it. Oshimugi (squashed barley) and setsudan mugi (cut barley) are cooked with rice, or on their own for a dish called *mugi-toro* (barley with grated yam). Mugi is usually available from health food stores.

NOODLES

Certainly among the most popular foods in Japan, noodles are one of the oldest, most widely eaten foods in all of South-east Asia, if not in the world. Noodle stores are dotted along every high street all over Japan and Japanese noodles are also becoming very popular in the West, with soba, udon and ramen all available at larger supermarkets.

Somen with tangy dipping sauce
This is a light, refreshing dish of chilled somen, perfect for lunch on a hot summer's day.

SERVES TWO

INGREDIENTS
   200g/7oz somen
   ice cubes
   watercress, sliced cucumber and
     tomato, and ice cubes, to garnish
   1 spring onion (scallion), finely
     chopped and grated fresh root
     ginger, to serve
For the dipping sauce (makes about
   200ml/7fl oz/scant 1 cup)
   2.5ml/½ tsp dashi
   45ml/3 tbsp shoyu
   15ml/1 tbsp mirin (or 10ml/
     2 tsp sugar)
   120ml/4fl oz/½ cup hot or cold water

1 Cook the somen in plenty of boiling water for 1–3 minutes following the instructions on the packet. Drain, then wash the outer starch from the somen under cold running water.

2 Place the cooked somen in a large serving bowl and add ice-cold water to cover well.

SOMEN

These are very fine noodles also made from wheat, but the dough is stretched with the help of vegetable oil to make very thin strips and then air-dried. There are two regions famous for their exceptional somen – Miwa in Nara and Ibo in Himeji – and the somen they produce takes only 1 minute to cook.

3 To make the dipping sauce, add the dashi, shoyu and mirin or sugar to the hot or cold water and stir. Divide the sauce between individual serving cups.

4 Garnish the noodles with some vegetables, such as watercress and sliced cucumber and tomato, and some ice cubes, if you like.

5 Serve the somen noodles in bowls with the chopped spring onion and grated ginger on small individual plates and the dipping sauce also in individual cups. Diners mix the spring onion and ginger in their sauce, then using hashi (chopsticks), dip the somen in the sauce, a few at a time, and eat.

SOBA NOODLES

This uniquely Japanese noodle is made of buckwheat flour mixed with ordinary wheat flour. To make buckwheat flour, the black-skinned seeds are first coarsely ground, then the outer skins are removed, and the flour is finely ground. As soba made from just buckwheat flour lacks elasticity and stickiness, wheat flour is usually added to act as a smoothing, binding agent. The colour ranges from dark brownish grey to light beige, depending on how the buckwheat seeds were ground.

Below: Dried somen noodles are available in packet form or in bundles.

There is also a green-coloured soba, called *chasoba*, to which powdered tea has also been added. The finest soba comes from Shinshu, the mountain area of central Japan. Fresh soba is available in Japan and most of the good soba shops make their own every day. It's also common to see a *soba-ya* (noodle store) every 10 yards or so on any high street in Japan, serving fresh soba, and other popular noodles. Cold soba noodles are often eaten in summer and served on a bamboo tray with a dipping sauce. The Japanese love the taste of the noodles themselves; the sauce enhances their flavour. Outside of Japan, prepacked dried soba is sold in bundles of fine strands at larger supermarkets and Asian stores.

Left: Soba noodles from Shinshu, central Japan, are considered to be the finest of all soba noodles produced.

Storage

Dried soba will keep for many months if kept sealed in the original packet, or in airtight containers. Soba, perhaps more so than other Japanese noodle, is considered a health food so makes an ideal store cupboard (pantry) item.

Below: Fine buckwheat soba noodles and green chasoba, *which get their distinctive colouring from the addition of powdered tea.*

Cooking dried noodles

1 Bring plenty of water to the boil in a pan and add the noodles. For each person use about 115g/4oz dried noodles cooked in at least 600ml/1 pint/2½ cups water.

2 Cook over a medium heat following the instructions on the packet. It normally takes up to 5–6 minutes for soba, 10–13 minutes for udon, 1–3 minutes for somen and hiyamugi, and 5–8 minutes for ramen. Lower the heat if the water starts to boil over.

3 When the noodles are half transparent, they are done. Remove the pan from the heat, drain and wash off the outer starch under running water. Drain again and serve in hot soup or with a dipping sauce.

Left: Usually white, these hiyamugi noodles have occasional brown and pale pink strands.

UDON

This is a thick wheat noodle, which is eaten all over the world and probably has the longest history. To make udon, wheat flour is mixed with salted water to make a dough, then rolled out and thinly sliced. Fresh, raw udon is available in Japan but in the West it is usually either dried or cooked and frozen to be sold in packets.

HIYAMUGI

These thin, white noodles are made in the same way as udon but cut very thinly. They take about 5 minutes to cook and are eaten in hot soup or with a dipping sauce. Dried and bundled hiyamugi is available in packets at Asian supermarkets.

Right: Dried and fresh udon noodles

RAMEN

Literally meaning stretched noodle, ramen originated in China, and is made of wheat flour with added eggs and what the Japanese call *kansui*, alkali water. The chemical reaction between them makes the wheat dough smooth and stretchable to create very fine noodles. Pure, naturally formed *kansui* is now hard to obtain and is often substituted with bicarbonate of soda (baking soda). Ramen is eaten with other cooked food with or without soup, and has been meticulously developed in Japan. Almost every county has its own version of the noodles, the soup and the ingredients. It has reached the point of a ramen phenomenon: there is now a museum dedicated to the noodle in Yokohama, south of Tokyo; a ramen village in Hokkaido, the northern island; and appreciation societies everywhere. The popularity has now spread to the West and in recent years many ramen shops have sprung up in big cities, run not only by the Japanese but also by the Chinese largely adopting Japanese-style cooking techniques.

Ramen is available fresh, dried or frozen at large supermarkets and Asian stores. There are also numerous kinds of instant ramen with various flavoured soups in packets. These are very popular as quick, healthy snacks and late-night suppers, especially among the young.

Right: Instant ramen noodles are usually sold with a flavoured soup sachet.

Culinary uses

All Japanese noodles can be cooked in hot dashi-based soup with a few added ingredients, or eaten cold with a dipping sauce. Somen is a useful ingredient because of its white, almost hair-like fineness and is often used in clear soup or as a garnish. Ramen is nearly always cooked in hot meat-based soup (mainly pork) with several added ingredients, or in summer it is eaten cold, topped with a few fresh ingredients.

General preparation and cooking tips

Whether fresh or dried, all noodles need to be boiled, and this should be done carefully to prevent them becoming too soft. Follow the instructions on the packet. Cut a strand in the middle to check the noodles are cooked. If the noodles are to be eaten in hot soup, boil them until they are still a little hard. If they are to be eaten cold, cook thoroughly. Once boiled, wash off the outer starch under cold running water.

All Japanese noodles except ramen are eaten simply, either on their own or with only a few added ingredients and rarely with meat. Ramen, on the other hand, tends to be cooked with an assortment of meat-based ingredients.

Storage

Fresh noodles keep for only a few days in the refrigerator. In dried form, they will keep for a few months if sealed in the packet and stored in a cool place.

Making handmade udon

MAKES 675G/1½LB

1 Sift 225g/8oz/2 cups plain (all-purpose) flour into a mixing bowl and make a well in the centre. Dissolve 15ml/1 tbsp salt in 150ml/¼ pint/⅔ cup water, pour into the well and gently fold in to make a firm dough.

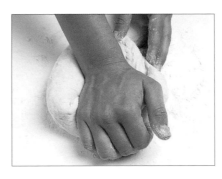

2 Turn on to a floured work surface and knead until smooth but still firm. Hit hard with a fist at least 100 times to remove any air pockets. Cover with a damp cloth and leave for 2 hours.

3 Roll out on to a lightly floured work surface to make a rectangular sheet, 3mm/⅛in thick. Dust with flour, then fold one long side into the centre.

4 Turn over, dust with flour again and fold the remaining third over the top. (If you look at the end of the folded dough, it will form an S-shape.) Fold the dough in half lengthways.

5 Using a sharp knife, cut the folded dough crossways into 3mm/⅛in thick strips. Separate the strands with your hands. The udon noodles can be frozen at this stage.

6 Bring plenty of water to the boil in a large, deep pan. Add the udon and cook for 25–30 minutes, adding some cold water each time it starts to boil, until the noodles are thoroughly cooked but still slightly firm.

7 Drain and wash well under cold running water to remove the outer starch from the noodles. When ready to eat, reheat in a soup or quickly plunge in boiling water, then drain and serve with dipping sauce.

COOK'S TIP
To check if the noodles are cooked, cut a strip of udon and if the core of the cut face is turning from white to grey, it's done.

VEGETABLES

In recent years an increasing number of exotic vegetables and fruits have been introduced to the West, and many Japanese varieties are now available, which makes Japanese cooking a lot easier. It is interesting to see, too, how Japanese and Western varieties of many ordinary vegetables, such as cucumber and pepper, differ in size, shape and taste.

As Japanese cooking is largely vegetarian oriented, due to Buddhist traditions, the Japanese painstakingly developed the best way to wash, cut and cook each vegetable in order to retain its natural flavour and texture. The following are some of the typical Japanese vegetables.

DAIKON

This long, white, dense vegetable, also known by the Indian name mooli, is a member of the radish family. Used widely in Japanese cooking, it is one of the oldest vegetables and its recorded use dates back to the 8th century. It is also one of the most versatile of vegetables: it can be cooked in soup, chopped for salad, shredded for a *sashimi* garnish or grated for use as a condiment. It is also made into takuan: bright yellow pickles often used for nori-rolled sushi.

As it is grown all over Japan all year round, there are numerous varieties with different shapes, sizes and hues. The one normally grown in the West (also most commonly available in Japan) is the green neck type, which

has the fading pale-green part at the top of the main body. The most flavoursome ones come on to the market in winter. The leaves are often pickled or cooked in miso soup.

Aroma and flavour

Daikon has an aroma similar to radish and a slightly pungent flavour which is not as bitter as radish. It can be eaten either cooked or uncooked, and is also useful for adding flavour when served as a condiment or in a dipping sauce. The raw texture is crunchy, and, when cooked, daikon becomes fairly soft but does not disintegrate.

Culinary uses

Daikon is used in Japanese cooking for its flavour and texture, and not for its nutrition; it is nearly 95 per cent water. If served raw, it is finely shredded and used as a crystal-white garnish for *sashimi* and other fish dishes. The shreds mixed with carrot shreds make a good vinegared salad. A subtly pungent dipping sauce is made with shoyu.

Daikon is also used for simmering in dishes with meat or poultry, since it withstands slow cooking, absorbs the flavour and juice of other ingredients, and does not easily disintegrate. Various pickles are made with daikon, too.

Above: Many vegetables that are familiar to Westerners may differ in size, shape or taste. Japanese cucumbers, for example, are smaller and thinner than Western ones.

Preparation and cooking

Select a firm daikon with a shiny, undamaged skin. When cut crossways, the cut surface should be smooth and watery. If the flesh has an opaque, snowflake-like spongy pattern, discard it. Always peel away the outer skin.

Daikon can sometimes be very hard and stringy; in such cases it will be too bitter to eat raw. Instead, cut it into chunks and use in a slow simmering dish, or dice it and put it in soup. Simmering daikon slowly lets it absorb the flavour of the other ingredients.

When cutting daikon into slices or cylinders, shave off the top edges so that they will not cook first.

Storage

Daikon keeps fairly well for a week or two in the refrigerator, but it is best used within three or four days.

Daikon and shoyu dipping sauce

This sauce goes well with grilled or pan-fried fish, meat and vegetables or with hotpot dishes, and serves two to four people.

1 Cut about 5cm/2in from the top of a daikon, then trim and peel. Finely grate the daikon, retaining the juice as well. Place in a small serving bowl.

2 Chop a spring onion (scallion) and add to the grated daikon.

3 Serve with lemon wedges for squeezing and a little shoyu in small individual bowls or plates. Each person mixes his or her own sauce using the daikon mixture, lemon juice, shoyu and a drop of chilli oil, if you like.

COOK'S TIP

It's sometimes difficult to find fresh, juicy daikon, though a reputable Caribbean grocer is a good place to try. A fresh daikon is at least 7.5cm/3in in diameter and sounds very dense and heavy when you pat it. Old daikon looks dehydrated and should not be used. Use fresh radishes instead.

Below: Daikon, a member of the radish family, resembles a very large, long, white carrot.

KABU

The turnip, originally grown in the Mediterranean coastal regions and Afghanistan, has been grown in Japan for over 1,300 years. Many types have been crossbred but the most commonly used, kabu, is a small, round-shaped one. This Japanese turnip is far smaller than Western varieties.

The kabu flesh contains sugar, protein, calcium, vitamin C and fibre.

Aroma and flavour

The smell of Japanese kabu is similar to that of a radish. It has a subtle flavour, and, when cooked, develops a slightly bitter-sweet taste.

Culinary uses

Both leaves and root are very good for pickles, and many regions have their own speciality kabu pickles. When kabu is cooked, the central part becomes soft fairly quickly but, just like daikon, it is protected by the hard outer layer so it does not disintegrate. Kabu is good for hotpot dishes as well as for soup.

Preparation and cooking

Although the outer skin is not as hard as daikon, kabu should also be peeled before cooking. However, it is not normally grated and eaten raw, as the flavour is not sufficiently pungent.

Storage

Kabu will keep well for a few days if stored in the refrigerator.

Right: Kabu (turnip)

Shredding daikon

1 Cut about 5cm/2in from the top of a daikon, then trim and peel. Place the daikon, cut side down, on a board. Using a sharp knife, cut off a thin slice. Continue until the daikon is too small to slice.

2 Put all the daikon sheets together, one on top of the other. Using the knife, cut the sheets crossways into thin shreds and place the shreds in ice-cold water. Drain and dry with kitchen paper.

SATOIMO

This small, oval-shaped potato, which originated in India, is one of the oldest vegetables used in Japan and is also very popular in China. Underneath its hairy, striped, dark skin there is a unique slipperiness, which makes the vegetable very easy to peel. It is widely available at Asian food stores. If you can't find it, taro can be substituted.

Aroma and flavour

Satoimo has a faint, potato-like aroma, but the flavour is much richer than ordinary potato and interestingly sweet and bitter at the same time. It also has a dense yet fluffy texture.

Culinary uses

Plain boiled or steamed satoimo, dipped in shoyu, is a popular snack in Japan. It is also excellent in simmered dishes, such as *oden* (hotpot), and winter soups.

Above: Satoimo, a member of the potato family, has a unique slippery coating under its hairy, striped skin.

Above and below: Satsuma-imo (sweet potato) can vary in its size, colour, taste and texture.

Preparation and cooking

To peel, boil whole, then the skin comes off very easily. Wipe off the sliminess with kitchen paper before using.

Storage

Satoimo keeps fairly well, for up to five days, if stored in a cool, airy place away from direct sunlight.

SATSUMA-IMO

Originating in Central America, the sweet potato was introduced to Japan via Spain, the Philippines, China and Okinawa. It first arrived in Satsuma, the southernmost area of Japan, hence its Japanese name, meaning satsuma-potato.

There are numerous types of sweet potato even among the Japanese varieties. The colour of the skin varies from scarlet red to mauve, and the flesh varies from a rich yellow colour to dark mauve. The varieties available in the West are generally tougher and less sweet than Japanese ones.

Aroma and flavour

It has a rich potato aroma and slightly sweet flavour.

Culinary uses

Sweet potato is most often used for simmered, steamed and fried dishes and is good for cooking on a barbecue. It can also be used as an ingredient in savoury cakes and desserts, and plain boiled or steamed satsuma-imo makes a tasty snack.

Preparation and cooking

As sweet potato contains a high percentage of water, it easily becomes over-soft and soggy. To avoid this, it is best to steam rather than boil sweet potato.

Storage

Sweet potato keeps well for up to one week if stored in a cool, airy place away from direct sunlight.

KABOCHA

This vegetable plays an essential part in Japanese cooking. Originally from Central America, this Japanese squash is the result of various crossbreedings over the last century. It has a dark green and ragged skin and is much smaller than Western squash varieties. The dense flesh is a rich yellow colour and, when boiled, becomes sweet and fluffy. Although it is highly calorific, kabocha is regarded as a health food for its nutritional content, containing both carotene and vitamin A. Along with many other varieties of the squash family, it is now widely available.

Aroma and flavour

Kabocha has a mild chestnut aroma, and the flavour is also similar to, but not as sweet as, the chestnut. The texture is dense, similar to a moist sweet potato.

Culinary uses

To appreciate its delicate flavour, this vegetable is best simply steamed or boiled. It is also used for frying in tempura, as well as for simmering with other vegetables and chicken. The seeds are full of protein, and can be dry-roasted and eaten as a snack on their own or as a tasty accompaniment to drinks.

*Above:
Kabocha has a
dark and ragged
green skin and the
flesh can range from
yellow to orange.*

Salt-steamed kabocha chips

This is a nutritious snack, much healthier than chips (French fries).

1 In a steamer, lightly steam whole kabocha over a high heat for 5–6 minutes until the outer skin becomes soft enough to peel. If using a pan, boil a little water, about 1cm/½in deep, then place the kabocha in it and cook for 3 minutes. Remove from the pan, and cut in half.

2 Using your fingers, take out the seeds from the centre and discard them. (Alternatively, the seeds can be dried, roasted and eaten.)

3 Place the kabocha on a chopping board with the cut-side down and, using a knife, scrape off about a third of the hard skin in strips.

Preparation and cooking

This is a very hard vegetable and not easily cut. It is therefore advisable to lightly steam whole kabocha first in

4 Cut into bitesize chunks, and place back into the steamer. Sprinkle over a pinch of coarse salt. Cover and steam over a high heat for about 8–10 minutes until the flesh can be pierced by a cocktail stick.

5 If using a pan, lay the kabocha pieces in the base of a shallow, flat-based pan, then add 45–75ml/ 3–5 tbsp water at the side (not on the kabocha) and sprinkle over a pinch of coarse salt.

6 Cover and cook over a medium heat for about 4 minutes. Reduce the heat to the lowest setting and cook for a further 8–10 minutes.

7 Remove the pan from the heat and leave the kabocha to settle, still covered, for about 5 minutes.

order to soften it slightly before cutting into large chunks. This is most easily done in a steamer, though a large pan will also suffice.

Although the skin is tough, do not remove all of it since the flesh closest to the skin is the tastiest part. Cutting off occasional strips of the skin will create a pretty marbled effect through the contrast of the outer green skin with the inner yellow flesh. This is a moist vegetable that easily disintegrates, so do not cook in too much liquid. An average kabocha will serve four to eight people.

Storage

Choose a heavy, dense kabocha with a dark green, hard, undamaged skin. It is a tough vegetable and keeps well for a week if stored whole in the refrigerator.

NAGA-IMO

This mountain potato, also known as yama-imo, meaning long potato, still grows wild in Japan, as well as being cultivated. The shiny, snowy white flesh is very slippery, and it is for this quality that it is most appreciated. Naga-imo is available in winter from Japanese supermarkets.

Aroma and flavour

Though naga-imo has little aroma, and has a bitter-sweet flavour, it is cherished by the Japanese for its rare, moist sticky texture.

Culinary uses

Among its many uses, the most popular is to grate the flesh to make a slimy thick soup that is eaten with barley rice. Naga-imo can also be shredded for use in vinegared salads, and sliced for frying.

Preparation and cooking

Naga-imo is mostly used uncooked, either grated or shredded. Once peeled, the flesh discolours, so eat immediately or sprinkle with vinegar or lemon juice.

Storage

Like most vegetables of this kind, naga-imo keep fairly well for up to one week in a cool, airy place away from direct sunlight. Once peeled, do not keep, as the white flesh turns an unappealing grey colour.

Left: Naga-imo has an unusual slippery flesh, so rub with a wet cloth after peeling for easy handling.

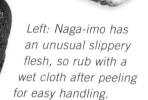

Below: Vacuum-packed gingko nuts

Right: Shelled and blanched gingko nuts

GINGKO NUT

The Japanese maple tree, *Icho*, bears the exquisite gingko nut, known as ginnan in Japan. It is a favourite delicacy and a traditional accompaniment to sake. The word gingko or ginkgo is a corruption of ginkyo, another Japanese name for the maple tree. Ginko nut is available either fresh in its shell, shelled in packets, or shelled and cooked in cans or jars. A dried variety is also available.

Aroma and flavour

Gingko nut has very little aroma but has a fairly prominent milky flavour with a hint of bitterness, which adds vivid freshness to simmered dishes.

Culinary uses

Fried or lightly roasted gingko nuts sprinkled with salt are often served as an hors d'oeuvre. They can also be used for fried and simmered dishes, and in soups.

Preparation and cooking

To break the hard shell, place the nut with the join part vertically on a chopping board and bang on top with a rolling pin. The thin brown membrane should be removed, and the nuts blanched before use in any dish. The best method is to boil the nuts in just enough water to cover them and rub off the thin brown membrane with the back of a ladle. If dried gingko nuts are being used, they need to be soaked in water for several hours before use. Drain before adding to soups and simmered dishes.

Storage

The whole gingko in an undamaged shell keeps for a long time, but once broken, use within a few days. Store unused soaked or canned gingko nuts in fresh water in the refrigerator for up to three days.

KURI

This Japanese variety of chestnut is grown throughout Japan and the southern Korean peninsula, and has a more triangular shape and smoother shell than the Chinese, European or American varieties. Kuri represents autumn and is a useful way to express the season in dishes for *kaiseki* (formal banquet) or tea-ceremony cooking. Apart from fresh kuri, peeled chestnuts are also available in cans, either cooked or uncooked.

Aroma and flavour

The transformation of kuri from its hard whitish raw state to a bright yellow jewel when cooked is quite striking. It is this golden yellow colour that makes it such a valued ingredient, along with its almost sesame-like aroma and subtly sweet, nutty flavour apparent in its cooked form.

Chestnut rice

With the golden colour of kuri against the simple white of rice, this is a beautiful, as well as delicious, dish.

SERVES FOUR

INGREDIENTS
   225g/8oz/generous 1 cup
     Japanese short grain rice
   90g/3½oz fresh chestnuts, shelled
     and peeled, or 150g/5oz cooked,
     peeled chestnuts
   5ml/1 tsp sea salt
   25ml/1½ tbsp sake or white wine
   10ml/2 tsp black sesame seeds,
     lightly toasted, to garnish

1 Wash the rice well, changing the water several times, until the water runs clear, then put the rice in a fine mesh strainer, and leave to drain for an hour. Put the rice in a deep pan.

2 If using fresh chestnuts, cut them in half and rinse in cold water. Drain and place on top of the rice.

3 Dissolve the salt in 300ml/½ pint/ 1¼ cups water and add to the pan. Add extra water, if necessary, to fully cover the rice and chestnuts. Pour in the sake or wine.

4 Cover and cook over a high heat for 5–8 minutes until the mixture begins to bubble. Lower the heat and simmer for 10 minutes until the water is absorbed.

5 Leave to stand, still covered, for about 15 minutes, then gently mix the chestnuts into the rice. Try not to break up the chestnuts as you mix them in. Serve in individual rice bowls sprinkled with the black sesame seeds.

Culinary uses

Kuri is one of the most useful and versatile ingredients found in Japanese cooking. It can be eaten just grilled (broiled) or boiled as a snack, or used as a means to express the season on hors d'oeuvres trays. It can also be mashed to make various sizes and shapes of sweet wagashi (Japanese cakes). *Kuri gohan* (rice cooked with chestnuts) is one

Left: Cooked sweet kuri (Japanese chestnuts)

of the more popular traditional dishes enjoyed by the Japanese each autumn. *Kuri kinton*, cooked and mashed kuri with added sugar made into a shiny sweet paste, is a better version of ordinary *kinto,* which is made with sweet potato, and is one of the dishes at New Year's celebration meals.

Preparation and cooking

Make a slit in the shell before boiling or grilling (broiling) to make peeling easier. When peeling, remove the outer shell and the thin brown membrane attached to the flesh, otherwise it will taste bitter.

Storage

Whole chestnuts keep well for a few weeks. Once peeled, use immediately.

Left: When purchasing hakusai, (Chinese cabbage), choose densely clinging, tall round ones with curly green, crisp leaves.

Aroma and flavour

Hakusai has a faint, fresh aroma and a very subtle cabbage flavour. The main quality of this vegetable is neither its aroma nor flavour but its crunchiness and versatility when cooked. As it absorbs the flavour of other ingredients, it is almost always cooked with meat, poultry, fish and other vegetables in a strong sauce.

Culinary uses

Salted hakusai is one of the usual dishes served to accompany plain cooked rice at the Japanese breakfast table. The salt takes the chill off the otherwise hard, iceberg texture of the thick, white core and brings out the colour. It is also used in simmered dishes, hotpots and steamed dishes: when cooked, the green part becomes more vivid and bright, and the white part translucent.

The straight, white trunk becomes flexible when cooked, so it can be rolled either on its own or with spinach, often with minced (ground) meat, poultry or fish stuffed inside, and then simmered. This succulent vegetable is very good for any soup dish: cook with chopped bacon and season with salt, pepper and a drop of shoyu. It's a very easy and delicious dish.

HAKUSAI

Although its origin can be traced back to the Mediterranean, Chinese cabbage is grown mainly in East Asia around China, the Korean peninsula and Japan. Introduced into Japan from China at the end of the 19th century, and developed to suit the local climate and tastes, it is now one of the most popular ingredients in Japanese cooking.

The Japanese variety, hakusai, meaning white vegetable, is larger and the outer leaves are in fact greener than the Chinese cabbage now widely available in the West. The leaves are also tightly crinkled and inside they are a bright yellow colour with a thick, white core. There are offsprings of this variety such as santo-sai and hiroshima-na, but these are not available in the West.

Hakusai is a winter vegetable and supplies otherwise scarce vitamin C during the cold months.

Preparation and cooking

Trim the base, then separate the leaves and wash thoroughly. The white part is very crunchy when raw, but when cooked it quickly becomes soft and stringy and not very easy to chew. So, always cut the leaves crossways against the fibre into bitesize pieces.

Storage

Tightly wrapped, this vegetable will keep well in the refrigerator for quite a long time. So, although it is a relatively large vegetable, a few leaves can be taken out as required over a period of up to two weeks.

KOMATSUNA

Among the numerous kinds of green vegetables, komatsuna is one of the most popular in Japan. It is a member of the radish family and has been crossbred in Japan. Unlike other radishes it does not grow a bulbous tuber. The leaf is smooth and soft, and the stem is thin and delicate. As it is resistant to cold weather, this deep green vegetable used to provide a good supply of winter leaves but today it is grown in the greenhouse all year round. It is not always available in the West but can be substituted by spinach.

Aroma and flavour

Komatsuna has a very subtle aroma and flavour. It is mainly used for its colour as well as for its vitamin content.

Below: Both komatsuna, front, and horenso (spinach), back, should be used on the day of purchase as the leaves wilt quickly.

Culinary uses

Although komatsuna can never take centre stage even in home cooking, it is a very useful green vegetable and commonly used in Japan. Cooked with meat, it provides balance to any fat, and in soup it gives a striking dark green background colour for other ingredients such as white tofu and pink prawns (shrimp). It is also used for pickles.

Preparation and cooking

Wash thoroughly before use and cook very lightly, otherwise the green colour quickly turns an unappetizing grey.

HORENSO

Originating in Western Asia, spinach can be classified into two main types: Eastern and Western. The Eastern variety was brought to Japan from China in the 16th century and commonly has a triangular, zigzag-edged leaf, which is pointed at the top, and a scarlet root. Western varities have a rounder leaf.

Horenso has thin leaves, a delicate texture and a mild, sweet flavour. Recently an East–West crossbreed has been developed, which is also now commonly available in Japan. Spinach is very rich in vitamins A, B_1, B_2 and C, as well as iron and calcium.

Aroma and flavour

Japanese spinach has a rich grass aroma and a sweet flavour with a hint of bitterness, particularly in the soft lower stem.

Culinary uses

The most popular use for horenso in Japanese cooking is *ohitashi* (cooked salad with dashi stock). Lightly cooked spinach is also tossed with seed and nut dressings.

Preparation and cooking

Wash thoroughly before use as spinach grows touching the ground and earth gets inside the stems. Always lightly boil first, to get rid of the slight bitterness, except those young spinach leaves that can be used in a salad.

Storage

As is the case with all delicate green vegetables, both komatsuna and spinach are best used on the day of purchase. Even if kept in the coolest part of the refrigerator the leaves will start to wilt almost immediately. There are canned or frozen cooked spinach on the market, but these are rather mushy and their use is limited.

SHUNGIKU

Chrysanthemum leaves are, contrary to what the name suggests, not actually leaves from the chrysanthemum flowers, but from the chrysanthemum vegetable. This vegetable plant has two to three shoots, on which grow several long, narrow zigzag leaves.

Originating in Mediterranean coastal areas, it has only recently become very popular in South-east Asia. It is full of calcium, iron, carotene and vitamin C. There are variations in leaf size and smaller ones can be eaten raw.

Shungiku is cut for eating when the plant reaches about 15–20cm/6–8in high and is brought to market with the stems intact; the stems are also very succulent when cooked.

Aroma and flavour

The leaves have a strong, herbal aroma, and a delicately bitter flavour. The yellowish green leaves turn bright green when cooked, and retain firm texture even if cooked for a long time.

Preparation and cooking

Wash shungiku well, particularly if it is to be eaten raw, and cut off the hard part of the stem. The most cherished quality of this vegetable is its unique aroma, so cook very lightly. To eat the leaves raw, pinch them from the stem.

Culinary uses

Shungiku is indispensable for Japanese hotpot dishes. Its exquisite aroma can also be appreciated in a warm salad, if cooked lightly and tossed in a dressing. It also can be simmered and even fried, as the leaves do not easily disintegrate.

Storage

This relatively tough vegetable keeps fairly well; it will store for up to three days, if kept in the refrigerator.

Left: Shungiku (chrysanthemum leaf); in Japan, medium-size leaves are the most valued, as they are the best for cooking.

Below: In keeping with its size, negi, a giant spring onion, has a robust aroma and flavour.

Preparation and cooking

Wash thoroughly and trim the base of the stem. Negi should be cooked very lightly, as when overcooked it has an unpleasant slimy texture. For sauces and soups, it is normally very finely chopped. For hotpots, cut crossways diagonally.

NEGI

This giant spring onion (scallion), which is 30–50cm/ 12–20in long and 1–2cm/½–¾in in diameter, is a unique Japanese vegetable and, even in Japan, is generally available only in the Tokyo area and eastern Japan. It may look like a slim leek, but the texture is a lot more delicate, rather like that of the spring onion, and it does not have a hard core like the leek. Although the long white part in preference to the green part is mainly used for Japanese cooking, the mineral and vitamin contents are much greater in the green. It is sometimes available at Asian supermarkets.

Aroma and flavour

Negi has a pungent aroma and also a strong onion flavour.

Culinary uses

In Japanese cooking this leek-type vegetable is mainly used finely chopped and added to sauces or soups as a herbal condiment. It gives a fresh, pungent final touch and a decorative look to plain shoyu or hot miso soup.

The white part, finely shredded, is also used to garnish *sashimi* or any other fish dish; the curled shreds, which resemble silver hair, make an interesting alternative to daikon shreds. It is used for grilling (broiling), in particular with *yakitori* (skewered grilled chicken) or any other meat. *Sukiyaki* (pan-cooked beef in sweet shoyu sauce) and *shabu shabu* (pot-cooked beef in soup) also usually include diagonally chopped negi.

For grilling in recipes such as *yakitori*, cut straight across into 3–4cm/1¼–1½in pieces, and cut other ingredients in the same way. For decorative curls, see below.

Storage

As with the spring onion, the green part starts to wilt and change colour within about two days even in the refrigerator, but the main white part keeps fairly well for up to three days.

Making spring onion curls

1 Choose small, slim spring onions. Trim off most of the green leaves to leave a 7.5cm/3in length.

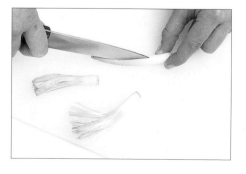

2 Shred the spring onions lengthways to within about 1cm/½in of the root end. Take care not to cut through the root completely.

3 Place the shredded spring onions in a small bowl of iced water and chill for 15–20 minutes, or until the shredded ends have curled.

RAKKYO

This bulb vegetable originated in the Himalayas and China. It grows in a bunch of six to seven small, thin oval-shaped bulbs, about 7.5cm/3in long. The body is milky white or with a faint purple hue. It is picked young, with each bulb weighing 2–5g/¹⁄₁₆–⅛oz, but some grow to 10g/¼oz after a year. Rakkyo is available in Japanese markets from late spring to early summer, when many households make rakkyo pickles to last throughout the year. When in season, it is available in Asian stores.

Aroma and flavour

Rakkyo is the Japanese equivalent of garlic; eat just one and the odour will linger on your breath for the rest of the day. It has an intense onion smell with a hint of garlic. Apart from the smell, its flavour is too sharp to eat raw, but once pickled, the brine brings out the high sugar content, which makes it not only more palatable but an ideal addition to hot rice.

Culinary uses

Rakkyo is almost always pickled, either in brine, in sweet vinegar or marinated for a shorter time in shoyu. It is served with rice or Japanese curry.

Preparation and cooking

Trim the root and the top, and wash thoroughly. If the rakkyo is very young, pickle immediately in brine; otherwise blanch quickly and then marinate in shoyu. It will be ready to eat after a week. The longer rakkyo is marinated the milder the taste becomes, but the smell always persists.

Storage

Like onions, the central core of rakkyo starts growing a green shoot after a while, and eventually the whole bulb dries out. It is best to pickle the vegetable immediately after purchase.

Right: Myoga

Above: Pickled rakkyo

MYOGA

This uniquely shaped vegetable is actually the flower bud of the myoga plant, which originated in tropical Asia. The bud grows directly from the root stem in summer in the wild, while cultivated buds are exposed to light twice before picking, to obtain their healthy red colour. Some varieties of the bud grow in autumn, and these usually have a richer flavour than the summer ones.

If the bud is left to grow, it forms a 50–60cm/20–24in long thin stem, which is eaten in winter. Myoga is one of the more unusual Japanese vegetables sometimes available in the West.

Aroma and flavour

Myoga smells and tastes more like a herb than a vegetable, and has a strong, piercing aroma. This crunchy vegetable has a bitter flavour making it unsuitable for eating raw. When pickled in brine for several weeks, the taste becomes milder and sweeter, but, like rakkyo, the sharp aroma remains.

Culinary uses

The most valuable quality of myoga is its unique aroma. It is used for dipping sauces and as a garnish to *sashimi* or other fish dishes. It is also used for cooked or vinegared vegetables, in soups or for tempura.

Preparation and cooking

Wash off the mud thoroughly. For pickling, use whole or cut in half, then finely slice when ready to eat. For all other purposes, it is better to slice thinly lengthways and use sparingly. Blanch first if using in a salad.

Storage

Myoga is not prone to wilting, but its distinctive aroma will soon fade if stored in the refrigerator. Store myoga at room temperature and use as soon as possible.

GOBO

This thin, brown burdock root was first introduced to ancient Japan from China as a herbal medicine, but it was soon developed by the Japanese into a form suitable for normal consumption. Raw gobo is inedible; when cooked, the grey flesh is quite stringy but it adds a unique texture and flavour to a dish. Its main nutritional content is sugar, but it is also high in fibre and calcium. Fresh gobo is sometimes available at Asian supermarkets, where frozen or canned, cooked gobo is also sold.

Aroma and flavour

Gobo has a unique sesame-like aroma and a slightly bitter flavour when raw. When cooked its sweetness becomes more pronounced.

Culinary uses

The most popular dish that features this root vegetable is *kinpira*, stir-fried shredded carrot and gobo with chilli and shoyu (soy sauce). It is also used for tempura, simmering dishes and in soups. It makes delicious rice-bran pickles, too.

Preparation and cooking

Scrub the thin outer skin, then shred with a sharp knife as if sharpening a pencil, and soak the root in water for 15 minutes to remove the bitterness. Alternatively, cut gobo into chunks and simmer slowly for a long time.

Storage

Gobo is a tough little root and keeps well even outside the refrigerator for several days.

TAKENOKO

Bamboo shoot is one of the popular vegetables in South-east Asia and is widely available in cans. The Japanese cherish the fresh young shoots, which are inevitably a very seasonal delicacy, only available from late spring to early summer. Most of the content of bamboo shoot is water and it has little nutritional value. Instead, it is appreciated for its pleasant, natural look and crisp texture.

The Japanese make use of the outer, hard brown barks for wrapping sushi or other rice-based lunches. Takenoko is also available pickled as *menma*, and cooked in jars and cans, or also in a dried form at Asian supermarkets.

Below: Takenoko (bamboo shoot) is available in a variety of forms; freshly peeled and cut, back, as a bark for wrapping sushi, left, and as dried strips, front.

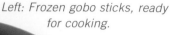

Left: Frozen gobo sticks, ready for cooking.

Aroma and flavour

Fresh takenoko has a very subtle, earthy aroma and a delicately bitter flavour, which improves with age. Whatever its age, the vegetable is capable of absorbing flavour from the sauce it is cooked with, while retaining its own taste.

Culinary uses

In Japanese cooking, takenoko is almost always slowly simmered, so that its delicate flavour will not be spoiled. Simply cooked fresh bamboo shoots in dashi sauce is one of the most popular dishes at Japanese restaurants. The young, tender shoot is also good for *takenoko gohan* (rice cooked with bamboo shoots), while the older shoots are best reserved for slow cooking with other vegetables and chicken, or for stir-frying.

Preparation and cooking

The already cleaned young shoot can be sliced or cut into bitesize chunks and cooked immediately, but older ones should be boiled before use. For this, it is advisable to use the milky water in which rice was washed, as the rice bran in the water reduces the bamboo shoot's bitterness. Canned bamboo shoots are ready cooked, so they just need to be rinsed and drained; dried bamboo shoots must be soaked in water for 2–3 hours before use.

Storage

Fresh, uncooked whole bamboo shoot keeps well in the refrigerator for over a week but it will gradually lose its moisture. Most of the fresh ones on the market are usually boiled, and do not last long, so use within two days. Canned, cooked shoots, once opened, should be stored in the refrigerator in fresh water that is changed daily, and used within a week.

Below: Fresh renkon (lotus root) is available in large quantities in winter at Asian supermarkets. Canned or frozen renkon are available all year round, and come peeled, sliced and cooked.

RENKON

Although renkon refers specifically to the lotus root, the lotus plant itself has a long association with Buddhism and has been a regular feature in temple ponds in Japan since ancient times. The first evidence of serving its roots as food was found in a book dating from AD 713.

The root normally has about four sections, and looks like a long, narrow balloon with a few knots, and although the outer skin is light beige, upon peeling it reveals a white, crispy flesh. Renkon has several vertical holes running through to the base, which reveal a flower-like pattern when the root is cut in cross-section, adding a unique look to any dish. Nutritionally, it contains mainly starch with 15 per cent sugar and little else.

Aroma and flavour

Renkon has very little aroma and flavour when raw.

Culinary uses

Renkon's crunchiness as well as its unique pattern is greatly appreciated in Japanese cooking. It is used for simmered dishes, tempura, sushi and for salads with vinegar dressing. It is always dressed or cooked with vinegar, which brings out its sweetness.

Preparation and cooking

Trim the hard part from both ends and peel. Cut into rings and plunge in vinegar and water (see right) to avoid discolouration. Cook in lightly acidulated boiling water. Do not use iron pans.

Storage

Select firm and undamaged renkon. Although the outer skin discolours quickly, the inside keeps fairly fresh for up to five days if stored in the refrigerator.

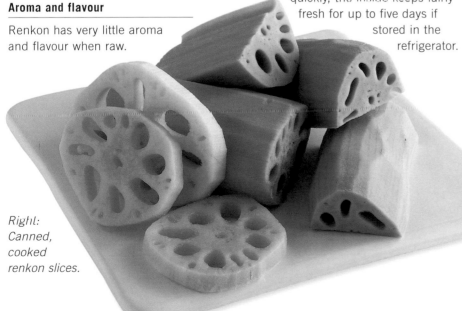

Right: Canned, cooked renkon slices.

Preparing renkon

When sliced and cooked with vinegar, renkon can be used in a salad or marinated in a mixture of rice vinegar, sugar and some salt.

1 Chop the renkon into sections, trim the hard part at the ends of the root and peel.

2 Cut into rings and immediately soak in a mixture of vinegar and water (120ml/4fl oz/½ cup water to 30–45ml/2–3 tbsp vinegar) to prevent discoloration. Allow to soak for about 5 minutes.

3 Boil enough water to cover the renkon, add 15–30ml/1–2 tbsp vinegar and the renkon rings, then cook for about 2 minutes until soft but still crisp. Remove from the heat and drain.

DRIED BEANS

As a major source of protein, beans have always been very important ingredients in Japanese cooking and, since the days of meat prohibition, the Japanese have developed numerous ways to cook with them.

Daizu, known as soya bean in the West, features prominently in Japanese cuisine, as do black and green beans, which are part of the same family. Also as popular are azuki, also known as aduki, which first became known in the West as a health food. In Japan they are known as "king of the beans" and they are reputed to be good for the liver and kidneys. Their use in Japanese cooking is far from healthy, however, as they are almost always made into an heavily sweetened paste for use in dessert or cake making.

Other beans such as kidney, haricot (navy), broad (fava), Burma and lima, and peas such as green, cow, chick and pigeon, all form part of the Japanese diet. These can be used in both fresh and dried forms. Many are cooked and eaten as snacks, and their appearance in the market is a welcomed signal of the new season.

Below: Black and yellow soya beans

Boiled soya beans
These simply boiled soya beans are not only delicious but also very nutritious and filling.

SERVES FOUR TO SIX

INGREDIENTS
  275g/10oz/1½ cups dried
    soya beans
  1 carrot, peeled and sliced
  5cm/2in square konbu
  2.5ml/½ tsp dashi-no-moto
    dissolved in 250ml/8fl oz/
    1 cup water
  2.5ml/½ tsp coarse salt
  22.5ml/4½ tsp sugar
  37.5ml/2½ tbsp shoyu

1 Soak the soya beans in 3–4 times their volume of cold water for at least 24 hours. Discard any beans that remain on the surface.

2 Drain, then boil the beans gently in fresh water, uncovered, for about 10 minutes. Drain again then rinse under cold running water.

3 Slice the carrot into rounds, par-boil in salted water, then drain.

4 Using kitchen scissors, cut the konbu into tiny squares, of a similar size to the beans.

5 Mix the dashi water, salt, sugar and shoyu in a large pan and bring to the boil. Add the carrot, konbu and the beans, and simmer, covered, over a medium heat for 30 minutes, or until almost all the liquid has been absorbed and the beans are tender. Stir the beans occasionally during cooking. Serve, hot or cold.

SOYA BEANS

Originally from China, where they were once considered sacred, the soya bean may not play a star role on the stage of Japanese cooking, but it is certainly the most vital ingredient backstage. It is the basis of the most important Japanese sauces, such as miso and shoyu, and, of course, tofu is made from it. There are numerous products all over the world that would not be the same without the use of soya beans for their flavour, texture, or simply as a binding agent.

Daizu, or soya bean, means big bean (as opposed to azuki meaning small bean), and there are basically three colours of the Japanese daizu family: yellow, green and black. Soya beans contain all the nutritional advantages of animal products but without the disadvantages. They are high in vegetable protein, sugar, fat and fibre and rich in vitamin B_1 and B_2. For this reason soya beans are called "the beef of the field" and are used to make meat substitutes as well. Yellow soya beans, the most commonly used variety, are available at health food stores as well as from some supermarkets.

Aroma and flavour

Soya beans have a distinctive roasted aroma, and a faint peanut-like flavour.

Culinary uses

The dried yellow beans are also called miso beans as their main use is for making miso. They are also used in the production of shoyu, natto (fermented bean) and tofu. The oil is useful for cooking, too. Soya beans can be simmered with other vegetables and chicken, or roasted to serve with drinks.

Dried green beans are used for their light green colour in Japanese sweets (candy), and black beans are mainly used for simmered dishes or they are roasted. The black soya bean is particularly appreciated for its shiny black colour, and is one of the ingredients for New Year's feasts.

Preparation and cooking

Except when intending to roast, dried beans should be soaked for 24 hours before cooking, then those that are still floating must be discarded.

Storage

Dried beans keep almost indefinitely if stored in a cool, airy place out of direct sunlight.

SOYA BEAN PRODUCTS

There are numerous soya bean products in Japan, from powdered to fermented and tofu. As tofu products play such an important part in Japanese cooking they are treated separately.

Right: Clockwise from left, black, yellow and green soya flour

Kinako

This is a yellow soya bean flour, although sometimes green soya beans are used to make green kinako. Mixed with the same volume of sugar and a pinch of salt, kinako is rolled in lightly boiled, soft mochi cakes to serve as a snack. Kinako is also used to make wagashi (Japanese cakes). This flour can normally easily be found at Japanese supermarkets.

Above: Natto (fermented soya beans), packed in a straw pouch. They are normally sold, particularly in the West, in a plastic container.

Natto

These fermented soya beans are rather smelly and slimy, and strange to the Western palate, but they go well with plain boiled rice. Mix some chopped spring onion (scallion), mustard and grated daikon with the natto, season with shoyu, and stir well. Put a couple of teaspoonfuls on hot rice and eat.

Storage

Soya flours should be kept in an airtight container in a cool, dry dark place. Keep natto in the refrigerator and eat within two weeks.

Cooking and soaking soya beans

• If you are short of time, the long soaking process can be speeded up: first, cook the beans in boiling water for 2 minutes, then remove the pan from the heat. Cover and leave for about 2 hours. Drain, rinse and cover with plenty of fresh cold water before cooking.

• Do not add salt to beans during cooking as this will cause them to toughen. Cook the beans first, then taste and season with a little salt and black pepper, if you wish.

AZUKI BEANS

Also known as aduki beans outside Japan, azuki (small beans) are probably the most popular Japanese variety of bean in the West. This bean has very high levels of starch (over 50 per cent), as well as protein and fibre, and some vitamin B1. It is regarded in Japan as a very healthy food.

There are various sizes of azuki, and colours include red, green, yellow and white. Most commonly used is the red variety, mainly for Japanese cakes and desserts. The green bean (mung bean), is used to make harusame (bean vermicelli) and beansprouts are grown from it. Azuki are widely available at supermarkets and health food stores.

Aroma and flavour

Probably due to the high starch content, azuki beans have a faint sweet aroma and a chestnut-like flavour.

Culinary uses

Azuki beans can be simmered in sauce or cooked with rice to make *sekihan* (red rice) for celebrations, but they are mainly used for making *an,* a sweet paste, for wagashi (Japanese cakes).

An, sweet bean paste

There are ready-made bean pastes in cans or they can be bought in powdered form to be reconstituted, but making fresh *an* from scratch is a far superior and easy option. This recipe makes *tsubushi-an* (crushed paste) and is used for making *o'hagi* (sweet, paste-wrapped, glutinous rice balls) and for stuffing mochi cakes. It is also very good spread on toast.

MAKES ABOUT 500G/1¼LB

INGREDIENTS
    200g/7oz/1 cup azuki or
      black beans
    200g/7oz/1 cup sugar
    salt

1 Put the beans in a large pan, add water to cover well and bring to the boil. Drain.

2 Return the drained beans to the pan, add 750ml/1¼ pints/3 cups water and soak the beans for about 24 hours. Discard any beans that remain floating. Place the soaked beans, still in the water in the pan, over a high heat and bring to a rolling boil.

3 Simmer over a very low heat, half-covered, for about 1 hour. Add water from time to time and stir frequently with a wooden spoon until the beans are very soft and the water is almost entirely absorbed.

4 Add the sugar and stir well. Keep stirring until the beans are thoroughly crushed. Add a pinch of salt and, using a large pestle or a rolling pin, mash into a smooth paste.

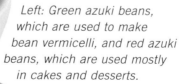

Left: Green azuki beans, which are used to make bean vermicelli, and red azuki beans, which are used mostly in cakes and desserts.

An also makes a rich addition to Western desserts, such as ice creams, fruit salads, and mousses. Simply arrange *an* around or on top of the dessert.

Preparation and cooking

Discard any damaged beans. For making sweet bean paste, soak the azuki beans in plenty of water for 24 hours before cooking, and discard those that remain floating. Do not soak if you are making dishes where you wish to retain the shape, colour and aroma of the beans, such as for a decoration for a dessert.

Storage

Azuki beans keep almost indefinitely if stored well away from direct sunlight.

FRESH BEANS

Young beans, such as eda-mame (green beans in the pod), soramame (broad/ fava beans), saya-ingen (green beans) and saya-éndo (mangetouts/snow peas), are often used in Japanese cooking. Eda-mame and soramame are also boiled and eaten as a snack.

Boiled eda-mame

This is a good way to appreciate young soya beans in the pod.

1 Separate the pods from the stalks if they are still attached. Trim off the stem end. Sprinkle the pods generously with salt and rub into the bean pods with your hands. Leave for 15 minutes.

2 Boil plenty of water in a large pan, then add the beans and boil over a high heat for 7–10 minutes, or until the beans inside the pods are tender but still crunchy. Drain immediately and refresh briefly under running water.

3 Serve hot or cold in a basket or a bowl with drinks. For extra saltiness, sprinkle with a little salt. To eat, it is acceptable to squeeze the pods with your teeth to push out the beans into your mouth.

EDA-MAME

In Japan, when fresh, young green beans in their hairy pods start appearing in the market, the people know summer has arrived. These beans are called eda-mame meaning branch beans as they are often sold still on the stalks. They are becoming popular outside Japan now, mainly through Japanese restaurants, and are available from summer to early autumn at some Japanese supermarkets.

Fresh young green beans in the pod are delicious boiled and are often served whole as hors d'oeuvres. Keep refrigerated and use within a few days.

Above: Eda-mame (young green beans still in their pods)

Green beans in walnut sauce

This nut-based sauce is a good way to add body and flavour to vegetables.

SERVES FOUR

INGREDIENTS
  250g/9oz/1⅔ cups green beans
For the walnut sauce
  65g/2½oz/2 cups shelled walnuts
  15ml/1 tbsp caster
    (superfine) sugar
  15ml/1 tbsp shoyu
  15ml/1 tbsp sake
  30ml/2 tbsp water

1 Trim the beans and then cut them diagonally into 4cm/1½in long nib-shaped pieces. Cook for 2 minutes in boiling water with a generous pinch of salt. Drain.

2 To make the walnut sauce, pound all but 2–4 walnut pieces to a fine paste in a mortar with a pestle.

3 When smooth, add the sugar and shoyu to make a fairly dry paste. Add the sake and water and mix to make a creamy sauce.

4 Put the green beans in a mixing bowl and add the walnut sauce. Stir well to coat the beans evenly.

5 Roughly crush the reserved walnut pieces. Serve the green beans and walnut sauce in individual bowls or on a plate, and sprinkle with the remaining walnut pieces on top. Serve warm.

COOK'S TIP

Other nuts, such as peanuts, or seeds, such as sesame seeds, may also be used to make a tasty dressing for boiled vegetables. For an extra smooth sauce, use a Japanese grinder and wooden pestle, rather than an ordinary Western mortar and pestle.

TOFU AND TOFU PRODUCTS

One of the oldest processed foods of South-east Asia, tofu has become more widely appreciated in recent years due to health-conscious trends around the world. Tofu came to Japan from China in the 8th century and has been one of the most important foods ever since.

As with many other foods, the Japanese developed tofu to a more refined form, as well as producing many new by-products to suit the subtlety and delicacy of Japanese cooking. Tofu is mostly made commercially nowadays, but there are still small tofu-making businesses in many residential areas of Japan, making fresh tofu at dawn everyday.

Left: Clockwise from front left, soft or silken tofu, lightly seared tofu and regular, firmer tofu

Pressing tofu

1 Wrap a tofu cake in kitchen paper or, alternatively, place a cake of tofu on a slightly tilting chopping board and place a smaller board on top.

2 If wrapped, place a large plate on top, so that the plate covers the tofu. Put a weight (such as a book) on it and leave it to press for up to 1 hour until all the excess water has been absorbed or has run down the tilted board.

TOFU

Highly nutritious and low in fat and sugar, tofu is made from soya beans, which are first boiled and crushed, then the milk is separated and made into curds with the help of a coagulant. The warm curds are set in moulds for a few hours, then released into a water tank to firm and cool further. A cotton cloth is laid across the base of the moulds to retain the curds while they set and to allow excess water to drain away. Tofu made in this way often has a distinctive cloth mark on its sides and is known as regular tofu. This tofu is called momen-goshi (cotton-sieved tofu), as opposed to the more delicate, softer kinu-goshi (silk-sieved tofu – sold as silken tofu in the West), which is made with thicker milk and without draining the excess water. Both are creamy white in colour.

Japanese tofu, both fresh and in cartons, is available from Asian supermarkets in the West, and is normally of a standard size, 10 × 6 × 4.5cm/4 × 2½ × 1¾in. There is also lightly seared tofu called yaki-dofu, which is available from Japanese shops and is mainly used in hotpot dishes. Other lesser-quality types of tofu are widely available from supermarkets.

The soya bean pulp, after exuding the milk, is not wasted. Called okara, it is used in vegetable cooking, and can occasionally be found at larger Japanese supermarkets.

Aroma and flavour

To the Japanese palate, little of the tofu available outside Japan has the real taste of tofu. Although some fresh tofu has a faint soya bean aroma and milky flavour, many varieties appear to be made of little more than milky water.

Culinary uses

Fresh tofu, silken tofu in particular, is best eaten as it is, cold or hot, with shoyu, chopped spring onion (scallion) and grated ginger, or in soups. The firmer cotton tofu is more suitable for cooking dishes such as *agedashi-dofu* (fried tofu in dashi sauce) and as tofu steaks. Tofu is also cooked with other vegetables, fish and meat, and used for making a white dressing for salads.

Preparation and cooking

Tofu is very fragile, so handle with care. Silken tofu is normally used as it is, but cotton tofu, if it is going to be fried or mashed to make a dressing, is normally pressed to squeeze out some water to make it a little firmer.

Storage

Fresh tofu should be kept in plenty of water in the refrigerator and can be kept for three days, if the water is changed daily. Follow the use-by dates on cartoned or vacuum-packed tofu.

KOYA-DOFU

Also known as kogori-dofu (frozen tofu), koya-dofu is believed to have been invented by Buddhist monks on the Koya mountain many centuries ago. It is a freeze-dried tofu, and is a quite different substance from regular tofu in texture, colour, flavour and size. It has a spongy texture and rich taste even after it has been soaked in water.

Today, koya-dofu is often available in packets of five pieces together with a powdered soup stock in which to cook it. When purchased this way it simply requires cooking in the soup provided. This modern version is readily available.

Aroma and flavour

Koya-dofu has a much stronger soya bean aroma and richer flavour than cotton or silken tofu. However, it is the unusual, spongy texture that strikes your palate. The beauty of this spongy tofu is that, however long it is cooked, it does not disintegrate.

Culinary uses

Because of its spongy nature, koya-dofu absorbs flavours well, so it is used for simmering with vegetables in a rich soup. It is also used for *shojin ryori*, Buddhist monks' vegetarian cooking.

Left: Koya-dofu (freeze-dried tofu)

Pan-fried koya-dofu in egg batter

The soup-cooked koya-dofu is coated with egg, then fried to make this crisp, delicious appetizer.

SERVES FOUR

INGREDIENTS
  2 cakes of koya-dofu with
    powdered soup
  10ml/2 tsp cornflour (cornstarch)
  2 eggs, beaten
  15ml/1 tbsp finely chopped
    fresh parsley
  oil, for frying
  salt

1 In a large pan, mix the sachets of powdered soup in the volume of water suggested on the packet and bring to the boil. Add the koya-dofu and simmer for 15 minutes. Turn a few times during cooking. Remove the pan from the heat and leave to cool for 10 minutes before lifting out the koya-dofu. Discard the soup.

2 On a board, squeeze out the liquid from the cooked koya-dofu, then slice horizontally into two thin pieces.

Preparation and cooking

If the packet does not contain sachets of powdered soup, koya-dofu needs soaking in hot water for 5 minutes before cooking. Use your hands to squeeze out the milky water a few times until the water becomes clear. However, most koya-dofu is now made so that it can be cooked immediately in the powdered soup provided in the packet.

3 Cut each piece into eight triangles.

4 Add the cornflour and salt to the eggs, stir well until the cornflour has dissolved, then add the parsley. Coat each triangle with the egg batter.

5 Fry the coated triangles in an oiled frying pan for 1–2 minutes on both sides. Drain, then serve.

Dilute the powdered soup in water following the instructions on the packet, lay the koya-dofu on the pan base and cook for the suggested time. Leave to cool, cut into appropriate sizes and eat, or cook again with other vegetables, herbs and flavourings.

Storage

Koya-dofu will keep for a long time stored in its packaging. Follow the use-by date on the packet.

Left: Yuba (dried bean curd skin) is available as flat sheets, rolled and cut, or in thick strips.

FRIED TOFU

There are various types of fried tofu commercially produced and commonly used for home cooking in Japan. They are, like tofu, freshly made every day by neighbourhood tofu makers and sold like freshly baked bread. In the West some deep-fried tofu are also freshly made and sold refrigerated at Japanese supermarkets.

YUBA

This is the dried soya bean skin that forms on the surface of the soya bean milk during the tofu-making process. Making yuba is simple, but requires considerable skill: a large pan of soya milk is brought gently to the boil, a thin layer of skin forms on the surface which is skimmed off with a stick in a single swoop, and this is hung up. When it dries, it forms a flat sheet; called yuba. Dried strips are made by rolling up the skin up while still warm, then leaving the strips to dry.

Yuba is a delicacy often used for *shojin ryori* (Buddhist monk's vegetarian cooking). Sold in packets, it comes in various sheet forms, including flat, rolled and cut, or in thick strips, and is increasingly available from many Japanese supermarkets.

Aroma and flavour

Once cooked in soup, yuba gives out a warm soya bean aroma and has a rich, milky flavour with a crunchy texture.

Culinary uses

Yuba is used mainly in clear soups and simmered dishes. It is one of Kyoto's specialities and is often used in their version of the *kaiseki* (formal banquet).

Preparation and cooking

Soften yuba in tepid water for 5 minutes before cooking. Although it does not disintegrate, cook only lightly.

Storage

Yuba will keep for several months if stored in an airtight bag in a cool place.

Below: Clockwise from left, atsu-age (thick deep-fried tofu), in cubes and blocks, abura-age (thin deep-fried tofu sheets), and gammodoki (deep-fried tofu balls with vegetables)

Preparing abura-age

1 Put the abura-age in a sieve and pour boiling water over to wash off any excess oil. Drain and gently pat dry with kitchen paper. If using fresh abura-age, par-boil in rapidly boiling water for 1 minute, then drain and leave to cool. Squeeze out any excess water.

2 Cut each sheet in half and place the pieces on a chopping board. Carefully pull each one open by rubbing the outside with the palm of your hand, in a back and forward motion, to ease apart. Use your fingers to open the bag fully, working your way carefully towards the bottom.

Deep-frying changes the texture and taste of somewhat plain, non-crunchy tofu and not only provides extra protein and oil but also gives the tofu some bite. As it has been fried in vegetable oil, fried tofu is suitable for vegetarians, and is also easier to handle and cook than regular tofu. It can be eaten either heated up or cooked with vegetables and meat.

Abura-age Thin deep-fried tofu is the most commonly used fried tofu in Japanese cooking. It normally comes in a standard size of 12 × 6cm/4½ × 2½in, and 1cm/½in thick, and is often used for cooking with other ingredients, mainly vegetables, and on its own as a source of vegetable protein.

The unusual feature of this fried tofu is that it can be slit open like a pitta bread and stuffed with vegetables or sushi rice. Pour boiling water over before use to reduce the oiliness. It is also used in soups and *oden* (hotpot) dishes. Abura-age is the only tofu product available in both frozen and fresh forms.

Atsu-age Thick deep-fried tofu is made of a whole coarse tofu and is available in the standard size 10 × 6 × 4.5cm/ 4 × 2½ × 1¾in. Only the outside is golden brown, while the inside remains white. It is sometimes cut into cubes first and then fried. Before use, pour boiling water over it and lightly press in kitchen paper to reduce its oiliness. It can be eaten lightly grilled (broiled) or pan-fried with sauce, as tofu steak. It is also good in soups and hotpot dishes, particularly in *oden* (hotpot) or in simmered dishes.

Gammodoki Deep-fried tofu with vegetables is another variety that is very popular in home cooking. It is made from chopped vegetables and seeds bound together with crumbled tofu and grated yam. The mixture is then made either into flat discs of about 8cm/3½in diameter or into small balls, and deep-fried. Gammodoki means "duck look-alike", probably due to its texture more than its look or taste. It is delicious on its own, as well as cooked with other vegetables and meat. It is also used in *oden* (hotpot dishes).

Home-made gammodoki
Plain soft tofu is transformed into a more substantial dish with added konbu and carrots. Konbu and hijiki can be substituted with shredded green beans.

MAKES ABOUT TWELVE BALLS

INGREDIENTS
    1 standard firm (cotton) tofu
    5 × 2.5cm/2 × 1in piece of konbu
        or 5–10g/⅛–¼oz dried hijiki
    ¼ carrot, peeled
    2 dried shiitake mushrooms,
        softened and stems trimmed
    8 green beans, trimmed
    1 egg
    salt, shoyu and mirin
    15ml/1 tbsp black sesame seeds
    vegetable oil, for deep-frying

1 Wrap a tofu cake in kitchen paper and place on a chopping board. Place a large plate upside down on top. Put a weight on it and leave it to press for about 1 hour until all the excess water has drained out.

2 Meanwhile soak the konbu or hijiki in tepid water for 30 minutes, then drain and chop roughly into 1–2cm/ ½–¾in long shreds.

3 Cut the carrot, shiitake and green beans into 1–2cm/½–¾in shreds.

4 Put the tofu in a suribachi (Japanese grinding bowl) or a food processor with the egg, a pinch of salt, and a dash each of shoyu and mirin. Grind or process to a very smooth consistency.

5 Transfer the tofu mixture to a large bowl. Add all the vegetable shreds and sesame seeds and mix well.

6 Heat the oil for frying in a deep frying pan to about 120°C/250°F. Spoon a heaped tablespoonful of the tofu mixture on to your wet palm and mould into a small oval shape about 2cm/¾in thick.

7 Place in the hot oil and deep-fry for 2–3 minutes, or until both sides are a light golden brown; drain on kitchen paper. Repeat this process until all the mixture is used up.

8 When all the tofu balls have been fried, reheat the oil to 170°C/340°F. Fry the balls again to make them crisp. Serve hot as an appetizer or main course, accompanied by some grated daikon with a little shoyu.

GLUTEN PRODUCTS

The gluten from various vegetables, such as potatoes, beans, gourds and wheat, is separated to produce long-lasting food that is quite different in shape, texture and flavour from the original vegetable. Initially developed as a way of preserving vegetables for the winter, gluten products are also appreciated for their unusual shapes and textures, important in Japanese cooking. Gluten products are mostly available in packets and in their dried forms at Japanese supermarkets.

KONNYAKU

An unusual, dense, gelatinous cake derived from the tough root of the konnyaku plant, a kind of yam potato. The thinly sliced root is dried, ground and the chemical compound, mannan, is separated; from this, konnyaku flour is produced. Next the flour is mixed with water, then hardened using lime milk as a coagulant and boiling water, to form cakes. This complicated process is said to have been brought to Japan from China, together with Buddhism, but is now only practised in Japan.

Since konnyaku is mostly water (97 per cent) and the main nutrient, gluco-mannan, cannot

Below: Konnyaku, a gelatinous cake made from flour produced from a yam-like root vegetable.

be digested, it is known to be a highly beneficial dietary food. However, due to its unusual appearance (it is also known as devil's tongue) and strange texture, it may need some getting used to before it can be appreciated.

There are many types of konnyaku products made commercially in Japan, such as fresh *sashimi* (raw konnyaku, thinly sliced), ito-konnyaku (string konnyaku), konnyaku balls and flavoured konnyaku. In the West only ita-konnyaku (standard konnyaku cake) in black (unrefined) or white (refined) and shirataki (fine filament) are

Below: Shirataki (fine white noodles made from the starch of the konnyaku plant) are sold in packets.

normally available from Japanese supermarkets. The standard size of the cake is about 15 × 8 × 4cm/6 × 3½ × 1½in and it is bought packed in water.

Aroma and flavour

Konnyaku has no aroma, nor flavour. It has a slippery, hard jelly-like texture, for which it is most appreciated.

Culinary uses

Fresh konnyaku is eaten raw like *sashimi*. When cooked, konnyaku is used with other vegetables and meat and also used for soups and hotpots, *oden* (fish cake hotpot) in particular.

Preparation and cooking

Konnyaku should be parboiled before use. Since it is quite soft, the cake can be torn with the fingers into bitesize pieces, cut into many shapes or made into decorative knots.

Konnyaku does not easily absorb flavours from the sauce or foods it is cooked with, so it is always simmered in a strongly flavoured sauce for as long a time as possible.

Storage

Once the packet is opened, store in plenty of water. Change the water daily, and keep for up to two weeks.

SHIRATAKI

The name shirataki means white waterfall. It is made from the konnyaku plant in the same way as konnyaku but only as a thin white noodle-like filament. Shirataki is sold in an inflated plastic bag filled with water or in cans and is available from Asian supermarkets. It is mainly used for hotpots, especially *sukiyaki* (table-top cooked beef and vegetables), and for salad dishes. Par-boil and roughly cut the long noodles before use.

Above: Harusame

tied around food, kanpyo is simmered with vegetables and meat. Before use it needs to be softened. Rub with salt and wash vigorously to break down the fibres and increase absorbency. It can then be boiled in water until soft and is normally cooked in a shoyu-based sauce, and used for sushi. Packets of 30–50g/1¼–2oz are available from Asian stores.

KANPYO

These dried gourd ribbons have an unusual role in Japanese cooking; they are used to tie foods together and look more like parcel string than food. The flesh of the calabah gourd, a member of the marrow family, is thinly shaved, then dried to a long ribbon, about 2cm/¾in wide, and whitened by smoking in sulphur. As well as being

FU

These gluten cakes are now used mainly as a decorative garnish. Wheat flour mixed with salt and water in a cloth bag is washed in water until the starch has seeped out and only the gluten is left. This is then steamed until firm to produce fresh fu, which is used instead of meat in Zen Buddhist cooking. Fu originated in China, but the Japanese have developed ultra-light dried fu in many colours, sizes and shapes to garnish soups and hotpots. It is not a pure gluten since wheat, glutinous rice powder and/or baking powder are added to the gluten before drying. Some dried fu is available from Asian stores.

HARUSAME

Meaning spring rain, harusame is a fine, translucent filament made from various starchy roots such as potato and sweet potato, or sometimes green beans. Starch, mixed with boiling water, is made into a gluey mixture, then extruded through fine holes into boiling water. It is then further boiled to harden it, cooled quickly and freeze-dried into crisp, fine filaments. It is available in dried form in packets from Asian supermarkets. Harusame is soaked in tepid water for 5 minutes and used for salads or soups. When the dried harusame is fried it expands to a fluffy white "bird's nest". To produce this effect, crush it into pieces, then use as a "batter" for frying fish and vegetables to make an unusual tempura. Store dried harusame in an airtight packet in a cool, airy place.

Above: Kanpyo (dried gourd ribbons)

Right: Fu (gluten cakes)

MUSHROOMS

The mushroom is a fungus whose developed offshoots grow in or under certain trees. In a relatively warm and wet country in which over 75 per cent of the land is covered by mountains, mushrooms grow in abundance and are used in everyday cooking. Apart from the most popular ones, introduced below, there are the Japanese equivalents of European mushrooms such as hiratake (oyster mushroom family), maitake (hen of the wood), amigasatake (morel), amitake (boletus) and anzutake (chanterelle), as well as numerous regional seasonal varieties available locally.

Most mushrooms consist primarily of water (about 90 per cent) but they are also rich in vitamins D and B2 and vegetable fibre. Some have a distinctive *umami* (rich taste), so are used for making vegetable soup stock.

FRESH SHIITAKE

Meaning *shii* (tree) mushroom, the shiitake is also known, incorrectly, as the Chinese mushroom, though it actually originated in Japan. Shiitake is a fungus that grows in the wild twice a year, in spring and autumn, under trees such as *shii* (*Pasania cuspidata*), oak and chestnut, though today it is also cultivated. It is recognized as a health food for its ability to reduce cholesterol in the blood.

Below: When buying fresh shiitake, look for ones with a dark brown, velvety cap.

There are various types of shiitake, but the ones with a dark brown, velvety cap of approximately 5cm/2in diameter, which are 70–80 per cent open, are regarded as being of the best quality. The variety called donko, meaning winter mushroom, which has a small, thick and dense, dark cap with crevasse-like deep lines on it, is the king of shiitake. It is also known as flower shiitake because of the pattern the lines create on its cap.

Although dried shiitake are widely available, due to increased effort in their cultivation, fresh shiitake are also more available outside of Japan – good news for Japanese cooking.

Aroma and flavour

Fresh shiitake have a distinctive woody aroma and slightly acidic flavour. The mushroom has a soft, slippery texture, which adds an exquisite quality. When dried the flavour intensifies.

Culinary uses

In Japanese cooking, fresh shiitake tend to be used for their subtlety – they absorb rather than override the flavours of the other ingredients. The shiitake is one of the regular ingredients for hotpot dishes containing meat, usually beef, and vegetables, such as *shabu shabu* or *sukiyaki*. They can also be simply grilled over a barbecue or battered and fried for tempura.

Grilled fresh shiitake with mustard

1 Wipe off the dirt from fresh shiitake with damp kitchen paper and use a small knife to trim off the hard parts of the stems.

2 Grill (broil) the mushrooms very lightly under a medium heat, or on a barbecue, for 1–2 minutes on both sides. Alternatively, heat a frying pan, add a little oil to just cover the base, and pan-fry the shiitake over a medium heat. Serve with mustard and shoyu.

Preparation and cooking

With a damp piece of kitchen paper wipe, rather than wash, off any earth and dirt, and trim off the hard part of the stem before cooking. When used whole, a decorative cross is often notched into the caps. Fresh shiitake can easily become too soft, so monitor the cooking carefully.

Storage

Choose fresh shiitake with the cap edges curled under. The caps flare out and become floppy within a few days. Store in the vegetable section of the refrigerator.

DRIED SHIITAKE

When shiitake are dried, their aroma and flavour intensify; it is for this enriched fungus flavour, coupled with the convenience of using dried shiitake, that they are most appreciated. The drying process also increases the fibre content to over 40 per cent.

The distinctive taste of shiitake suits Chinese cooking better than Japanese, hence the widely held belief that it is a Chinese mushroom. There are many types and grades of dried shiitake available in packets, but the small, thick donko (winter mushroom) is the most highly rated.

Above: Various dried shiitake; on the far right are dried donko, which are considered the most flavoursome.

Aroma and flavour

Dried shiitake have a pleasantly strong, roasted aroma and intensified fungus flavour. The increased fibre content gives it more bite than fresh ones.

Culinary uses

In Japanese cooking, dried shiitake are usually cooked in a seasoned liquid, then used for dishes such as simmered vegetables with chicken, mixed sushi and soup noodles.

Storage

Dried shiitake last almost indefinitely if stored in an airtight plastic bag. They can also be frozen, which is a better way of retaining flavour.

ENOKITAKE

Also known as yukinoshita, meaning under the snow, this bundle of tiny berry-cap mushrooms with thin stems grows in the wild on the stumps of *enoki* (hackberry), poplar and persimmon trees in winter. The wild enokitake has brownish orange caps, about 2–8cm/¾–3½in in diameter, but these days is now widely cultivated at a low temperature, without light, to produce bundles of snowy white caps with a maximum diameter of 1cm/½in and long slender stems. Cultivated enokitake is often marketed outside Japan as a new nutritious salad ingredient to be eaten raw.

Aroma and flavour

Enokitake has a very delicate, fresh flavour and a delightfully crisp texture.

Culinary uses

They are one of the regular ingredients for hotpot dishes, such as *shabu shabu*, and are also delicious in seasonal salads and in soups. Because they do not have an overpowering flavour, they go well with almost anything, and can be wrapped in foil with fish or poultry for cooking on a barbecue. They can also be eaten raw in salads.

Preparation and cooking

Cut off the spongy root, 2.5–5cm/1–2in from the bottom, and wash under cold running water. Use cooked or raw. They cook in no time, so be careful not to overcook. Enokitake are the easiest mushroom to handle, and they give a refreshing, pretty character to dishes.

Storage

Choose shiny white bundles and store in a sealed bag in the refrigerator. Enokitake keep well for up to a week.

Below: Cultivated enokitake

Preparing dried shiitake

1 Quickly wash off any dirt under running water and soak in cold water. Dried shiitake must be soaked in tepid water for about 2–3 hours, or overnight. If you are short of time, soak for at least 45 minutes, with a little sugar sprinkled over, before cooking.

2 Remove the shiitake from the soaking water, and gently squeeze out the water. Using your fingers or a knife, trim off the stem and then slice or chop the caps to use in cooking. Use the stems in soups. Don't discard the soaking liquid; rather drain through muslin (cheesecloth), then use in soups or for simmering.

MATSUTAKE

This relatively large, dark brown fungus with a thick, meaty stem is usually picked before the cap spreads open. Matsutake means pine mushroom and signifies autumn to the Japanese. For connoisseurs autumn never goes by without tasting *matsutake gohan* (rice cooked with matsutake) or *dobin-mushi* (teapot soup with matsutake).

Matsutake grow only in the wild in undisturbed stands of red pine trees. The mushroom is sometimes compared with European cep or porcini, but it is much more delicate and a great deal rarer, and thus inevitably much, much more expensive. It is truly the king of Japanese mushrooms. Unfortunately, matsutake are never dried, so they are very difficult to obtain outside Japan. Fresh matsutake have, however, occasionally been seen at large Japanese supermarkets at the height of the season. They may be worth looking around for.

Aroma and flavour

The matsutake is eaten for its distinctive pine fragrance and exquisite flavour. The thick stem has a slippery but unusually crunchy texture.

Culinary uses

Matsutake should be only very lightly cooked, otherwise the delicate fragrance will be lost. The most traditional method is to grill (broil) the mushroom briefly over a charcoal fire, then tear apart with the fingers and eat with a citrus-flavoured dipping sauce. They can also be steam-grilled: wrap in foil with a little sake and cook over a barbecue.

Other light cooking methods include plunging in a clear soup, *dobinmishi* (teapot steam) and cooking with rice, such as *matsutake gohan*, a luxuriously flavoured rice dish.

Right: Shaka shimeji are a popular variety of shimeji due to their striking and distinctive appearance.

Preparation and cooking

Do not wash; instead, wipe with a damp cloth or rinse very quickly. Trim off only the hard part of the stem, about 1–2cm/½–¾in from the bottom. Unlike other mushrooms, matsutake are eaten with the thick stem intact, so slice or tear, lengthways. Take care not to overcook.

Storage

The longer matsutake are kept, the less fragrant they become, so they should be used immediately, or at least within three days of purchase.

SHIMEJI

The shimeji is another popular Japanese mushroom and grows in autumn in bunches or in circles under trees such as *nara* (Japanese oak) and red pine. There are many varieties, but the most common has a light grey cap and grows to 2.5–10cm/1–4in in diameter. One

Above: Oyster mushrooms have a similar texture to shimeji, and can be substituted if the latter are not available.

of the varieties, called shaka shimeji, sports small caps with short stems that grow stuck together at the lower end giving it a unique appearance and greater popularity. It is this variety that is most commonly available in the West from Asian supermarkets.

Aroma and flavour

The shimeji has little aroma and an undistinguished flavour. Rather it is valued for its fresh, meaty texture which is similar to that of oyster mushrooms.

Preparing shimeji

Wash the mushrooms and cut off the hard base. Separate any large blocks of fresh shimeji into smaller chunks with your fingers.

Culinary uses

This mushroom's fresh and unassuming character suits most delicate Japanese cooking, such as *shimeji gohan* (rice cooked with shimeji), clear soup, and grilled (broiled) and fried dishes. It is also a popular hotpot ingredient.

Preparation and cooking

Trim off the spongy part about 2–2.5cm/ ¾–1in from the bottom and quickly rinse the shimeji under cold running water. Using your fingers, separate the stem and cook lightly.

Storage

Shimeji keep fairly well for up to a week if stored in the vegetable compartment of the refrigerator. They can be stored dried, frozen and pickled, but nothing is better than fresh.

NAMEKO

Meaning slippery mushroom, nameko grows in Japan in autumn on the stumps and fallen trunks of broadleaf trees, such as beech. It has a small, 1–2cm/½–¾in diameter, orange-brown button cap covered by a very slippery, gelatinous substance, hence the name. Its thin stems, which are about 5cm/2in long, are bunched together at the bottom. Nameko is now largely cultivated

and those grown artificially on trees are regarded as better quality than those cultivated on wood chips.

This is one mushroom that is available only in jars or cans even in Japan. Fresh nameko has a very short life, so it is preserved in brine. Nameko in cans or jars is widely available at Asian supermarkets.

Aroma and flavour

Although it is covered by a thick slippery brine, nameko has an unmistakable fungus aroma and faintly sweet flavour. However, it is this soft slipperiness for which it is most prized by the Japanese. This feature may be very strange to Western palates but well worth trying.

Above: Nameko mushrooms

Culinary uses

The most popular use of the nameko is in miso soup; among all the possible combinations of ingredients nameko, together with tofu, makes the tastiest miso soup. Nameko is also used for clear soup and for hors d'oeuvres.

Preparation and cooking

Very little preparation and cooking is required as the mushroom comes soaked in brine in cans or jars. Just drain off the brine before use.

Storage

If canned or sealed in jars, these mushrooms will keep almost indefinitely. Once opened and drained, however, they should be used immediately.

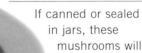

Right: A wide range of Japanese mushrooms is available in cans, including, clockwise from top, shiitake, enokitake and shimeji.

SEAWEEDS

The Japanese have been enjoying the bounty of their surrounding seas since ancient times, whether for fish, shellfish or seaweeds. Over thirty varieties of seaweeds plus the numerous products developed from them are regularly used in Japanese cooking.

Most seaweeds contain a surprisingly high percentage (above 50 per cent) of the type of carbohydrate that aids digestion. They also contain iron, calcium, phosphorus and iodine and are rich in vitamins A and C. Seaweed and seaweed products are generally available in dried forms.

KONBU

This giant kelp is an indispensable ingredient in Japanese cooking. It is used on its own and also provides a subtle flavour to numerous dishes as one of the basic ingredients of dashi (fish stock). It contains a large amount of glutamate acid, the source of its intense flavour, and is rich in iodine, calcium and vegetable fibre.

Konbu grows in the northern seas off the Japanese coast, and Hokkaido, the northernmost island, is known as the biggest producer of dried konbu. There are many varieties of kelp; the size alone ranges from 5cm/2in to 30cm/12in wide and some grow to over 20m/60ft long. They are all dried and graded, classified by their uses, either for eating or for making dashi stock. The lower and thicker part of the konbu stem is the best in quality.

Left: Tsukudani *is made by slowly simmering konbu pieces wtih shoyu, giving it a salty flavour.*

Dried konbu is also commercially processed to make numerous konbu by-products, such as cut konbu for savoury snacks and *tsukudani* (a slow-simmered savoury). Other popular konbu products include tororo and oboro, both of which are shaved from fresh konbu. Tororo konbu is a pile of fluffy, very thin threads shaved lengthways and is eaten with rice and in a clear soup. Oboro konbu is a thin, almost transparent, sheet used for wrapping rice and other food mostly for decorative purposes.

Aroma and flavour

Dried konbu has a distinctive ocean aroma and intense flavour. It has a pleasantly moist texture.

Culinary uses

The most important role dried konbu plays in Japanese cooking is in making dashi stock, together with katsuo-bushi (dried skipjack tuna flakes). It is also used to provide extra flavour to boiled rice, in sushi, and for simmering with vegetables, fish and meat.

Preparation and cooking

Dried konbu is usually covered with a fine white powder, a natural by-product of the drying process. Do not wash or rinse off; instead, wipe with damp kitchen paper. In cooking,

Left: Oboro konbu (dried konbu sheets)

in soup or a hotpot, dried konbu sheet is made into decorative knots or rolled. Use the soaking water in a stock or soup.

Storage

Unopened packets of dried konbu keep well for several months if stored in a cool, airy place.

Knotting and rolling konbu

1 To knot konbu, soak a sheet of konbu in tepid water until soft. Cut crossways into 16cm/6¼in sheets, then lengthways into 2–3cm/¾–1¼in wide strips. Make a knot in the centre and cook.

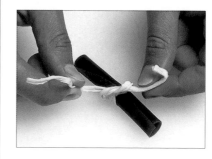

2 To roll knobu, cut a soaked konbu sheet crossways into 5cm/2in sheets and roll up tightly. Carrot, an anchovy fillet, or meat such as ham or sausage, can be rolled inside, if you wish. Secure by tying with a thin strip of konbu.

NORI

The most famous seaweed product is nori, a dried paper-thin sheet of asakusa-nori, a laver, which is a small orange-brown, film-like marine algae. It grows up to 25cm/10in long and about 5cm/2in wide. The laver is washed in fresh water, laid in thin sheets and then sun-dried on bamboo or wooden frames.

Nori is rich in vegetable protein, vitamins and minerals. It is packaged in a standard size of about 20 × 18cm/ 8 × 7in for rolling sushi, usually in packets of five or ten sheets. Mini nori sheets, about 8 × 3cm/3½ × 1¼in are also available. These are used for wrapping rice, most notably served at a traditional breakfast, and some are ready-toasted or coated with a shoyu-based seasoning. Standard nori sheets are widely available from most large supermarkets and other types of nori can be found at Asian supermarkets.

Aroma and flavour

Although it has a light, smoky flavour, nori is mainly appreciated for its subtle ocean aroma. Dark, shiny nori has much more flavour than the cheaper reddish types.

Culinary uses

Nori is mainly used with rice for rolling sushi and wrapping *onigiri* (rice balls) and mochi (rice cakes). It is also crumbled or shredded for use as a garnish on mixed sushi or soba noodles.

Preparation and cooking

To bring out the aroma and make nori crispy, quickly toast it on both sides before use by holding a single sheet horizontally over a low heat. Move it about as you toast it so that it heats evenly. It will be very crisp within 2–3 seconds. Do not grill (broil). One side of nori is shinier than the other, so when you roll sushi, make sure you place the nori shiny-side down on the makisu (sushi rolling mat) so the dull side is inside the roll.

Storage

Nori will keep almost indefinitely in an airtight bag placed in a container. Under no circumstances let it become moist.

WAKAME

This is a brownish orange algae and grows up to 1–2m/3–6ft long on rocks under the sea from early winter through to early summer. Wakame is mostly dried or salted, and there are various types, sizes and grades of wakame readily available.

The fact that it is full of vitamins with absolutely no fat content makes it a useful health food. Fresh wakame is available only in Japan, but processed wakame has been successfully developed in recent years. Cut wakame, which softens almost instantly, is sold in packets and is widely available.

Aroma and flavour

This seaweed has a delicate aroma and a very refreshing flavour. It is slightly slippery but has a pleasant vegetable crispness.

Culinary uses

Wakame is one of the most popular soup ingredients and is also delicious served as a salad with a vinegary dressing. It is often simmered with other vegetables.

Preparation and cooking

Dried wakame must be softened before use. If using a whole wakame with the stem intact, soak in tepid water for 15–20 minutes before cutting it out. If using instant wakame, soak in plenty of water for about 5 minutes before use. Drain and pour boiling water over it, then immediately plunge into cold water to enhance the green colour. Some types of dried wakame can be put directly into the soup.

Storage

Store dried wakame in an airtight bag in a cool place away from direct sunlight. It will keep almost indefinitely if stored in this way.

Above: Dried and cut wakame, at front.

HIJIKI

Very popular among health-conscious eaters, hijiki is a twiggy black marine algae that grows up to 1m/3ft long all around the Japanese coast. It is full of vitamins, minerals, including calcium, and fibre, and contains no fat. Hijiki is cooked and dried, and sold in packets. It can be bought from Asian food stores.

Aroma and flavour

Hijiki has little aroma and a faint ocean flavour. It has a fairly tough texture.

Culinary uses

Hijiki is normally shallow-fried and then simmered in a shoyu-based sauce with other vegetables. It is often used with abura-age (fried thin tofu). It is also used to garnish rice dishes, such as mixed sushi and *onigiri* (rice balls), as its black, small twig-like shape provides an attractive contrast to the white rice.

Preparation and cooking

Soak dried hijiki in tepid water for 15–20 minutes until softened. It will normally expand to 7–10 times its dried volume. It is a tough seaweed and withstands vigorous cooking. It goes well with oil, so it is often shallow-fried and then simmered in dashi-based soup seasoned with shoyu, mirin and sugar.

Storage

Dried hijiki will keep well if stored in an airtight container.

Right: Hijiki seaweed

KANTEN

Also known as agar-agar, kanten is taken from tengusa, a burgundy-coloured, fern-like seaweed that grows in the Indian and Pacific oceans. Freeze-dried, it becomes a pure form of gelling agent that has many advantages over conventional gelatine.

Kanten makes a slightly opaque jelly, which sets at above room temperature, so does not require refrigeration. It does not have gelatine's rubbery texture, so it is easier to cut, and its texture is firmer, so it will fall from its mould more easily. Above all, it has a refreshing texture and is a healthier option than gelatine. It has no nutritional value although it contains vegetable fibre, which helps digestion. Freeze-dried kanten comes in three forms: sticks about 25cm/10in long, filaments of a similar length, and a powdered form.

Aroma and flavour

Kanten has no aroma or flavour, which makes it a perfect gelling agent. It will, however, absorb the flavourings with which it is prepared.

Culinary uses

It is mainly used as a setting agent for making desserts and cakes.

Preparation and cooking

If using a stick or filament, soak for 30 minutes in water until softened, then squeeze out the water and tear the kanten into small pieces. Cook in hot water until melted, add sugar and when dissolved, strain. Return the liquid to the pan and cook for 3 minutes more. Pour into a wet square mould, leave to cool, then chill. When set, remove from the mould by pressing with your fingers round the sides, and cut into tiny cubes with a knife. Check the packet, but as a guide, 5ml/1 tsp powder will set 300ml/½ pint/ 1¼ cups of liquid.

Storage

Freeze-dried kanten keeps well for a few months if kept in a cool, dry place.

Left: Kanten is available in various forms; sticks and filaments are the most commonly used, and are easily found in Asian food stores.

HERBS AND SPICES

Unlike European cooking, where herbs and spices are cooked together with the main ingredients, Japanese cooking uses them mainly for additional aroma and flavour, often sprinkled on dishes or mixed with a dipping sauce.

Shiso, ginger and wasabi are some well-known examples, but there are also various wild plants called sansai, meaning literally mountain vegetables, which are used as herbs and spices for their unique aromas and flavours. These are, unfortunately, difficult to find outside of Japan.

SHISO

Although originally from China, Burma and the Himalayas, shiso has been cultivated in Japan for centuries, and is now used predominantly in Japanese cooking. It is a member of the mint family but has a subtle basil flavour.

There are basically two types, green and red (known as the beefsteak plant in the United States), and the whole shiso plant from berries to flowers is used as a herb or garnish for Japanese dishes. The green variety is used for its exquisite flavour and the red for colouring as well as its aroma. As the plant is hardy, it is now widely cultivated and available in the West, but the aroma and flavour of shiso grown other than on Japanese soil somehow lacks richness. Green leaves in packets are sold all year round at Asian stores.

Aroma and flavour

Shiso has a very distinctive, pungent aroma and rich but subtly piercing flavour, more like basil than mint.

Culinary uses

Normally only green shiso is used as a herb and garnish for dishes such as *sashimi*, tempura and vinegared salads. Red shiso is used for making umeboshi (dried and salted Japanese apricot) and other pickles. The berries, stems and flowers of both types are also used to garnish *sashimi*, soup and sauces.

Above:
Shiso leaves

Preparation and cooking

Simply use as it is or cut into required shapes. For tempura, only the underside of the leaves should be battered and fried very quickly.

Storage

Shiso leaves are very thin and do not keep long, so store in a plastic bag in the refrigerator and use within three days.

Below:
Mitsuba

MITSUBA

This herb has three light green, coriander-like leaves (hence the name, meaning three leaves) on top of thin whitish stalks, about 15–20cm/6–8in long. A member of the parsley family, it is cultivated outside Japan and is available from Asian stores.

Aroma and flavour

Mitsuba has a relatively strong grass aroma and a faintly bitter flavour.

Culinary uses

Mitsuba is used for its unique aroma, so only a few leaves are put into clear soup, thick egg soup or used in hors d'oeuvres. It is also used for hotpot dishes and the stalks can be fried. The most attractive use is to tie food with the stalks as if it were a ribbon. For this, quickly plunge the stalk part only into boiling water to make it flexible.

Preparation and cooking

This is a very delicate herb so requires only very light par-boiling.

Storage

Store mitsuba in a plastic bag in the refrigerator.

*Above: Young
ginger shoot*

SHOGA

Fresh ginger, or shoga, is one
of the oldest, most universal
ingredients and dried root ginger is
widely available all the year round. For
Japanese cooking, however, only fresh
ginger is used and often only the
extracted juice. In addition to shoga,
(root ginger), so-called ha-shoga (ginger
shoot), and mé-shoga (ginger sprout),
are available in summer in Japan.
Ginger shoot is picked young with the
short stalks still attached to it, and
ginger sprout is a whole ginger plant
with a small young root at the bottom.
Ginger is highly valued not only for
cooking but also for its medicinal
properties; it is believed to warm the
body, help digestion and prevent motion
sickness, for example. It is also
available as pickled ginger slices in
packets or jars.

Aroma and flavour

Fresh ginger has a subtly pungent
aroma, reminiscent of citrus, and
a pleasantly sharp flavour.
Young ginger is tender and
mild enough to be cooked
as a vegetable while older
roots become fibrous
and more
pungent.

Culinary uses

Apart from
pickled ginger to
accompany sushi, root
ginger is almost always grated and only
the juice is used in Japanese cooking.
Ginger shoot is also pickled and used
as a garnish for grilled (broiled) fish
dishes. Ginger sprout, on the other
hand, is fresh and mild enough to eat
raw with miso, or to use for tempura.

Preparation and cooking

Always peel off the outer skin. To
extract the juice, use a Japanese grater
or fine cheese grater to finely grate the
ginger, then squeeze out the juice.
To make pickled ginger, use very fresh
young root ginger, or ginger shoot.

Storage

Choose a shiny, pale beige, smooth-
skinned root. Stored in a cool, airy
place away from direct sunlight, shoga
will keep well for up to two weeks.

*Below: Pickled thinly sliced ginger, gari,
is available in packets or jars, but can
also be made at home.*

Obtaining juice from fresh root ginger

For best results, use a Japanese
grater specially designed to catch
juices in a curved tray at its base.

Peel the fresh root ginger, then
finely grate. Using your fingers,
squeeze the juice from the grated
ginger, then discard the pulp.

Homemade pickled ginger

Easy to make, pickled ginger will
keep for several months.

MAKES 475ML/16FL OZ/2 CUPS

INGREDIENTS
200g/7oz fresh root ginger or
  ginger shoot
5–10ml/1–2 tsp salt
250ml/8fl oz/1 cup rice vinegar
120ml/4fl oz/½ cup water
45ml/3 tbsp sugar

1 Peel the fresh root ginger thinly
or scrape the ginger shoot. Lightly
rub salt on to the peeled ginger
and leave for 24 hours.

2 In a small bowl, mix the vinegar,
water and sugar, and stir until the
sugar has dissolved. Rinse and
drain the ginger and add to the
vinegar mixture. Leave to marinate
for a week. (The ginger will turn
pinkish in the vinegar mixture.) To
use, slice the ginger thinly along
the grain, cutting only as much as
you require.

WASABI

For over a thousand years, Japan's somewhat moderately flavoured cooking has been given an unusual pungency through the addition of wasabi. Meaning mountain hollyhock, it is sometimes introduced as the Japanese equivalent of Western horseradish, though the two are not related. Wasabi grows in the wild in clear mountain streams, but is now mostly cultivated at wasabi farms using pure running water diverted from nearby rivers.

Grated fresh wasabi has a milder fragrance and less sharp pungency than horseradish. However, freshly grated wasabi is a rarity even in Japan and the root is more commonly used in its powdered and paste forms, which are

Right: Sansho powder

now widely available all over the world, largely due to the sushi phenomenon. When grated, fresh wasabi reveals a vivid green flesh.

Aroma and flavour

Freshly grated wasabi has a refreshing, radish-like aroma and subtly pungent flavour. Interestingly, to give it a little more kick, white horseradish is also included, among other ingredients, to make the powders and pastes.

Culinary uses

Wasabi and raw fish are an inseparable combination and wasabi paste is always used for *sashimi* and sushi. Wasabi is also used for pickling vegetables and in salad dressings.

Preparation and cooking

If you are lucky enough to find fresh wasabi, use a small sharp knife to peel the tough skin then finely grate from the top end, which is more pungent. To make a paste from powdered wasabi, mix water with the powder (see left).

Storage

Fresh wasabi does not keep long; this is one of the reasons it is not available outside Japan. Powdered wasabi keeps almost indefinitely, if kept well sealed in its can. Once opened, the wasabi paste that comes in a tube should be stored in the refrigerator and used within a few weeks.

Making wasabi paste

Put about 5ml/1 tsp powdered wasabi in an egg cup and add the same volume of tepid water. Stir vigorously to make a firm, clay-like paste. Place the dish upside down on a board to stand for at least 10 minutes before use. This will prevent the wasabi paste from drying out and at the same time helps it develop its distinctive sharp flavour.

Left: Powdered wasabi and the prepared paste.

SANSHO

This plant, whose name means mountain pepper, is not actually a pepper plant but a prickly ash tree; it grows in Japan, along the Korean peninsula, and China. Sansho is a very useful and important plant in Japanese cooking and its refreshingly piercing fragrance is used to mask the strong smells and balance the taste of fatty foods.

Sansho is so versatile that many Japanese households have this plant in their garden, and use it at every stage of its growth from spring through to autumn. The delicate young sprouts, called kinome, appear first, then the tiny greenish yellow flowers, hana-zansho, occur throughout spring, and the bitterly pungent berries, mi- or tsubu-zansho, appear in early summer; all are carefully hand-picked and used in daily cooking. Finally, the ripened seedpods are dried in autumn, and when the pods split open, the bitter seeds are discarded, and the pods powdered to make kona-zansho. The dried split pods can be ground at home, but are usually bought powdered.

Powdered sansho in small jars and cans is widely available from Asian supermarkets. In Chinese cooking, only the dried seedpods, called Sichuan pepper, are used.

Aroma and flavour

Sansho is not as pungent as pepper and has a soothing, minty aroma and faintly acidic flavour.

Culinary uses

Powdered sansho is used as a condiment, most famously for *unagi kabayaki* (grilled eel fillet) and other grilled (broiled) dishes such as *yakitori*. It is also one of the ingredients for shichimi togarashi (seven-spice chilli pepper). Fresh kinome and hana-zansho are used uncooked as a garnish for simmered dishes, dressed salads, grilled fish and soups.

Storage

Powdered sansho in jars and cans will slowly lose its fragrance once opened. Use within a few months.

GOMA

The sesame plant grows in tropical and subtropical regions all over the world, and the sesame seeds, goma, are used all over the world in cooking and for making fragrant oil.

The oval-shaped seed pods have four compartments, each bearing numerous tiny flat seeds. The shades of colour vary from white through to black, but in Japanese cooking mainly white and black seeds are used; the choice depending on the dish.

Sesame seeds are nutritionally beneficial – they are rich in oil, protein and amino acid, and also contain calcium, iron and vitamins B_1 and B_2. The washed raw seeds are too hard to

digest and have a slightly unpleasant smell, so they are normally roasted before coming to market in Japan. They are called iri-goma or atari-goma and can be bought in packets from larger Asian supermarkets.

Aroma and flavour

Sesame seeds come alive as soon as they are heated. For this reason, they are always lightly toasted again before use to bring out the unmistakable, nutty aroma and rich, crunchy flavour needed for Japanese cooking.

Culinary uses

Whole black seeds mixed with salt are used for sprinkling over rice and for mixing into sushi rice. The seeds make a very good paste for dressing cooked vegetables and are also used for making *goma-dofu* (tofu with sesame seeds). A simple dressing can be made with red and white miso sauce, mirin and sugar, which is used to coat boiled and simmered daikon slices.

Preparation and cooking

Always lightly toast before use. Heat a small dry pan, add the seeds and toast over a medium heat, moving the seeds in the pan constantly, for 30 seconds to 1 minute until just turning golden. Half-crush the toasted seeds using a mortar and pestle to bring out more flavour.

Storage

Sesame seeds keep well for several months if stored in an airtight container or sealed bag in a cool, dry place away from direct sunlight.

Left: Black and white goma (sesame seeds)

White sesame dressing

Add a rich flavour to lightly boiled vegetables such as spinach and green beans with this dressing.

1 Heat a small, dry pan, add 45–60ml/3–4 tbsp white sesame seeds and toast over a medium heat, moving the seeds in the pan constantly, for about 1 minute until just turning golden. Take care not to burn the seeds.

2 Immediately transfer the seeds to a suribachi (Japanese grinding bowl) or a mortar and pound vigorously with a surikogi or a pestle until the seeds become flaky and paste-like.

3 Add 5–10ml/1–2 tsp shoyu, 30 45ml/2–3 tbsp water and 15ml/1 tbsp mirin, and mix well.

Left: Whole, dried red chillies

DRIED RED CHILLIES

This South American hot spice is not a natural Japanese ingredient and is only used in foreign-influenced dishes. Although the Japanese have traditionally taken great pride in using very fresh home-grown ingredients, they normally only use dried chilli.

Chilli was introduced into Japan in the 16th century, and fresh chilli has been a rarity until recently. Its Japanese name, togarashi, meaning Chinese mustard, suggests it came through China. The long, thin variety most often used in Japanese cooking is called takanotsume, meaning hawk's claw. This variety, usually dried, is probably three times hotter than fresh chilli, so should be used sparingly.

Japanese seven-spice chilli powder, shichimi-togarashi, is made with powdered, dried chilli mixed with other seeds, usually sesame, poppy, hemp, shiso and sansho seeds as well as nori. The dried powder made from chilli only, called ichimi, is also available. They are both used as condiments and sprinkled over soups, noodles, *yakitori* and other grilled meat and fish, and are

Right: Chillies are available dried, in a powdered form and as an oil.

widely available in small jars from Asian supermarkets. Rayu, chilli oil, is also made from dried chilli. The heat of the chilli is exuded quickly when the oil is very hot, and is used with Chinese-influenced foods such as ramen and dumplings.

Aroma and flavour

Only when dried chilli is heated does its piquant aroma become evident. Even unheated it is very hot tasting, especially the seeds. It is generally known that the larger and fatter the chilli, the milder it tends to be, although there are some exceptions to this rule.

Culinary uses

Takanotsume is used for making *momiji-oroshi* a dipping sauce with grated daikon, and served with hotpot dishes such as *shabu shabu*. It is also used in piquant marinades such as *Nanban* sauce, a Portuguese-influenced hot-and-sour marinade for fried fish.

Preparation and cooking

Chilli seeds are extremely hot, so always remove from the pod. First, trim off the stem and shake out the seeds. If this is

not successful, soak the pod in water until it becomes soft enough to handle and, using the back of a knife, push out the seeds. In Japanese cooking, the pod is often cut into thin rings, which look pretty sprinkled on food.

Storage

Stored in an airtight bag, in a cool, dark place, dried chilli will keep indefinitely.

Momiji-oroshi (red maple grated daikon)

This recipe takes its name from the beautiful autumn-leaves colour of the grated chilli-stuffed daikon.

1 Seed 3–4 red dried or fresh chillies. If using fresh chillies, cut into fine strips.

2 Cut a 5–6cm/2–2½in long piece from a large daikon and peel off the hard outer skin. Using a hashi (chopsticks), make 3–4 deep holes lengthways in one end and push some chilli into each hole.

3 Leave for 5 minutes, then grate the chilli-stuffed daikon using a sharp grater. If intending to use in a dipping sauce, always make with a Japanese grater.

FRUIT

From north to south, Japan covers vast latitudes and so is blessed with a variety of fruits, ranging from apples and pears in the north to various citrus fruits and the Japanese loquat in the south. Mikan, known as satsuma, is probably the most popular Japanese fruit in the West but kaki (persimmon) and nashi (pear) are also making their way into Western supermarkets. The beautiful reddish orange colour of kaki makes it ideal to use in cooking, since it expresses both the fruit season itself and the autumnal colour of the leaves.

Citrus varieties, such as yuzu and sudachi, are all used to add flavour to Japanese cooking.

YUZU

Among the many varieties of citrus fruits used in Japanese cooking, yuzu is the most popular. It is about the size of a clementine with a firm, thick yellow skin and is in season throughout winter. Apart from culinary uses, yuzu is used in the bath in Japan; a hot citrus bath is good for your skin and for warming up your whole body. Yuzu is occasionally available in season from Japanese supermarkets, although lime can be substituted if it cannot be found. A citrus flavouring called ponzu is made commercially to resemble the aroma of yuzu and is available in jars.

Aroma and flavour

Yuzu has an unique, sharp and strong, penetrating aroma, which makes it too sharp tasting to eat fresh.

Culinary uses

Yuzu is used almost entirely for its exquisitely aromatic rind. Tiny pieces and slivers from the bright yellow skin are scraped and used to garnish soups, salads, simmered dishes, pickles, relishes and desserts. Although the fruit is not edible, the juice can be used in salad dressings and dipping sauces. The whole outer skin, after the flesh has been removed, is often used as a cup in which to serve hors d'oeuvres.

Left: Yuzu

Below: Sudachi

Preparation and cooking

Using a very sharp knife, cut small pieces just before serving each time the yuzu is used. A few tiny pieces of the rind, up to 5mm/¼in in diameter, will be sufficient to garnish each dish.

SUDACHI

This is another of the many varieties of citrus fruits used in Japanese cooking. Sudachi is a little smaller than yuzu, weighing 30–40g/1¼–1½oz, and has a firm thick green skin and light yellow, moist flesh with relatively large seeds. The juice is not as sharp as that of yuzu, so it is used mainly to garnish *sashimi* (prepared raw fish), and grilled (broiled) fish and hotpot dishes. The most notable combination, however, is with matsutake (pine mushroom) and the juice is always sprinkled over dishes such as lightly grilled matsutake or steamed matsutake teapot soup. The rind is also finely grated and used as a flavouring for dipping condiments. It has only a short season, appearing in late summer. Sudachi is not normally available outside Japan but lime, or even lemon, make an acceptable substitute.

Right: Kaki, the Japanese persimmon, whose arrival at market heralds the coming of autumn for the Japanese.

KAKI

Also known as Japanese persimmon, the kaki has been grown in Japan for centuries. There are as many as 800–1,000 varieties and those that are available in the West are normally fuyu or jiro. The kaki grows to about 10cm/4in in diameter and has a hard, smooth reddish orange skin and dense but crunchy flesh. It tastes very similar to Sharon fruit, one of the persimmon family. It has a regular, flower-like pattern at the core and can contain eight seeds although it is often seedless, which makes this fruit useful as a decorative garnish.

Kaki fruit in a dish signifies autumn as its reddish colour is suggestive of autumn leaves. It is also used in dressed vegetable dishes and salads. There are some bitter varieties, which are not suitable for eating unprocessed and these are often dried like dates.

MIKAN

Known in the West as satsuma or mandarin, mikan grows in the warmer regions of Japan, particularly on the south and west coasts facing the Pacific Ocean. The English name for mikan, satsuma, comes from the old name for the western coastal region of the southernmost island, Kyushu, from where mikan was first exported.

Mikan is a winter fruit, which is one of the most juicy and sweetest of orange varieties and is also a good source of vitamin C and beta-carotene. Fresh mikan are widely available in the West, and it is also possible to buy canned, peeled whole mikan in syrup.

Aroma and flavour

Mikan has a faint citrus aroma and a sweet, juicy flavour.

Culinary uses

Apart from being eaten raw, mikan is used mainly as a dessert with kanten (agar-agar) or other fruits. After removing the flesh, the intact skin can be used as a cup in which to serve hors d'oeuvres.

Left: Nashi (Japanese pears)

Right: Japanese apples are much larger than Western types – these ones are about 10cm/4in in diameter.

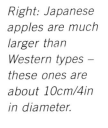

APPLES

Originally from Central Asia, apples are some of the most common fruits grown all over the world: there are said to be more than 10,000 varieties. In Japan up to 1,500 types have existed in the country, though usually only about 20 varieties are commercially grown. Modern varieties of apples are relatively new to Japan; they came from America in 1872. However, Japan has since developed many new varieties and is now exporting its own crossbreeds, such as Fuji, to the West. Japan has also developed varieties that contain what is called honey – a sweet, almost transparent part – found around the core. These types are not normally available outside of Japan.

Fuji is a cross between Kokko and Delicious and is regarded by some as one of the best apples in the world. It is juicy, yet the flesh is dense with a rich aroma and sweet flavour. It keeps well.

NASHI

Simply meaning pear, nashi is a round, russel-coloured Japanese pear now widely available in the West. There are about ten Japanese or crossbreed varieties and popular ones include chojuro and nijusseiki. Since nashi contain 84–89 per cent water, they have a very watery, crunchy texture and are not noticeably sweet. They have an almost transparent flesh and can be used for jam but are mostly eaten raw as hors d'oeuvres or in salads.

UME

Also known as Japanese apricot, ume is one of the oldest fruits grown in Japan. There are about 300 varieties, which are roughly divided into two categories: flowering trees and fruit-bearing trees. Like an apricot, the pale green fruit turns yellow with reddish patterns on it when ripe. It grows to about the size of a golf ball and is harvested from June through to July. Ume is an unusual fruit since you are not supposed to eat it fresh. Not only is it too sharp to eat but the unripe fruit contains prussic acid at its core, which can cause stomach upsets. Instead, it is processed into umeboshi (salted and dried ume), jam, umeshu (ume liqueur) and confectionery.

Below: Unpleasant to eat fresh, the Japanese have developed a number of ways of preparing ume. They can be salted and dried, or made into jams and liqueurs, and even confectionery.

Pickled ume or apricot

This is a simple method for pickling ume (or apricot), which retains the crunchiness of the fruit. A healthy dish, it is good eaten with rice.

MAKES ABOUT 1KG/2¼LB

INGREDIENTS
   1kg/2¼lb unripe ume or young
     small apricots
   15ml/1 tbsp rice vinegar or white
     wine vinegar
   115g/4oz/1 cup salt
   shochu or brandy

1 Wash the ume or apricots and soak in plenty of water for at least 1 hour. Drain and pat dry with kitchen paper.

2 Trim the stem part using a cocktail stick (toothpick) and place the fruit in a freezer bag. Sprinkle the vinegar over the fruits, then add two-thirds of the salt. Holding the bag in one hand, roll the fruit around to distribute the salt.

3 Put half of the remaining salt in a sterilized non-metallic bowl and add the contents of the freezer bag. Sprinkle the rest of the salt on top.

4 Using a cloth dampened with shochu or brandy, wipe the inside of the bowl, then cover the fruits with a shochu- or brandy-sprayed plate and place a clean 1.6kg/3½lb weight on top. Wrap the bowl, plate and weight with clear film (plastic wrap) and cover with a lid.

5 Leave to pickle for a week, during which time unwrap, take the weight off and shake the pan to spread the liquid around the fruits twice daily.

Pickling ume

Properly done, pickled ume will last for several months in the refrigerator and is a healthy stand-by snack or light meal if eaten with boiled rice. When pickling, (see above) it is important to ensure sterile conditions are maintained at all times: once placed in the freezer bag, do not touch the fruit unnecessarily. During the week when it is necessary to shake the pan containing the fruit, again make sure that the prepared fruit and equipment never come into contact with unsterilized items.

Once the fruit has been allowed to pickle, remove the clear film and transfer the ume or apricots to a sterilized bottle together with the liquid from the bowl, cover and store in the refrigerator. They will mature in about a week and be ready for eating then, though will keep for several months if properly sealed.

Home-made umeboshi

Umeboshi, salted and dried ume, is a unique Japanese pickle, usually eaten with rice for breakfast. It is regarded as having a tonic quality, aiding digestion and keeping the intestinal tract clear. It is often pickled with red shiso leaves for flavour as well as for its bright red colour. The following is a very basic method for salting ume or alternatively young small apricots.

MAKES ABOUT 2.5KG/5½LB

INGREDIENTS
    2kg/4½lb ume or young apricots
    120ml/4fl oz/½ cup shochu or
       white wine
    360g/12½oz salt

1 Wash the ume or apricots carefully and soak in plenty of water overnight.

COOK'S TIP
After drying in the sun for three days, the fruits are ready to eat, but will mature in one year and their flavour will improve with keeping.

2 Drain and, using a cocktail stick (toothpick), remove the stem part. Pat each fruit dry with a clean cloth, place in a large freezer bag and sprinkle three-quarters of the shochu or white wine evenly over the fruit.

3 Add three-quarters of the salt and roll the fruit around in the bag so the salt is evenly distributed.

4 Put half the remaining salt in a deep non-metallic bowl, then transfer all the ume or apricots to the bowl and evenly sprinkle the fruit with the remaining salt. Thoroughly spray the inside of the bowl with the remaining shochu or white wine.

5 Place a plate over the fruits inside the bowl and put a 4–5kg/9–11lb weight on top. Seal the bowl with clear film (plastic wrap), then cover tightly with a cloth or paper.

6 Leave in a cool place away from direct sunlight for about 10 days or until the liquid rises above the level of the plate.

7 Reduce the weight on top of the fruits by half and leave wrapped for another 10–15 days. Drain.

8 Spread the salted fruits on a flat bamboo strainer and air-dry in the sunlight for three days.

BIWA

The loquat originated in China, though it commonly grows in South-east Asia. Biwa bears yellowish orange, slightly dense fruits, the size of a small egg. and has a faintly acidic, not very sweet flavour and firm texture. The loquat is called biwa, after the guitar-like Asian instrument, which its oval shape resembles. When ripe, biwa peels well to reveal underneath a smooth and shiny surface.

In Japan, the loquat grows along the Pacific coast to Kyushu, the southern island, and is in season in early spring. It is generally consumed fresh, but because of its beautiful yellowish orange colour and small size, biwa is sometimes used decoratively as part of hors d'oeuvres trays to represent the arrival of spring. It is also sometimes used for desserts with jelly or kanten (agar-agar).

ICHIGO

First introduced by the Dutch traders in the middle of the 19th century, the strawberry is a relatively new addition to what is now a huge Japanese fruit industry. Many varieties from the USA, England and France have been cross-bred and Japan now produces various firm, sweet strawberries in differing sizes, such as Toyonoka and Joho. The huge, almost square shaped Fukuwa Ichigo, formerly the favourite in Japan, is now declining in popularity due to the influx of new varieties.

Ichigo, which are rich in vitamin C, are available all year round in Japan due to the favourable climate and the use of technology in cultivation.

Below: Smaller Western types of ichigo (strawberries) are now more popular in Japan than the traditional large variety.

FISH

There is no doubt that the Japanese are the world's biggest fish eaters. They deal with 3,000 kinds of fish and shellfish daily at the Tokyo fish market, the world's biggest fish market by volume of trade. Choices are far greater in Japan than anywhere else in the world and housewives go shopping for fresh fish every day. The following are some of the essential fish for Japanese cooking.

MAGURO

A member of the mackerel family, maguro or tuna has become widely available in the West. There are several kinds of tuna: blue-fin (black tuna in Japan), big-eye, yellow-fin, long-finned and southern blue-fin. Katsuo, skipjack tuna, although in the same family, is a different group of fish.

The blue-fin is the king of tuna, with deep red meat. It inhabits warm seas around the world reaching the southern coast of Hokkaido, the northernmost island of Japan. In summer it weighs about 350kg/770lb and has a 3m/10ft

Below: Maguro intended for sashimi *is classified according to which part of the fish it is from and its oiliness. O-toro, front, is oilier than* chu-toro, *middle, though both are from the lower part of the fish. Akami, back, is from the upper part of the tuna and is less oily.*

long body. The most commonly fished tuna is the big-eye, which grows to 2m/6ft in tropical seas. The lesser-quality long-finned one is usually processed and canned or used as steaks. The southern blue fin is now becoming as popular as the blue-fin.

Tuna is often sold already skinned and sliced as steaks or in chunks, which can make it sometimes difficult to tell which tuna you are buying.

In Japan, tuna is normally displayed cut into thick rectangular pieces – convenient for *sashimi*. There are usually two kinds, akami and toro, depending on which part of the fish the flesh comes from. Akami, red meat, is from the main, upper part of the body and toro, oily meat, is from the lower. It is sometimes classified by the degree of oiliness into *chu-toro*, middle toro, or *o-toro*, big toro. Akami was more popular than toro before World War II, but now it is generally thought that toro is superior in taste to akami and it is thus priced accordingly.

Aroma and flavour

Maguro has a delicate, sweet flavour and a dense, smooth texture.

Culinary uses

Maguro is most often used for *sashimi* and sushi, dressed salads, salt grilling (broiling), *teriyaki*, and simmered dishes. Long-finned tuna is not used raw, but is sold canned as steaks.

Preparation and cooking

Always use fresh fish and avoid any that is discoloured. Trim off any veins.

Storage

Tuna that is to be eaten raw should be used straight away, or stored in the refrigerator for up to two days. It can also be frozen.

Slicing fish for sashimi and sushi

Fish that can be eaten raw include tuna, skipjack tuna, salmon, mackerel, turbot, sea bass and sea bream. Use absolutely fresh fish and avoid ready-cut steaks or filleted fish. Also, do not eat defrosted frozen fish raw.

Slicing tuna, skipjack tuna or salmon

Buy a chunky piece, avoiding the part with veins. Cut the chunk into 2–3cm/¾–1¼in thick, 6–7cm/2½–2¾in wide fillets. To cut for sushi, cut 5mm/¼in thin slices crossways, placing the knife's blade slightly at an angle against the chopping board.

For *sashimi*, slice 1cm/½in thick pieces, again keeping the blade slightly at an angle.

Slicing smaller or flat fish

Using a sharp knife, fillet and skin the fish carefully, then remove all bones from the fillets. Cut flat fish fillets in half down the centre, then slice very thinly, inserting the blade diagonally.

KATSUO

Skipjack tuna is one of the most important and versatile fish in Japanese cooking, but it is not usually available fresh in the West, since once killed it goes off very quickly. It grows to about 1m/3ft long and weighs up to 20kg/44lb in tropical to subtropical seas, coming up on the warm current in large shoals to the Japanese coasts in spring. Katsuo is a handsome fish, with a deep blue-mauve back and silvery white belly with a few black stripes. In the same katsuo group are frigate mackerel, round frigate mackerel and striped bonito; these are slightly smaller than skipjack tuna.

In Japan, katsuo caught at the beginning of the season – in spring to early summer – is called hatsu-gatsuo (first katsuo), and is regarded as a delicacy. The autumn katsuo are known as modori-gatsuo (returning katsuo) as they are on their way back south. They have a richer flavour and firmer texture.

Aroma and flavour

Katsuo has dark red flesh, much darker than tuna, and a slightly fishy aroma.

Culinary uses

Katsuo is famous for its *tataki*, seared carpaccio eaten with ginger, garlic and other herbs. It is also dried whole to make katsuo-bushi, a hard fish block that is shaved to make the fish flakes used as the base of Japanese dashi stock. Processed and canned skipjack tuna is available outside Japan.

SAKE

While sake refers to salmon only, salmon and trout are categorized in the same group of fish although, rather confusingly, some salmon such as chinook (*Onorhynchus tshawytscha*), cherry (*O. masou masou*) and pink (*O. gorbuscha*) are regarded as trout in Japan. There are also some species such as coho salmon (*O. kisutch*) and blue-back (*O. nerka*) that the Japanese call trout as well as salmon. The king of salmon in Japan is chum salmon (*O. keta*), which has a perfect silvery body. It comes back to the river of its birth for spawning from September to January in Japan and some are caught for artificial insemination to be later released. Ishikari, a region on Hokkaido, the northernmost island, is famous for its salmon fisheries.

Left: Me kajiki (swordfish) is usually sold in blocks or steaks.

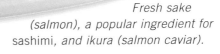

Above: Fresh sake (salmon), a popular ingredient for sashimi, *and ikura (salmon caviar).*

Culinary uses

Salmon is used for *sashimi* in the West but, due to parasite infestation, not in Japan. For *sashimi*, ask the fishmonger to cut fresh from a big chunk of salmon rather than use ready-cut steaks.

In Japan, salmon is traditionally often salted and wrapped in an aramaki (straw mat). Fresh salmon is used for grilling (broiling), frying, *saka-mushi* (sake steaming), hotpots and soup dishes. *Ishikari-nabe* is a salmon hot-pot dish in miso soup. Salmon is also processed to make canned and smoked salmon. Other products from salmon include sujiko (salted whole ovary) and ikura (salmon caviar).

KAJIKI

Also known as kajiki maguro, kajiki is the general term for a group of fish, the two most important examples being ma-kajiki (striped marlin) and me-kajiki (swordfish). They all have a long sword-like beak and a big fin on the back. These fish inhabit subtropical to tropical seas and grow to 3–5m/10–16½ft, some weighing over 500kg/1,100lb.

Aroma and flavour

Kajiki have a taste and firm texture similar to tuna. Ma-kajiki is considered the best and it has a light pink flesh.

Culinary uses

Kajiki is used for processed foods but can also be eaten as *sashimi* or *teriyaki*.

Right: Whole and filleted suzuki (sea bass)

SUZUKI

The sea bass grows to about 1m/3ft long and tastes better when over 60cm/24in. It is a handsome fish with big round eyes, a blue-grey back and silvery white belly. The pinkish white flesh, together with the delicate flavour and the chunky texture, adds a pleasant freshness to *sashimi* and sushi.

If suzuki is to be cooked, it should be done so very lightly with sauce, in soup, steamed or in a hotpot. The flesh is too delicate to be fried.

Sea bass are available all year round, as whole fish or as fillets. They are at their best in spring and early summer, before they spawn. The tastiest specimens are wild, but farmed suzuki are an acceptable alternative.

Below: Red and black tai (sea bream). The flavour and texture of black tai is similar to red, but not as fine.

TAI

In Japanese cooking, sea bream, or tai, has a special place as a celebratory fish simply because the ending of the Japanese word for "celebration" sounds the same. The largest tai grow to 1m/3ft long but it is the 30–50cm/12–20in fish that is used whole for grilling (broiling). For special occasions, the fish may be shaped before it is grilled with the use of skewers to make it look as if it is still alive and moving to symbolize a vibrant figure bravely swimming through troubled waters. Red tai has a silvery red skin, which becomes redder when grilled, and red is regarded as a cheerful, festive colour in Japan.

The flesh of tai is milky white and flaky when it is cooked so it is used for making soboro (fish flakes). It is also used for *sashimi* and sushi – such as oshizushi (pressed sushi) – as well as in soups and rice dishes.

Filleting and skinning round fish

1 Scale and gut the fish, cut off the head and wash under running water. Pat dry with kitchen paper and place the fish flat on a chopping board.

2 Insert a sharp knife as close as possible to the backbone. Cut along the back towards the tail keeping the knife flat to the bone.

3 Turn the fish over and repeat to fillet the other side.

4 Place one fillet at a time skin-side down on the chopping board and insert the blade between the skin and meat at the tail end. Press the skin firmly down with one hand and push the blade along the skin towards the head to remove the skin.

KAREI

There are more than 100 species of the karei family worldwide, including plaice, sole, halibut and flounder, and 20 of these inhabit the seas around Japan. Karei look very similar to hirame (see below) except chiefly for the location of the eyes: karei have eyes on the right-hand side of the body and hirame on the left. Karei also have a smaller mouth. Depending on the species the texture and flesh can vary greatly. Sole is arguably the finest fish of the group, with a firm, delicate flesh and superb flavour. The best halibut has a fine, meaty texture and is usually sold whole, though larger ones may be prepared as steaks or fillets. Flounder has a soft texture and less distinct flavour.

The season for karei varies according to the species, and komochi-garei (pregnant karei) is the most sought after type. Karei are a very versatile fish and are used for *sashimi*, as well as frying, simmering and grilling (broiling).

HIRAME

A type of flounder, hirame is a flat fish with its eyes on the back. The skin on the back is shiny black; on the belly it is opaque white. It is one of the most commonly used fish in Japanese cooking, being used for *sashimi* and sushi as well as for frying, simmering and steaming, and in vinegared vegetable dishes and dressed salads. The thin, broad chain-like frill on the edges of the fish, called *engawa,* is regarded as a delicacy and is used for *sashimi,* simmered and grilled dishes. You can substitute turbot or lemon sole, if you wish.

Filleting and skinning flat fish

1 Place the fish on a chopping board and, using a sharp knife, make slits in the centre on the bone and both sides just inside the fins.

2 Inserting the blade horizontally between the flesh and the bones, carefully run the top of the blade along the bones separating the meat. Gently pull back the flesh as you proceed, handling the fish with care as you cut.

3 Repeat this procedure to remove the three other fillets, two on either side of the fish.

4 Place a fillet with the skin-side down on the chopping board and insert the blade between the flesh and skin. Start from the tail end of the fillet. Firmly pressing the skin down on the chopping board with the fingers of one hand, run the blade along the skin separating the flesh from the skin. Repeat this with three other fillets.

Above: The fish known in Japan as karei is in fact a family of fish that includes plaice, sole, halibut and flounder.

Left: Whole saba (chub mackerel)

SABA

An attractive streamlined fish, saba (chub mackerel) is a red-meat fish and should be used on the day it is caught, since it goes off very quickly. To check its freshness, make sure the eyes are clear, the skin shiny and that the intestines do not smell. A small saba is better than a large specimen. Saba is a relatively fatty fish, usually with 16 per cent fat, although this increases to over 20 per cent in autumn when it is in season, and 20 per cent protein.

Aroma and flavour

Saba has a succulent flavour but has a fishy smell, which can be moderated through the use of salt. It also goes well with miso and vinegar. In *sashimi*, eat dipped in a little shoyu with grated fresh root ginger.

Culinary uses

For sashimi, very fresh saba is first salted and then marinated in vinegar. Saba should not be eaten unmarinated due to the risk of parasite infestation. This method of marinating, called *shime-saba*, meaning firming saba, clears parasites. Saba is often fried, though it is not used for tempura as its flavour is quite different from other tempura ingredients and much stronger.

AJI

This is the general term for about 50 species of a group of fish ranging from horse mackerel to scad, which are now often available at good fishmongers in the West. Aji can grow up to 40cm/16in, but is normally caught young at 10–20cm/4–8in long. Shima-aji (striped jack), grows to about 1m/3ft. Aji is regarded as a high-quality fish, and is mainly reserved for *sashimi*. Ordinary aji is a grey, firm fish with a sharp, saw-like line of spiky scales on both sides of its lower body; these should be cut out, otherwise they may hurt you when you handle the fish. The season runs from spring to autumn.

Culinary uses

Very fresh aji is made into *tataki*, finely chopped flesh eaten with shoyu and grated fresh root ginger. It is also used for grilling (broiling), simmering, and in vinegared dishes. Smaller fish is good for frying whole. Aji is also famous for its dried products such as *hiraki-boshi* (the whole body is opened and dried) and *mirin-boshi* (a whole opened body dried with mirin) and *kusaya* (a strong smelling, opened dried body). Dried aji are available from Asian supermarkets.

Below: Whole aji

Shime-saba (salt and vinegar cured mackerel)

1 Fillet a very fresh mackerel but leave the skin intact. Place the two fillets flesh-side down on a thick bed of salt in a large, flat dish and cover them completely with more salt. Leave for at least 30 minutes, ideally for 3–4 hours.

2 Wash the fillets and pat dry with kitchen paper, then remove all the bones, with tweezers, if you wish.

3 Put about 120ml/4fl oz/½ cup rice vinegar or white wine vinegar in a flat serving dish. Lay the fillets flesh-side down in the dish and sprinkle more vinegar over them. Leave the fillets to marinate for 10 minutes, then drain.

4 Pat dry with kitchen paper and carefully remove the transparent skin with your fingers, working from head to tail, leaving the silver pattern on the flesh intact. For *sashimi*, cut the fillets crossways into 1–2cm/½–¾in thick slices.

Left: The firm, chunky flesh of ankoh makes this fish ideal for most forms of cooking.

ANKOH

Monkfish or anglerfish, known as ankoh in Japan, is highly symbolic of winter in Japanese culinary terms. Fugu and puffer are similar winter fish.

Culinary uses

A popular fish, ankoh is cooked in a hotpot at the table in restaurants as well as at home. It has a firm, chunky meat, not flaky even when cooked, so it is suitable for simmering, frying or grilling.

All the parts of the ankoh, including the liver, stomach and ovaries, are eaten but the liver is regarded as a particular delicacy and is often compared to foie gras. The liver is normally marinated in a vinegar sauce.

IWASHI

Sardines, iwashi, are the most commonly used fish in Japan, and they account for 25 per cent of the total catch by the sea fisheries. Along with the main species, there are a number of other varities also considered part of the same group, including ma-iwashi (Japanese pilchard), urume-iwashi (big-eye sardine) and a smaller species, katakuchi-iwashi (Japanese anchovy). Ma-iwashi has a blue-green back and silvery white belly with dark dots on both sides of the body. It grows up to 25–30cm/10–12in long. Katakuchi-iwashi grows to about 15cm/6in long. Iwashi is best in winter but is available all year round.

Culinary uses

Fresh iwashi is eaten grilled (broiled), in vinegared dishes, in mixed sushi, fried and minced (ground) into fish balls. However, it is mostly processed to make canned and numerous dried products such as niboshi, which is used for

Below: Beheaded and gutted iwashi (sardines) are packed raw, with their backbones, in oil; the canning process cooks them.

making dashi stock, and mezashi, four to six small half-dried iwashi strung together in a row with a piece of straw. Tiny fries under 3cm/1¼in long are normally dried to make shirasu-boshi (see Fish Products). In the past, export of these fish has been limited due to differing food regulations, but some are now produced in the West and are available from Japanese supermarkets.

SAMMA

Also known as saury, this long, narrow fish has a blue-black back and shiny silver-white belly. It inhabits the seas around North America and Russia, coming down towards Japan in autumn, the best time to eat it since by then it has acquired its maximum fat content of 20 per cent.

Preparation and cooking

In autumn, samma is best grilled (broiled) or pan-fried whole and eaten with a little grated daikon and shoyu to moderate its fishy smell. Dried samma is also very popular. In other seasons when it is less oily, fresh samma is used for making vinegared salads or sushi.

Fresh samma is sold in season at high-quality fishmongers, and cooked samma in cans is often available.

Below: Samma

SHELLFISH

Along with fish, shellfish have always been an indispensable ingredient in Japanese cooking, and Japan probably consumes the widest range of shellfish in the world. Most types are used for *sashimi* and sushi as well as in other forms of cooking. The following are some of the most popular shellfish used in Japanese cooking that are also widely available outside Japan.

Note: In the US all prawns are called shrimp, then differentiated according to size: small, medium, jumbo. The Japanese, however, use both shrimp and prawn, so US equivalents in brackets will not be provided, to avoid confusion.

EBI

Among the numerous kinds of shellfish used in Japanese cooking, the prawn has the largest market share. If you want to eat prawn sushi, for instance, at a sushi restaurant in Japan, you need to specify which prawn you would like from among at least five kinds likely to be available. Kuruma-ebi (tiger prawn) has a light reddish shell with brown or blue-red stripes and grows to about 20cm/8in long. Ushi-ebi (black tiger prawn) has a dark grey shell with black stripes and, along with kuruma-ebi, supposedly has the best flavour. Both are best eaten raw when very fresh but are also used for grilling (broiling), simmering, frying and in soups.

Below: Ushi-ebi (black tiger prawns) are considered the most flavoursome type of prawn.

Right: Pink shrimps

Korai-egi (Chinese prawn), also known as taisho-ebi, has a light grey shell and is used for tempura and other frying dishes, stir-frying or simmering.

Japanese shrimps, such as shiba-ebi and botan-ebi, are used mainly for cooking, and hokkoku aka-ebi, also known as ama-ebi, is a delicious sushi topping. Tenaga-ebi (freshwater shrimp) has long tentacles and is often used for simmering and frying, while even smaller shrimps, sakura-ebi, are mostly dried. Unfortunately, many of these are not available outside of Japan.

Preparation and cooking

In Japan all prawns and shrimps are available fresh, sometimes still alive, but in the West they generally come on to the market frozen. One advantage of prawns is that they are available all year round. They become bright red or pink when cooked, thus providing colour to a dish. When cooking prawns, leave them in their shells so that they won't lose too much of their flavour.

Ensuring straight prawns

When heated, prawns curl up. For tempura, grills or griddles where you do not wish the prawn to curl, skewer it lengthways with a cocktail stick (toothpick) before cooking and carefully remove it afterwards. If it proves difficult to remove the stick without spoiling the shape of the prawn, for instance when preparing tempura, another option is to hold the unskewered, battered prawn by the tail and lower it into the hot oil very slowly so that it heats section by section. Take care not to touch the hot oil.

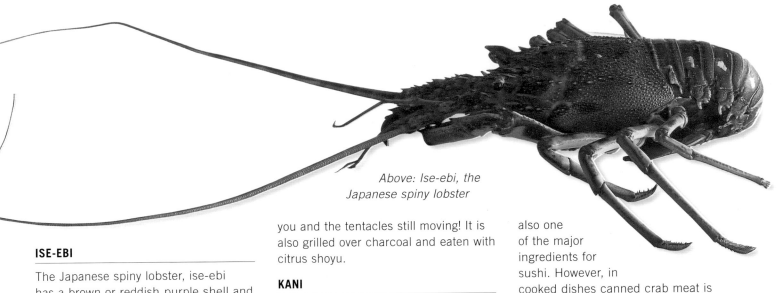

*Above: Ise-ebi, the
Japanese spiny lobster*

ISE-EBI

The Japanese spiny lobster, ise-ebi
has a brown or reddish purple shell and
smaller claws than most American and
European lobsters. It grows off the
Pacific coast of west Japan to about
35cm/14in, though it also inhabits the
seas around the Caribbean, Australia
and Africa. Ise-ebi is traditionally used
for celebratory meals because the red
colour, when cooked, signifies
happiness in Japan.

Culinary uses

Lobsters have a uniquely firm, sweet
flesh with a delicious flavour. Fresh
ones are nearly always eaten as
sashimi. At fish restaurants they are
often kept in a tank and the chef makes
a dish called *iki-zukuri* (live *sashimi*)
from your choice of lobster in front of
you. But beware, the *sashimi*
will be arranged on the
dissected shell with
the head intact,
its sad eyes
looking at

you and the tentacles still moving! It is
also grilled over charcoal and eaten with
citrus shoyu.

KANI

There are about 1,000 different crabs
inhabiting the seas around Japan alone.
The commonest are tabara-gani (king
crab), kegani (horsehair crab) and
zuwai-gani (snow crab). As its intestine
goes off very quickly, kani is always
boiled or steamed, often as soon as it is
caught on board the fishing boat, before
going to market.

King crabs look like gigantic spiny
spiders, but are very good to eat. A
mature male king crab can weigh up
to 12kg/26½lb and measure almost 1m/
39in across. Their triangular bodies are
bright red, with a pale cream underside.

Culinary uses

The claw flesh is the main part eaten,
most often fresh with citrus shoyu, in
salads, in grilled (broiled) and fried
dishes, or in hotpots. Crab meat is

*Left: Tabara-gani (king
crab) claws*

also one
of the major
ingredients for
sushi. However, in
cooked dishes canned crab meat is
more usually used. Be advised that
crab sticks or seafood sticks do not
usually contain crab meat.

Japanese delicacies

Kani-miso Crab intestine
mixture, is considered a delicacy
in Japan and is most often served
as part of an hors d'oeuvres tray
or as an accompaniment to sake.
Kani-miso is available canned.

Snow crab The sweet-tasting flesh
of this crab is usually sold frozen
or canned. The snow crab itself
has a roundish pinkish-brown
body and long legs. It is also
known as the queen of the crabs.

IKA

Squid is a common shellfish in Japan and several types are used in cooking. Which squid is selected for which dish is determined by taste, texture, colour and seasonal availability.

Surume-ika (Pacific flying squid), also known as Japanese common squid, has a dark, red-brown skin. It grows to about 30cm/12in long with tentacles as much as 20cm/8in long, and is in season throughout summer to autumn. Yari-ika (spear squid) grows to about 40cm/16in with relatively short tentacles and has a faintly reddish body with a pointed head. This squid is most commonly available in the West from winter to late spring.

Above: The flesh of larger cuttlefish, such as kaminari-ika, is delicious finely sliced and used in sashimi.

Kensaki-ika (swordtip squid) is very similar to yari-ika, but with a sharper, pointed head, and it is in season from spring to summer. Aori-ika (board-mantle squid) looks like a big cuttlefish, over 40cm/16in long with 50cm/20in tentacles, but without the calcareous shell and although it is available in summer it is not very common. Koh-ika (cuttlefish) has a round body about 18cm/7in long and 20cm/8in tentacles,

with a hard inside shell and thick flesh. Its season runs from the beginning of autumn to late winter. Kaminari-ika, available at the same time, is a large cuttlefish with tentacles that can grow up to 45cm/18in. Hotaru-ika (firefly squid) is unique. It has a luminous body that grows to a mere 5–7cm/2–2¾in and has an almost transparent skin. It inhabits the seas around Japan and is available from spring to summer. Aka-ika (flying squid) is a large squid with a dark reddish brown skin and a thin, gluey bone inside. It is commonly used for making a range of dried, smoked and marinated squid products.

Culinary uses

Fresh squid is used for *sashimi* only when it is very fresh. Prepared squid can usually be bought in Japanese supermarkets. Always cook very lightly as overcooked squid is unpleasantly tough and chewy. Whole squid is also used for making *ika-zushi* (ika stuffed with sushi rice).

Preparing squid

1 Rinse the squid thoroughly under cold running water. Put your fingers inside the body, grab the tentacles, together with the soft central bone and intestine, and gently pull out of the cavity.

2 Separate the two flaps from the body so that the white flesh comes away from the skin attached to the flaps. Gently peel off the skin from the flaps and discard.

3 Cut away and discard the intestine. Cut off the tentacles from the head of the squid and rub off the skin.

4 For *sashimi*, cut the body flesh in half lengthways and then slice each piece crossways into thin strips to reduce its chewy texture. These strips are called ika somen (squid noodles).

5 For geso (tentacle *sashimi*), divide the ten tentacles into five equal pieces or separate individually, and cut the two long feelers in half.

6 For tempura, pan-frying and grilling (broiling), make criss-cross slits on the skin side of the body and cut into pieces.

COOK'S TIPS
• The tentacles can be tough when fried, so chop the tentacles finely and fry with vegetables.
• To make squid "flowers", make delicate, diagonal criss-cross slits across the inside of the flesh and cut into small pieces. Use in quick frying dishes.

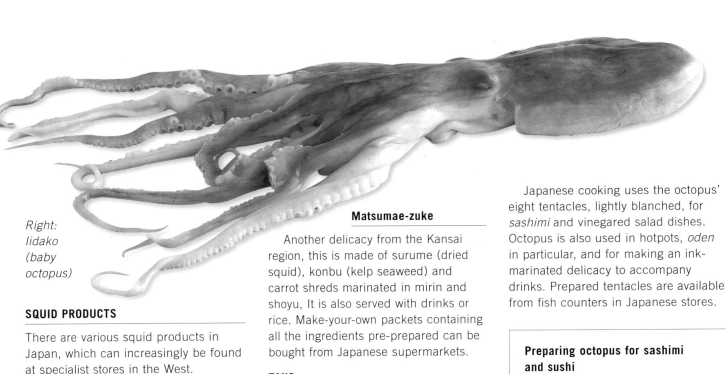

Right: Iidako (baby octopus)

SQUID PRODUCTS

There are various squid products in Japan, which can increasingly be found at specialist stores in the West.

Surume

This is whole squid opened up and dried, and is one of a number of delicacies served to accompany drinks. It is normally grilled (broiled) whole, torn crossways with the fingers into fine shreds, and eaten sprinkled with a little shoyu. Kensaki-ika (swordtip squid) with its fine, tender flesh, is the best. It is available, whole or shredded in packets, from Japanese supermarkets and the Chinese version is generally available from Asian supermarkets.

Shiokara

This is raw squid, marinated in its own ink and salt. It is served with drinks or rice and is available in jars.

Matsumae-zuke

Another delicacy from the Kansai region, this is made of surume (dried squid), konbu (kelp seaweed) and carrot shreds marinated in mirin and shoyu, It is also served with drinks or rice. Make-your-own packets containing all the ingredients pre-prepared can be bought from Japanese supermarkets.

TAKO

The octopus' contrasting colours of milky white flesh and dark red skin (once heated, octopus skin turns red), together with the unusual round shape of its sliced tentacles, adds interesting character to Japanese cooking. There are over ten types of octopus caught all over the world and their sizes vary from Idako (baby octopuses), which are less than 10cm/4in, to ones over 3m/10ft. The most common octopus are in the *ma-dako* family.

Above: Surume, dried squid, is made from kensaki-ika (swordtip squid), and is ranked first in terms of quality.

Japanese cooking uses the octopus' eight tentacles, lightly blanched, for *sashimi* and vinegared salad dishes. Octopus is also used in hotpots, *oden* in particular, and for making an ink-marinated delicacy to accompany drinks. Prepared tentacles are available from fish counters in Japanese stores.

Preparing octopus for sashimi and sushi

1 Clean an octopus weighing 675g/1½lb, and separate the head and tentacles. Discard the head or reserve for use in another dish.

2 Bring plenty of water to the boil in a large, deep pan, add a halved lemon, 5ml/1 tsp salt and the octopus; bring back to the boil.

3 Cook over a medium heat for 5–6 minutes, taking the octopus out and plunging it back into the boiling water so that all the skin comes into contact with the hot water. Remove from the heat, drain and allow to cool.

4 For *sashimi* and sushi, use only the cooked tentacles. Separate the tentacles and chill for no more than 15 minutes. Using a sharp knife, slice diagonally into 5mm/¼in thick rings.

Left: Large hamaguri (common hard clams) and asari (Manila clams) are just two of the many clams used in Japanese cooking.

Above: Dried hotate-gai (scallops) are soaked in a little sake and steamed to make them soft and easy to handle. This process also brings out their distinctive flavour.

HAMAGURI

Clams are one of the oldest foods in Japan as is evident from the remains of the shells found in all the prehistoric settlements excavated. They are still a very important ingredient, and many varieties are used for Japanese cooking such as aka-gai (ark shell), asari (Manila clam), tori-gai (cockle), baka-gai or aoyagi (hen clam) and hokki-gai (surf clam). They are all used for sushi and *sashimi* as well as for all other

Below: Clockwise from top left, fresh cockles, hokki-gai (surf clam), tori-gai (cockle) and aka-gai (ark shell)

methods of cooking. Hamaguri (hard clam) is the most common and is in season from winter to early spring. It is grilled (broiled), steamed or simmered in soup still in the shell and is also somtimes used shelled for cooking with rice or in hotpots. Clams should be left in salted water to extract the sand in the shell before cooking. They are available fresh, dried, or cooked in cans.

HOTATE-GAI

The scallop is a very versatile shellfish because of its size and fish-like texture. There are several members of the scallop family available in Japan, including hotate-gai, the scallop most often sold in the West; itaya-gai

Below: Kaki, pacific oysters

(Japanese scallop), tsukihi-gai (saucer scallop) and hiogi-gai (noble scallop). All varieties are regular, indispensable ingredients for sushi and *sashimi*. They are used for vinegared salads, or can be salt-grilled, simmered, fried or used in soups. The thin ribbon around the scallop's flesh and the red intestine are not wasted, but are used in soups. Dried scallop is available from most Asian supermarkets and some larger stores.

KAKI

A few Pacific oysters are available in Japan. The most common kaki (giant Pacific oyster) is oblong in shape, about 8cm/3½in long and 5cm/2in wide in contrast to the round European native oyster. It is available all through the year but is at its most flavoursome from November to March.

To eat oyster raw, Japanese-style, dip in a little citrus shoyu. *Kaki-fry* (fried breaded oyster) is another Japanese speciality. Oysters are also used in clear soups, hotpots and cooked with rice. Kaki are known to cause food poisoning so when eaten raw they should be very fresh. Always buy fresh oysters from a reputable fishmonger.

FISH ROES

The Japanese use all parts of the fish, and its eggs, in particular, are regarded as a delicacy. Since the eggs are normally heavily salted to preserve them, they go well with plain boiled rice. They are also regular ingredients in sushi and are used for making hors d'oeuvres.

TARAKO

Cod ovaries, called tarako, are available at the fish counters of supermarkets in Japan. Sold in pairs, cod ovaries are usually simply grilled (broiled) to eat with boiled rice. Mentaiko is a salted version and karashi mentaiko is a pungent chilli type. Tarako are normally coloured slightly red with vegetable colouring to make them look more attractive. Tarako is used for *norimaki* (nori-rolled sushi) and also for making hors d'oeuvres.

IKURA

In Russia, all fish eggs are called ikura, but the name is used only for salmon eggs in Japan. Ikura is already salted to preserve it, so it normally keeps for a short time. It is mainly used for sushi, eaten with grated daikon and shoyu, and also for making hors d'oeuvres. It is widely available in jars at supermarkets. Salted whole salmon ovaries called sujiko are available only in Japan.

KAZUNOKO

Salted and dried herring ovaries, kazunoko, were once abundant but are now so scarce that they have become a

rare delicacy. Soak in water overnight to soften and remove the salt before use. Kazunoko is usually eaten as it is with a little shoyu and katsuo-bushi, dried skipjack tuna flakes. It is one of the special items that constitute the New Year's day celebration brunch and is also used as a sushi topping. It is rarely available outside Japan, but most sushi restaurants have it on the menu.

UNI

The Japanese sea urchin, or uni, is a dark spiky, round sea creature that varies in size, depending on type, from 3 4cm/1¼ 1½in to over 10cm/4in in diameter. Only the ovaries are eaten. Fresh uni is one of the regular items for sushi toppings and is also used for making hors d'oeuvres. It provides an interesting golden coating for some

Above: Kazunoko (salted and dried herring ovaries)

Above: Uni (Japanese sea urchin ovaries)

Left: Ikura (salmon

seafood, such as squid, that is to be grilled and also an unusual dressing for many shellfish. Salted uni is also available.

Preparation and cooking

Look for urchins with firm spines and a tightly closed mouth (on the underside). To open, wear gloves and use a purpose-made knife, though sharp scissors can also be used. Cut into the soft tissue around the mouth and lift off the top to reveal the coral. Alternatively, slice off the top like a boiled egg. Remove the mouth and innards, which are inedible, but retain the rich juices for use in sauces. Scoop out the bright orange coral.

Below: Tarako (cod ovaries) are usually just slightly red, front, though they turn a brighter red colour when prepared with chilli, back.

FISH PRODUCTS

Numerous fish products are used in Japanese cooking and many are available in the West, fresh or frozen. They are easy to use and very useful as a flavouring in home-cooking. The following are some of the items that are increasingly available from larger Japanese supermarkets.

KATSUO-BUSHI

Katsuo, skipjack tuna, is cooked and dried whole to a hard block called katsuo-bushi and then shaved for use. Once it was the housewife's job, first thing in the morning, to shave katsuo-bushi, but today ready-shaved kezuri-bushi or hanagatsuo in various graded packets is widely available. This is one of the main ingredients in dashi stock and it is also used for sprinkling on vegetables or fish as an additional flavouring. Mixed with a little shoyu, it makes a delicious accompaniment to hot boiled rice or stuffing for *onigiri* (rice balls).

Culinary uses

Kezuri-bushi can be sprinkled on dashi-marinated boiled spinach, or on finely sliced onions; with a little shoyu added, this makes a good accompaniment to drinks. Another option is to mix with shoyu and sprinkle on hot boiled rice or use to stuff rice balls.

Right:
Various sizes and grades of ready-shaved dried fish are now readily available.

Home-made dashi stock

Dashi, fish soup stock, is probably the most frequently used ingredient in Japanese cooking. First dashi stock is used for soups; clear soup in particular. Second dashi stock is for simmering vegetables, meat and fish.

MAKES FOUR BOWLS OF SOUP

INGREDIENTS
    600ml/1 pint/2½ cups water
    10cm/4in standard konbu
    20g/¾oz or 3 × 5g/⅛oz packets
    kezuri-bushi

1 Pour the water into a pan and add the konbu. Leave to soak for 1 hour.

2 Place, uncovered, over a medium heat and bring almost to boiling point. Remove the konbu and reserve it for use in the second dashi stock. Bring the water to the boil.

3 Add about 50ml/2fl oz/¼ cup cold water and immediately add the kezuri-bushi. Bring back to the boil and remove the pan from the heat. Do not stir. Leave the kezuri-bushi to settle to the base of the pan.

4 Strain the mixture through a fine sieve and reserve the kezuri-bushi in the sieve to make a second dashi stock. This first dashi stock liquid is now ready for use.

Second dashi stock

MAKES 600ML/1 PINT/2½ CUPS

INGREDIENTS
    reserved konbu and kezuri-bushi
    from first dashi stock
    600ml/1 pint/2½ cups water
    15g/½oz or 3 × 5g/⅛oz packets
    kezuri-bushi

1 Put the reserved konbu and kezuri-bushi from the first dashi into a pan with the water. Bring to the boil, then simmer for about 15 minutes, or until the stock is reduced by a third.

2 Add the kezuri-bushi to the pan and immediately remove the pan from the heat. Skim any scum from the surface and leave to stand for 10 minutes. Strain.

COOK'S TIPS
• Freeze-dried granules called dashi-no-moto can be used to make a quick dashi stock, if preferred.
• Dashi stock can be frozen.

TATAMI-IWASHI

Tiny fry sardines are stuck together and dried into a thin sheet shaped like nori (dried seaweed sheet) to make tatami-iwashi. It is then lightly grilled before serving, and makes an excellent accompaniment for drinks as well as for hot boiled rice. Tatami-iwashi is mildly sweet with a rich flavour. It is not normally available outside Japan.

CHIRIMEN-JAKO

A speciality of the Kansai region (Osaka and surrounds), these are another form of dried shirasu (white fry sardines), which have been cooked and often flavoured with shoyu. They are eaten as are and make a good accompaniment for hot rice or in *ochazuke* (cooked rice in tea). Shoyu-flavoured ones are fairly salty. They are available in packets.

TAZUKURI

Dried small sardines, tazukuri are lightly roasted in a small pan before serving as an accompaniment for drinks or as a snack. They have a distinctive *umami* (rich flavouring). At New Year's time they are coated in sugar and served as part of the savoury celebration hamper. They are not only delicious but also very nutritional as they are full of calcium, which is highly beneficial, especially for growing children. Tazukuri are another fish product available outside of Japan.

Above: Unagi no kabayaki, grilled eel

MEZASHI

Meaning eye-pierced, mezashi is made from half-dried whole sardines strung together, four to six at a time, by a piece of straw pierced through the eyes, hence the name. It is just lightly grilled and eaten with hot boiled rice or to accompany sake. The whole sardine including the head, bones, tail and intestines can be eaten, so it is highly nutritional, full of protein and calcium, yet a cheap everyday food. A visually striking dish, and largely new to the Western palate, mezashi is sometimes available at larger Asian food stores.

SHISHAMO

This small, 10–15cm/4–6in long, narrow, pinkish silver fish is unique to the north Pacific and Atlantic oceans. Shishamo is considered one of the best Japanese delicacies to eat with sake, especially *komochi-shishamo* (shishamo with eggs), and is priced accordingly.

NIBOSHI

These hard, dried sardines are used for making a strong-flavoured dashi stock. In contrast to the delicate flavour of kezuri-bushi, niboshi is boiled for about 5 minutes to exude the flavour and make a more robust stock. Hence niboshi stock is used for making rich soups such as miso soup and the soup for soba and udon noodles.

UNAGI NO KABAYAKI

Filleted eel is steamed, then grilled (broiled) with a thick, sweet shoyu sauce. This soft fish does not resemble, or taste, like eel. It is placed on top of hot boiled rice with the accompanying sauce sprinkled with seven-spice chilli powder, or sansho. Unagi no kabayaki is available ready-to-eat in packets, frozen or vacuum-packed.

HIDARA

This dried cod fillet can be grilled, then torn into pieces with the fingers and eaten with rice. It is also used for making snacks to go with drinks, and is available in packets.

SHIRASU-BOSHI

Tiny white fry sardines, shirasu are used to make many dried products. Shirasu-boshi are a soft, plain dried shirasu, which are eaten as they are mixed with other ingredients such as grated daikon and shoyu. They make a good accompaniment for hot boiled rice and are also often used as an hors d'oeuvres and as a stuffing for *onigiri* (rice balls). Shirasu-boshi are not often easily available outside of Japan.

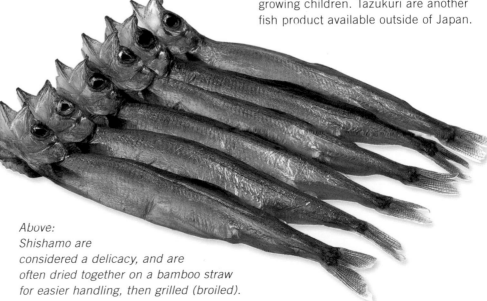

*Above:
Shishamo are considered a delicacy, and are often dried together on a bamboo straw for easier handling, then grilled (broiled).*

FISH PASTES

Numerous puréed fish products are used in Japanese cooking, among which the following are the most common. They are normally available frozen from Japanese food stores and are the main ingredients for *oden* (fish pastes and vegetables cooked in dashi-based soup).

KAMABOKO

Puréed white fish is mixed with a binding agent and made into various shapes and sizes then steamed, boiled or grilled (broiled) to produce kamaboko. The standard product is called ita-kamaboko; a small fish paste cake, about 4–5cm/1½–2in thick and 15cm/6in long, stuck on a wooden board. It can be coloured pink around the outside. Eat finely sliced with shoyu and mustard as an hors d'oeuvre to accompany drinks, or use in soups, hotpots, and with noodles.

SATSUMA-AGE

This is deep-fried kamaboko and is normally shaped into an oval disc measuring about 7.5 × 5cm/3 × 2in. Pour boiling water over the paste to reduce the oil before use. It can be eaten as it is with shoyu, or lightly grilled. It is also used for simmering with vegetables, in soups, hotpots, and in noodle dishes. There are many sizes and colours of

Above: Clockwise from left to right; chikuwa, narutomaki, satsuma-age and hanpen puréed fish products

deep-fried kamaboko and even stuffed and rolled versions as well. Ika-maki is a fried kamaboko roll with squid inside and gobo-maki is stuffed with burdock. Both of these together with ordinary satsuma-age are popular ingredients for *oden* (fish paste hotpot), and are available, mostly frozen, at Japanese and Asian supermarkets.

CHIKUWA

Puréed fish is moulded around a stick, then steamed and grilled, and the stick removed. Chikuwas normally measure about 15cm/6in long with the hole running this length. The outer skin is seared an attractive uneven brown. It can be eaten just sliced as is, or use for simmering with vegetables or in hotpots.

NARUTOMAKI

This is a kind of kamaboko with a decorative pink swirling pattern inside. It is one of the regular ingredients for ramen, Chinese-style noodles, and is also used in udon noodles and soups.

HANPEN

This puréed shark's flesh is mixed with grated yam and egg whites, shaped into a 7–8cm/3½–3¾in square cake about 1cm/½in thick and then boiled. It has a light, fluffy texture and can be eaten grilled with shoyu and mustard, and is also used for hotpots and soups.

SHINJO

There are many types of ready-made fish balls available in Japan, including *yuba-shinjo* (shinjo rolled in a sheet of dried soya bean skin). There are also flower-shaped ones in various colours used as garnishes. Some shinjo may be available at Japanese stores.

TSUMIRE

This greyish coloured fish ball is made from red meat fish such as sardines and mackerel and, though firm, has a soft texture. It is a flat disc with a "crater" in the centre so that it heals quickly and evenly. It is used in soup, oden and hotpot dishes and is available frozen.

Above: Ita-kamaboko, white fish paste on a wooden board

MEAT AND CHICKEN

The eating of meat was banned in Japan for many years, first due to Buddhism and later by the Shogunate for 300 years until 1868. However, game, such as wild boar, hare and mountain birds have always been eaten by some communities. It was only after World War II that meat, mainly beef, pork and chicken, became a part of the general diet. It is still only sparingly used; nearly always thinly sliced or shredded and cooked with vegetables, or minced (ground).

BEEF

There are four types of wagyu, (Japanese beef): black, reddish brown, hornless and short-horned. Black beef is the most common. Matsuzaka beef, also known as Kobe beef, omi beef and yonezawa beef, are the top-quality meats. They are massaged with beer, which helps to distribute the fat, so making the lean meat more tender, and wagyu meat is pink rather than red. The attention the Japanese give to their beef is highly labour intensive, which accounts for its ferociously high price. Wagyu is not available in the West but you can use sirloin or fillet instead. For *sukiyaki* and *shabu shabu*,

Right: Thinly sliced pork

Below: Chicken is used in various ways; minced for making meatballs, skewered for teriyaki, *and the thigh for barbecuing.*

Above: Finely sliced beef for shabu shabu *and* sukiyaki

where almost transparent slices are required, choose a roasting joint without a bone, or fillet. If a joint is used, trim off the fat completely and cut into 4–5cm/1½–2in thick oblong pieces, then freeze for two or three hours. Remove to the refrigerator, leave for

1 hour to half thaw and then slice into paper-thin oblong pieces. Ready-sliced *sukiyaki* beef is generally available. Trim off any excess fat, if necessary.

PORK

Since ancient times pork has been eaten, even during the period when meat was banned, and it remains popular today. It is thinly sliced, pan-fried and mixed with grated fresh root ginger and shoyu, or else chopped and used as a flavouring in vegetable dishes. Long-simmered pork is delicious with ramen.

CHICKEN

Native regional chickens, called jidori, are popular in Japan, though there are also many mass-produced broiler chickens. *Nagoya kochin* is one such jidori, with a pinkish golden, firm meat. Minced chicken is often used for making meatballs, sauces or as a flavouring for simmered vegetables. *Yakitori* is chicken pieces threaded on a bamboo skewer, then grilled (broiled) with sweet taré sauce. Boneless chicken thighs marinated in *teriyaki* sauce and then grilled are ideal for barbecues. Chicken is also used for hotpots.

SAUCES FOR FLAVOURING AND DIPPING

Shoyu and miso are the two oldest and most important flavouring sauces in Japanese cooking. Although their strong, distinctive flavours means they are used more as condiments for dipping or as flavouring for cooking, rather than as a sauce for coating food. The two also have a preservative quality and are good for marinating raw fish, meat and vegetables.

The Japanese have also developed ready-mixed sauces for certain popular dishes such as *sukiyaki* and *yakiniku* (barbecue), as well as Japanese vinegar and mirin, both made from rice.

SHOYU

Japan's ancient seasoning was called hishio, and consisted of a preserve of what was at that time very scarce and precious salt fermented with animal or vegetable protein and fibre. Grain hishio, fermented with grains such

as rice and wheat, and also beans, was developed into miso and its exuded liquid became shoyu. (The present-day sushi is also thought to derive from the ancient fish hishio, raw fish fermented with salt and rice.)

Using new techniques, introduced from China, Japan soon developed its own type of soy sauce, shoyu, made from daizu (soya beans), wheat and salt. First a mixture of soya beans and wheat is made into a culture called koji, helped by active mould; this is then mixed with salt and water, and the mash is left to ferment and brew slowly for one year. After this time it is compressed to exude the liquid, which is then refined. (Mass-produced shoyu does not follow this authentic process but instead uses chemicals to hasten it.)

Shoyu is now widely available from supermarkets, but Japanese shoyu is quite different in aroma and flavour from Chinese varieties.

Aroma and flavour

Shoyu is quite salty, although less salty now than it used to be, due to recent warnings about the role of salty food in heart disease. There are basically two types: usukuchi (light), and koikuchi, (dark). The usukuchi is an all-purpose shoyu, clearer but slightly saltier than koikuchi, which is used for making sauces such as taré for *teriyaki*. There are also many grades, depending on the grade of soya beans, which are priced accordingly. Tamari is made from soya beans only without wheat, so it is similar to the liquid obtained during the making of miso.

Light shoyu (soy sauce), left, has a lighter colour but saltier flavour than regular shoyu, far left.

Above: Light and dark shoyu. Use light shoyu, left, for flavouring, such as in clear soups, and dark shoyu, above back, in simmered dishes.

Culinary uses

Shoyu is without doubt the single most important ingredient in Japanese cuisine and is used in almost every recipe. When just a drop is added to ingredients, they do not take on the colour of the shoyu; this is called *kakushi-aji* (hidden flavour). It is often used as a dip on its own for sushi, *sashimi*, pickles and many other dishes. Tamari is a dark shoyu used for making taré sauce and is suitable for those on a wheat-free diet.

Cooking techniques

To avoid the strong colour of shoyu dulling fresh ingredients, add the sauce towards the end of the cooking time, except for long-simmered dishes. For a dip, use shoyu sparingly by pouring only 15–30ml/1–2 tbsp at a time into a small sauce dish. If, for instance, you plunge your sushi into a large bowl of shoyu, it will become too salty or else a lot of shoyu will be left at the end of the meal.

Storage

All manufactured shoyu is pasteurized, with preservatives added. Bottled shoyu, except natural or organic varieties, normally keeps fairly well for a long time. However, the flavour deteriorates gradually, so once opened it is best to use it within three months. Natural, preservative-free shoyu should be kept in the refrigerator. If a thin layer of mould forms on the surface, filter the sauce. Though harmless, do not eat.

MISO

Although lifestyles are rapidly changing, for many Japanese the day still starts with a bowl of miso soup for breakfast. Miso is one of the oldest traditional Japanese ingredients – it was already being made in the 12th century – and its origin can be traced back to the ancient seasoning called hishio, a preserve of salt fermented with grains and beans. Today, boiled daizu (soya beans) is crushed, then mixed with a culture called koji, which is made with wheat and rice, barley or beans. The fermented mixture is allowed to mature for up to three years.

Numerous kinds and brands of miso are available in supermarkets, even outside Japan. They are categorized into three basic grades according to strength of flavour and colour: shiro-miso (white, light and made with rice), aka-miso (red, medium and made with barley), and kuro-miso (black, strong and made with soya beans).

Aroma and flavour

Miso is quite salty and has a strong fermented bean flavour. Shiro-miso is the lightest in saltiness and flavour, aka-miso is of medium flavour, and the strongest is kuro-miso. There are less salty brands for the health conscious.

Culinary uses

Miso is a versatile ingredient and can be simply diluted with dashi stock to make soups, including the soup for miso ramen. It is used as seasoning for simmered dishes or dipping sauces, and also as a marinade for meat and fish. Shiro-miso (white) is a speciality of Kyoto, thus often referred to as Saikyo miso, and is particularly good for soups, dressings and marinades. Shinshu (in central Japan) and Sendai (in the north-east) are also well known for miso production and they produce both light and medium miso. Aka-miso (red) is good for soups and for meat marinades. Hatcho miso, the best kuro-miso (black), is rich and salty, and is good for dipping sauces and soups. It is often used mixed with another lighter miso.

Cooking techniques

If miso is overcooked it loses its subtle aroma, so add the paste towards the end of the cooking time. In soups, use sparingly. Dilute a little with some of the liquid and mix it into the soup. Check the taste and add more if needed.

Storage

In a tightly covered jar, miso will keep for a long time in the refrigerator, but the flavour gradually deteriorates.

Above: Clockwise from top left, aka-miso, shiro-miso, hatcho-miso and kuro-miso

Miso-marinated flat fish or steak

Flat fish such as plaice and turbot are used for this dish, which involves marinating the fish in shiro-miso, a kind of white miso.

1 On a large plate spread a thin layer of shiro-miso (use aka-miso for meat). Cover with kitchen paper and press lightly so that the paper absorbs the miso.

2 Place fish fillets, flesh-side down, or meat on the paper and cover with another piece of paper.

3 Using a knife, press a thin layer of miso on top of the paper so that the paste covers the fish or meat. Marinate fish for about 3 hours; meat can be marinated overnight.

4 Remove the fish or meat from the marinade and grill (broil).

READY-MADE SAUCES

A number of ready-to-use ingredients have been developed in recent years and Japanese cooking is much easier as a result. The following ready-made sauces are available in the West.

MEN-TSUYU

This is a dashi-based condensed sauce for soba and udon noodles. It is made of dashi stock, shoyu, salt, sugar and other ingredients, and is used as a dipping sauce or soup for noodles. The instructions on the packet will state how much water should be added to make a dip for soba and somen, or soup in which to cook udon and soba. It is usual to dilute 1:1 for a dip and 1:8 for soup. Store in the refrigerator.

TONKATSU SAUCE

Tonkatsu (pork cutlet) is one of the most popular dishes in Japan, and this thick brown sauce is the ideal accompaniment, together with shredded cabbage and mustard. It is made of fruits, spices and seasonings. You can easily make your own *tonkatsu* sauce by mixing a fruit sauce, such as ketchup, and Worcestershire sauce.

TEN-TSUYU

This tasty dipping sauce for tempura is made of dashi stock, shoyu, mirin and a number of seasonings. Ten-tsuyu is normally used undiluted together with a little grated daikon and finely shredded fresh root ginger.

YAKINIKU NO TARE

This Japanese version of barbecue sauce is made of shoyu, spices and various seasonings. It is slightly sweeter than the Western barbecue sauces and is also used for griddled food.

SUKIYAKI SAUCE

This is a sweet shoyu sauce for cooking *sukiyaki*, made of dashi stock, sugar, sake and seasonings. First thinly sliced beef is pan-fried, then some of this sauce is added, together with vegetables.

Making simple sauces at home
Most Japanese have a number of sauces in their repertoire that can be easily made on the day of use.
Yuan sauce This sauce gives a subtle flavour to rather bland ingredients such as white fish, and enhances the flavours of stronger-flavoured varieties, such as salmon. Mix together 5 parts mirin, 3 parts shoyu to 2 parts sake and 2 parts lime juice. Marinate the fish in the sauce for at least 15 minutes, before frying or cooking over a barbecue.
Tonkatsu sauce Delicious with fried pork, mix together 1 part Worcestershire sauce to 5 parts tomato ketchup. Coat pork slices in flour and beaten egg and deep-fry. Dip into the sauce and eat.

Below: The numerous types of Japanese ready-made sauces include, from left, tonkatsu sauce, sukiyaki sauce, men-tsuyu sauce, ponzu, men-tsuyu sauce for somen and yakiniku no tare.

PONZU

Made of citrus juice, vinegar and seasonings, ponzu is used mixed with shoyu and spices for hotpot dishes.

CURRY ROUX

Japan was first introduced to curry in the middle of the 19th century, not directly from India but via England, where curry powder was concocted and exported. Since then, curry has become one of the most popular daily foods in Japan. The Japanese, as with many introduced ingredients, further developed the powder into an instant curry sauce roux, mixing together all the necessary ingredients such as herbs and spices, fruits, soup stock, sauces and seasonings. It comes in the form of a soft slab, resembling a chocolate bar, in a sectioned plastic tray. All you need to do is boil the fresh ingredients such as meat or shellfish, potato, onion and carrot, and add some of this sauce mix. There are degrees of hotness: mild, medium, hot and very

hot. There are also separate roux for meat and fish. An average packet normally serves 12, but remember that a Japanese portion is very small and it really makes enough for only six to eight adult appetites, particularly if eaten on its own.

Japanese curry is quite sweet, even the very hot type, and usually contains a lot of MSG (monosodium glutamate). If you are unsure of the flavour peculiar to MSG, which can make you a little thirsty afterwards, use this product sparingly.

Left: Many types of curry roux are stocked at Japanese supermarkets. Available in boxed form, they resemble a chocolate bar and are graded by hotness (mild, medium, hot and very hot).

Homemade Japanese curry
Using a ready-mixed roux, a tasty and filling curry can be cooked in less than 30 minutes.

SERVES FOUR

INGREDIENTS
  2 onions, thinly sliced
  30ml/2 tbsp vegetable oil
  500g/1¼lb prawns (shrimp), peeled or any meat, cut into bitesize pieces
  1 carrot, peeled and chopped
  1–2 potatoes, peeled and roughly chopped
  750ml/1¼ pints/3 cups water
  125g/4¼oz (½ packet) curry roux
  15–30ml/1–2 tbsp shoyu or Worcestershire sauce, to taste (optional)
  rice, to serve

1 In a deep pan, gently stir-fry the onion slices in the vegetable oil until the onions become slightly brown. Add the prawns or meat and continue to stir-fry for 1–2 minutes.

2 Add the carrot and potatoes and stir-fry for another 1–2 minutes. Add the water and bring to the boil. Lower the heat and simmer for 5–10 minutes, more if meat is used, until the prawns and vegetables are cooked.

3 Remove from the heat. Add the roux, broken into small pieces, and stir well until all the roux pieces have melted into the soup. Place the pan back over a medium heat and gently simmer for about 5 minutes, stirring continuously, until the soup thickens.

4 To slightly reduce the sweetness of the curry, add a little shoyu or Worcestershire sauce. Serve with hot boiled rice.

VINEGAR AND MIRIN

Unlike shoyu and miso, Japanese vinegar and mirin (sweet cooking sake) are delicate tasting and good for adding subtle flavours to Japanese cooking. Both are made from rice.

RICE VINEGARS

Unless labelled yonezu (pure rice vinegar), most Japanese vinegars, called su or kokumotsu-su, normally contain other grains besides rice. If less than 40g/1½oz rice was used to make 1 litre/1¾ pint/4 cups of vinegar, it is labelled as kokumotsu-su (grain vinegar). There is also a cheap, mixed product, gohsei-su, which consists of brewed (about 60 per cent) and synthetic vinegar. Rice vinegar and other vinegars and vinegar products can be found at Japanese supermarkets.

Aroma and flavour

Japanese rice vinegar has a mild, sweet aroma and is less sharp than ordinary wine vinegar.

Culinary uses

Vinegar has many qualities. It can be used to refresh and soften saltiness, it acts as an antiseptic, and is a coagulant for proteins. It also prevents food from discolouring, helps to wash off slimy substances from food and to soften small fish bones. It is, therefore, useful from the preparation stage of food to the final seasoning. There are numerous vinegared dishes, such as cucumber and wakame salad, vinegar-cured raw fish, and gari (pickled ginger) to accompany sushi.

Cooking techniques

The slightly mild, subtle, acidic flavour of Japanese vinegar disappears quickly, so add to hot dishes at the last minute.

MIRIN

This amber-coloured, heavily sweetened sake is used only in cooking. It is one of Japan's ancient sake and is made from shochu (distilled sake). Shochu, mixed with steamed glutinous rice and koji (a yeast-like culture made from rice), is brewed and compressed to absorb the liquid, and then filtered. There is a synthetically made, cheap mirin-like liquid available called mirin-fuhmi (mirin flavouring), as opposed to hon-mirin (real mirin). The alcohol content of hon-mirin is 14 per cent and mirin-fuhmi only 1 per cent. These two types of mirin are available in bottles of 300ml/½ pint/1¼ cups or 600ml/1 pint/2½ cup from Asian supermarkets.

Culinary uses

Mirin has a faint sake aroma and syrupy texture, which adds not only a mild sweetness to food but also an attractive shiny glaze and slightly alcoholic flavour. It is used for simmered dishes and in glazing sauces such as taré (for yakitori). Other uses include mirin-boshi (a mirin-coated dried fish), and daikon is pickled in mirin pulp.

Left: Yonezu (rice vinegar) and kokumotsu-su (grain vinegar)

Cooking techniques

Use mirin towards the end of the cooking time to add a subtle sweetness and depth to the flavour of the dish. It is not meant to be used as a sweetener, but if you must, you can use 5ml/1 tsp sugar in place of 15ml/1 tbsp mirin.

Storage

Both vinegar and mirin keep well for a long time if stored in a cool place away from sunlight. The flavour of vinegar will deteriorate gradually, once the bottle is opened, so should be used as soon as possible. Once a bottle of mirin is opened, a white sugary substance will form around the cap, which is the residue after the alcohol evaporates. This is harmless but keep the bottle clean. It is best to use mirin within the shomi-kikan (appreciative period), since the flavour deteriorates and after several months it will become mouldy.

Below: When buying rice vinegar, look for hon-mirin, left, rather than mirin-fuhmi, right, which is a cheap imitation.

DRIED FLAVOURINGS

Ever on the look out for tasty accompaniments to rice, the Japanese have developed a number of flavourings, known as tsukudani.

TSUKUDANI

Various foodstuffs, such as konbu (kelp seaweed), shiitake, matsutake, dried herring, clams, beef and even whale meat are made into tsukudani. Konbu is the most popular. It is cut into small pieces and then simmered with shoyu for a long time. It is sometimes cooked with other foods, such as shiitake or matsutake, and fish flakes. Tsukudani is fairly salty and goes well with hot plain boiled rice. An assorted tsukudani set is a popular gift during the traditional gift seasons at the middle and the end of each year. Konbu tsukudani is usually available in packets from Japanese supermarkets all year round.

FURIKAKE

Consisting of various types of granulated fish and vegetable extracts, furikake are popular sprinkled on hot boiled rice. They are also used for making *onigiri* (rice balls), either mixed with rice or used as a stuffing. Various sprinkles in packets or jars are available from Japanese supermarkets.

Above: Assorted furikake (seafood and vegetable granules)

Above: Ochazuke no moto (flavourings for leftover rice)

Left: Sushi mixes

OCHAZUKE NO MOTO

A favourite Japanese way of enhancing leftover rice is to pour boiling water with added flavouring over it. There are many different flavours of ochazuke no moto available, including salted salmon, cod roe, umeboshi (salted and dried Japanese apricots) and nori, and they are available in individual packets.

SUSHI MIX

This is a packet or jar of pre-prepared ingredients for *chirashi-zushi* (mixed sushi), made by stirring the packet's contents into the rice. The garnish of shredded nori is also included in the packet. The flavour is sweet and it contains MSG (monosodium glutamate).

PICKLES

For the Japanese, rice and tsukemono (pickled vegetables) have gone hand in hand since ancient times. There are many varieties of tsukemono, also known as oshinko, preserved in all sorts of ways, and different regions have their own speciality. Barrel after barrel of freshly made tsukemono are displayed in the food hall of any department store in Japan and you can sample them before buying. The Japanese do not use vinegar as a pickling agent, instead, rice bran, miso, sake or mirin pulps, mustard, koji (rice malt) or shoyu, together with salt, are used. Salting takes away the coarseness of the hard vegetables and makes them soft and digestible as well as preserving them. It also adds more character and depth to the taste and improves the nutritional content. The following are some of the popular pickles available in packets from Japanese supermarkets.

Above: Naturally pickled daikon, front, and a commercially produced example, back. The latter is darker due to the addition of yellow food colouring.

TAKUAN

Fresh, just harvested daikon are hung for two to three weeks, then salted and pickled in nuka (dry rice bran) and salt. It takes two or three months to mature and the end result is a soft but crunchy, delicious yellow daikon. This tsukemono is said to have been invented

by the Buddhist monk Takuan in the 17th century, hence the name. Salty with a hint of sweetness, it is good on its own with hot boiled rice. It is also a regular ingredient for *nori maki* (nori-rolled sushi) and other rice dishes. Most of the manufactured takuan has bright yellow food colouring added, so for naturally pickled daikon, look for the paler ones and check the label first.

SHIO-ZUKE

This is the general term used for all salted vegetables, and many vegetables, including cucumber, aubergine (eggplant), daikon, hakusai and mustard leaves, are used. Japanese cucumber and aubergine are a lot smaller and more delicate in flavour than Western varieties, so look particularly for those.

NARA-ZUKE

This tsukemono is a speciality of Nara, the ancient capital of Japan. The pulp that mirin is exuded from is used to pickle various vegetables, and nara-zuke (salted daikon pickled in mirin pulp) is one such pickle. It has a sweet flavour with a hint of alcohol. Eat with hot boiled rice.

Above: Shio-zuke (salt-pickled vegetables) can refer to a number of vegetables including, from left, aubergine, radish and cucumber.

Left: Nara-zuke (mirin pulp pickles)

Making a pickled turnip flower

Serve these attractive flowers as an hors d'oeuvre or as an easy garnish for sushi.

1 Trim and peel five small turnips and place, one at a time, between a pair of hashi (chopsticks) on a cutting board. Insert a very sharp blade down into the turnip, across the hashi, and make parallel cuts until the blade touches the hashi.

2 Turn the turnip 90 degrees, and cut across the first series of cuts.

3 Repeat with the remaining turnips, then place them in a large bowl. Sprinkle with 5ml/1 tsp salt and rub in lightly. Cover with a small plate, place a weight on top and leave for 30 minutes.

4 Mix 250ml/8fl oz/1 cup rice vinegar and 150g/5oz/¾ cup sugar in a deep bowl and stir until the sugar has dissolved. Drain the turnips and pour the vinegar mixture over them. Leave to marinate and soften overnight.

NUKA-ZUKE

This is a traditional method of pickling and each house-hold used to keep a tub of nuka-miso (rice bran mash), which resembles miso and from which it takes its name. Nuka (dry rice bran) is mixed with warm, strong brine into a mash, in which vegetables such as aubergine (eggplant), carrot, cucumber, daikon, hakusai or turnips are buried and left to pickle. It is ready to eat the next day. This makes the vegetables mildly sweet and enriches the flavour, but not without paying the price of its strong odour. The mash must be stirred every day, ideally with bare hands. Although long-serving dutiful wives were once fondly called nuka-miso (smelling wife), today not many wives wish to be appreciated for their smelly hands! Nuka for pickling is available from Japanese stores, although ready-pickled nuka-zuke in packets is more popular.

MISO-ZUKE

The saltiness and strong flavour of miso are the two ideal qualities for making pickles. Red or white miso can be used on its own or often flavoured with mirin and sake to make miso-doko (miso mash). Fish and shellfish, poultry and beef can be marinated before grilling (broiling) and vegetables that have been marinated are then eaten as pickles. All crunchy vegetables are suitable for pickling in miso but gobo (burdock root), is probably better than anything else for pickling in miso. Ready-to-eat gobo miso pickles are usually available in packets at Japanese supermarkets.

RAKKYO

To make rakkyo, spring onions (scallions) are first salted and then pickled in heavily sweetened vinegar. This is traditionally served with curry.

Making rice bran pickles

Nuka-zuke is a traditional pickling method for vegetables such as carrot, daikon and cucumber, and is an old Japanese favourite.

1 Following the instructions on the packet of nuka, mix the water and salt in a pan and bring to the boil. Remove the pan from the heat and leave to cool. The ratio is usually 3 parts nuka to 1 part of salt mixed with 2½ parts of water.

2 Put the rice bran in a large mixing bowl, then add the salted water and mix well. Seal well or transfer the wet nuka to a large container with a tight-fitting lid. Leave to settle for 5 days, stirring well 1–2 times a day.

3 Wash and trim the vegetables (cut big vegetables into smaller sizes), then push them into the bran bed. Softer vegetables are ready within 24 hours and harder ones, such as daikon, within 2 days. Adjust the saltiness by adding more salt or rice bran. Stir the bran well every day even when nothing is being pickled. The bran can be used indefinitely.

BREAD AND BUNS

Bread, called pan in Japan, was first introduced by the Portuguese in the 16th century. However, it wasn't part of the general public's diet until after World War II. In recent years it has become very popular and, although rice still remains the staple food, toast is taking over at the breakfast table in many households. Younger generations now prefer easy-to-make sandwiches to the more elaborate and heavy rice lunch box and the Japanese have developed their own, very fine loaves and unique buns. Today, Japanese bakeries, *yamazaki-ya*, produce many of them abroad. Here are some of the popular ones.

SHOKU PAN

There are two types of Japanese standard loaf: the square loaf and Igirisu-pan (English loaf). Japanese breads are all very soft and wet with a faintly sweet, delicate flavour. They are similar to English milk bread in both

Below: Shoku pan, the Japanese version of a traditional English cottage loaf, can be bought whole or sliced.

taste and texture though the Japanese shoku pan is a little fluffier. Unlike the real English loaf, the Igirisu-pan's cook's hat shape is rather exaggerated and too perfect. All loaves are available in half or whole, and are often ready-cut into six or eight thick slices per half. To keep the softness it should be stored in its cellophane bag and eaten within two to three days, or else refrigerated for up to five days. It can also be frozen.

Left: An pan (red bean paste filled bun)

BUDO PAN

Also known as reizun pan, this raisin bread normally comes as a loaf, weighing about 500g/1¼lb. It is fairly sweet in flavour and has a slightly dense texture but it is not as dense as Western raisin breads. Budo pan should be eaten within two to three days or kept wrapped in the refrigerator for no more than five days. It is available at Japanese supermarkets.

KOPPE PAN

This is an individual-size soft loaf, normally 20–25cm/8–10in long and 7.5–8cm/3–4in wide, and has a faintly sweet flavour. The word, koppe, supposedly comes from a German word, kuppe, meaning the summit. This bread is usually served at school lunch in Japan. It should be eaten within a day or two, or kept in the refrigerator for up to four days. Koppe pan is not often available outside Japan.

AN PAN

A soft round bun about 7–10cm/3–4in in diameter, stuffed in the centre with a sweet azuki paste, called *an* in Japan. There are two types of azuki paste: a coarse one with the azuki skin mashed in and a smooth one without. An pan stuffed with coarse paste has sesame seeds sprinkled on top to distinguish it from the other one. It is a strange combination of Western

Below: Custard-filled cream pan

Right: Melon pan

bread and Japanese sweet *an* with a dense texture and tastes more like a cake than a bun. But for young and old alike in Japan it's an all-time favourite snack. It's best eaten as soon as possible but keeps for a few days. It is available at Asian stores.

FRANCE OGURA

This is what Japanese bakers consider French-style *an* pan, approximately 10cm/4in in diameter and 2cm/1in thick. The bread is slightly drier than ordinary *an* pan, more like a brioche and has more bite. Ogura is the name of a mountain in Kyoto where the original *an* (coarse azuki paste with skin mashed in) comes from, but this France ogura has a less sweet flavour than ordinary *an* pan. It is normally available at Japanese stores along with *an* pan.

CREAM PAN AND JAM PAN

The cream pan is a triangular or oval-shaped bun stuffed with custard. It has a light and fluffy texture and the flavour is less sweet than *an* pan. It should be eaten on the day of purchase and it is available at Japanese supermarkets. Jam pan have a slightly rounder shape, to distinguish them from cream pan without having to break it open.

CHOCO KORUNE

This is a spiral-patterned, corn-shaped bun with chocolate cream in the centre. The texture of the bun is firm enough to hold the chocolate cream and it's quite sweet. It should be eaten on the day of purchase. It is not often available outside Japan.

MELON PAN

This is a yellow fluffy bun, with sugar coating on top. It is called melon pan because of the colour and shape, and has nothing to do with the taste. It has a crisp sugary texture outside but light bread inside, and a sweet flavour. It's best eaten while the exterior is still crisp, but keeps for up to three days if kept in the cellophane bag.

CURRY PAN

An oval-shaped, fried bread stuffed with curry; this is the most unusual of all Japanese buns. The curry inside is a rather sweet Japanese curry sauce and does not contain many ingredients other than tiny bits of minced (ground) meat, carrot, onion and potato. As it is fried it will keep for up to three days.

AN DOUGHNUT

This popular doughnut has sweet azuki paste inside. As it is fried, the bread is drier than normal Japanese buns and is coated with sugar, so is doubly sweet. It is

Above: Curry-filled Japanese buns

CAKES AND SWEETS

Wagashi (Japanese cakes) are an art form in themselves. They are extremely beautiful creations of both ingenuity and observation of nature that only the Japanese could dream up in such a meticulously detailed way. Flowers, petals, foliage and birds are all featured in wagashi from season to season. There are basically three types of wagashi available at Japanese wagashi shops: namagashi (raw, wet cakes) are made of fresh ingredients that do not keep long; han-namagashi (half raw cakes) made of fresh ingredients that are hardened by long cooking, so keep well for a few weeks; and higashi (dry cakes and sweets), which are made from sugar, bean flour or jellies and keep well for a few months. Namagashi and han-namagashi are very dense and sweet, and mostly made of glutinous rice flour, azuki or other bean paste, chestnuts, sweet potatoes and kanten (agar-agar). Higashi are blocks of sugary bean flour and come in many shapes.

The wagashi are eaten not as dessert but as an accompaniment at the tea ceremony as well as at teatime. As they are all freshly made, they harden and go off quickly, particularly namagashi.

The namagashi served at formal tea ceremonies are specifically called omogashi (main, fresh cakes) and are served with koicha (thick matcha tea). With usucha (thin matcha tea), higashi (dry cakes) are normally used.

Wagashi are only available at wagashi shops except for some popular ones consumed daily that can also be frozen. The following are some of the wagashi for daily consumption rather than for the tea ceremony, and are normally available at Japanese wagashi shops or maybe at large supermarkets.

KUSA MOCHI

This is a glutinous rice cake stuffed with azuki paste, but the mochi is mixed with pounded yomogi (mugwort – a wild leaf, which gives it a light green colour). If real yomogi is used, it should contain bits of grass and have a grassy aroma and flavour. However, those normally available at supermarkets are only coloured green, hence have no such aroma and flavour. Unlike daifuku, kusa mochi is a thick mochi cake, which makes it more filling. It is either covered by light flour or wrapped in a leaf to prevent it from sticking. Kusa mochi hardens quickly but, because of its thickness, it keeps for up to three days.

DAIFUKU

This simple cake, made of glutinous rice cake stuffed with sweet azuki paste, is an all time favourite among old and young alike. The glutinous rice flour is steamed, then made into a very smooth dough and stretched to a thin, almost transparent dough that is wrapped around the azuki paste. It's very sticky, so is sold rolled in light flour. It hardens quickly, losing the soft stickiness, so should be eaten within three days. It is available frozen; thaw then eat.

KASHIWA MOCHI

This kashiwa (oak leaf) wrapped glutinous rice cake is a speciality for the Children's Day (Boy's Festival) on 5th of May. There are two kinds: one stuffed with sweet azuki paste and the other containing a sweet miso paste. The latter cake is normally coloured cherry pink to distinguish from the former, and both are wrapped with a fresh oak leaf, which is not supposed to be eaten though edible ones are available.

OHAGI

A mixture of ordinary rice and glutinous rice is pounded to make a rice ball, which is then covered by a thick layer of sweet an (azuki paste). This is the most common wagashi eaten at celebrations, and can be made at home.

Above: Assorted wet and semi-hard wagashi, left and middle, plus kushi dango, skewered rice balls coated in sweet azuki paste, right.

Green and yellow layered cakes

The Japanese name of this colourful two-tone dessert is derived from the preparation technique: *chakin-shibori*, in which *chakin* means a pouch shape and *shibori* means a moulding action.

SERVES SIX

INGREDIENTS
For the yolk mixture
    6 small (US medium) hard-boiled
      (hard-cooked) eggs
    50g/2oz/¼ cup sugar
For the pea mixture
    200g/7oz/1¾ cups frozen peas
    40g/1½oz/3 tbsp sugar

1 Make the yolk mixture. Shell the eggs, cut them in half and scoop the yolks into a sieve placed over a bowl. Using a wooden spoon, gently press the yolks through the sieve. Add the sugar and mix well.

2 To make the pea mixture, cook the peas in salted boiling water for 3–4 minutes, until softened. Drain, place in a mortar and crush with a pestle.

3 Transfer the paste to a pan. Add the sugar and cook over a low heat until thick. Stir constantly so that the mixture does not burn.

4 Spread out the pea paste in a shallow dish so that it cools as quickly as possible. Divide both mixtures into six portions.

5 Wet a piece of muslin or thin cotton and wring it out well. Place a portion of the pea mixture on the cloth and put a similar amount of the yolk mixture on top. Wrap the mixture up and twist the top of the cloth to join the mixtures together and mark a spiral pattern on the top. Unwrap and place on a plate. Make five more cakes. Serve cold.

SAKURA MOCHI

This is also a kind of glutinous rice cake stuffed with azuki paste, but the dough for this one is made of domyoji (finely cracked glutinous rice), which gives sakura mochi an elegant covering of tiny grains. The domyoji is coloured cherry pink and the cake is wrapped with a cooked edible cherry leaf, which also prevents it from sticking. The sweet leafy aroma and flavour of cherry leaf provides a good balance against the underlying sweetness. This rice cake hardens very quickly, so it's best eaten on the day of purchase.

KUSHI DANGO

Three or four glutinous rice balls, each the size of a quail's egg, are skewered together by a bamboo stick topped with either sweet azuki paste or a thickened clear sauce flavoured with a hint of shoyu. The rice ball is dense but not as sticky as mochi cakes and is not flavoured. The clear shoyu sauce version has a unique flavour combined with a little sweetness. Dango, meaning rice ball, is always eaten at feasts held during the cherry blossom viewing season in early April.

Right: Rakugan, a type of higashi, or dry cake. Made of a mixture of flour (soya or wheat) and sugar, they are made in moulds of birds, shells and trees.

DORA YAKI

Sweet azuki paste sandwiched between two small pancakes is called dora yaki (meaning little "gong"), and is one of the most popular and longest standing Japanese cakes. The pancakes have a spongy texture and rich egg flavour with a light sweetness through the addition of maple syrup; this combines well with the dense sweetness of the azuki paste. They are sold at Japanese supermarkets as well as cake shops but are also easily made at home.

YOKAN

This hard block of sweet azuki paste is a han-namagashi (half-raw wagashi), so keeps for several months. There are various flavours and textures but two basic types – ogura-yokan (made using coarse paste) and neri-yokan (a smooth paste) – are available at Japanese supermarkets. Yokan normally comes in a rectangular-shaped block about the size of a pencil case. Flavour variations include one with citrus flavouring and another with matcha tea, and there are also yokan mixed with sweet chestnut pieces. Yokan is a very popular sweet to serve with Japanese tea, such as sencha.

TEA

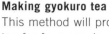
Below: Gyokuro (jewel dew) tea, which is made from fresh young tea leaves and is the very best quality tea.

The Japanese have been drinking tea since ancient times, although principally as a herbal remedy until it became popular among the aristocracy and the warrior class during the 13th and 14th centuries. The rise in the popularity of tea-drinking coincided with the spread of Zen Buddhism, out of which developed the rituals of the formal tea ceremony.

The tea that is drunk daily in Japan is green tea, in contrast to the brown or red tea of China and India. Green tea contains more thiamine (vitamin B1), which gives it its delicious *umami* (rich flavour). Freshly picked tea leaves are immediately steamed to prevent fermentation and blackening, then dried by rolling and crumbling, and finally by hot air. The quality of the tea is judged by the colour and shape of the leaves, and the colour and flavour of the brew. Green tea should not be brewed with boiling water. The better the quality of tea, the less hot the water should be. Several kinds of Japanese tea are available from Asian supermarkets and the following are listed in order of quality.

Right: Sencha tea

GYOKURO

Translated as jewel dew, this is the best leaf tea made from young leaves picked in early spring. The dried leaves are very finely rolled and are a shiny, deep green colour. The tea should be brewed in warm water, at about 50°C/122°F, in a small quantity, and drunk on its own or with wagashi (Japanese cakes). It is extremely fragrant and mellow, and the quality is reflected in its price.

SENCHA

Literally meaning infused (steeped) tea, this is the middle-range leaf tea made from good, young leaves. If you visit a Japanese household, this is the tea you will be served, along with wagashi. Each year, shincha (new tea) comes out in the summer. Brew this tea in the same way as gyokuro but in hotter water.

Making gyokuro tea

This method will provide enough tea for four people.

1 Fill a kyusu or small teapot with freshly boiled water, then use this water to fill four small teacups and leave to cool for about 5 minutes, until it reaches a temperature of 50–60°C/122–140°F.

2 Empty the teapot and add 20ml/ 4 tsp gyokuro. Pour the warm water in the cups back into the pot and let it brew for 2 minutes.

3 Shake the pot a few times, half-fill the cups, then top them up in turn so that the infusion of the tea is evenly distributed. For second cups, pour slightly hotter water into the pot without changing the leaves or adding more.

Left: Clockwise from left, hojicha, genmaicha and bancha teas

HOJICHA

This is a roasted bancha and brews a slightly bitter brown tea. Freshly roasted hojicha can be made by tossing bancha in a dry frying pan over very high heat for 3 minutes. The roasting infuses (steeps) a smoky aroma and adds character to the basic banch flavour.

GENMAICHA

A mixture of bancha and roasted rice grains, which adds aroma and a mild flavour.

MATCHA

This is a powdered tea, used mainly for the formal tea ceremony. Steamed tea leaves are dried flat and made into a powder that retains the vivid light green colour and fragrant aroma. The tea is made by whisking the powder in hot water in individual cups with a whisk rather than brewing in a pot. Only a tiny amount, 5–10ml/1–2 tsp per 120ml/4fl oz/ ½ cup water per person, is used.

BANCHA

This coarse tea used for daily consumption is made from larger leaves and stems, and brews a yellowish green tea. It is best drunk with meals and is the tea freely served at Japanese restaurants and offices. There are many grades of bancha and the lower the grade the more stems and twigs are included. Brew bancha just as you would ordinary tea.

Right: Powdered matcha tea – once opened it should be stored in the refrigerator.

Above: Mugicha, roasted barley, is now available in tea bags.

MUGICHA

This is not actually tea but whole grains of roasted barley. Mugicha is drunk cold in summer. To make mugicha, boil plenty of water in a large pan and add 120–250ml/4–8fl oz/½–1 cup mugicha to 2 litres/3½ pints/8¾ cups boiling water, depending on how strong you like it. Bring back to the boil, lower the heat and simmer for 5–10 minutes. Strain, discard the barley, then transfer the mugicha to a bottle and chill.

Making matcha
Eat wagashi or something sweet before you drink this tea to best appreciate the flavour of the tea. If you don't have a bamboo whisk use a small fork instead.

1 Warm a large cup (a rice bowl is ideal) with hot water. Soak the tip of a bamboo whisk in the hot water so that the matcha won't stain it. Empty the cup.

2 Put 5–10ml/1–2 tsp matcha, to taste, in the cup and add about 120ml/4fl oz/½ cup hot water.

3 Using the bamboo whisk, first stir, then whisk vigorously until frothy and the powder dissolves.

ALCOHOLIC DRINKS

Until quite recently sake and its variations had been the sole drinks in Japan. The first available record for a Japanese alcoholic drink was in a Chinese book written around AD 280, wherein the Japanese were said to "grow rice and hemp", "drink sake, and dance with music and drink". However, sake has long been superseded by beer, predominantly lager, as the drink of choice in Japan and may now have given way to whisky or even to wine in popularity. Despite this, sake is still the most respected drink of all. It is increasingly popular outside Japan along with Japanese food and cooking and is readily available.

Beer, whisky and grape wine were all introduced to Japan after the country was forced to open its markets to the world towards the end of the 19th century but only became popular with the general public after World War II. Lager is particularly popular due to the long, warm, humid spring and summer seasons (nothing is more suitable than a glassful of ice-cold lager to combat the climate) and a thriving beer industry has been developed. Many Japanese beers are now exported to the West. On the other hand, grape wine, while very popular, is more difficult to establish as a' domestically produced product, so consequently remains a relatively small industry.

SAKE

The Japanese have drunk sake since prehistoric times and it has played a vital role in the development of Japanese cuisine. In the past decade or two, however, the consumption of wine in Japan has increased more than ten-fold, and more and more people now drink wine with their daily meal. Despite this rapid change of habit in Japan, sake remains the drink for Japanese meals such as *kaiseki* (formal banquet) and as such is developing into more of a connoisseur's rather than a daily drink. There are reputedly about 6,000 brands of sake produced by about 2,000 makers in Japan, ranging from mass-produced nationwide brands to smaller regional, exclusive names. Since each brand has a few different types, there are in total a bewildering 55,000 different kinds of sake sold in Japan. Regional sake, known as jizaké, are seeing a rise in popularity over the often inferior mass-produced ones.

How sake is made

Sake is made from rice, but the rice used for making it is a harder variety than the rice used for eating. The rice is first intensely refined by shaving off the husk made of fat and protein, reducing the grain to just its core. How far it is refined (50, 60 or 70 per cent) determines the quality of the end product. The rice is then soaked in water and steamed at a high temperature. After cooling, it is transferred to a vat and left to turn into koji (rice malt) over a 48-hour period. More steamed rice, a yeast-like agent and water are added and stirred to make a mash, to which steamed rice, koji and water are again added. The mash is finally left in a tank to ferment. It will attain an alcohol content of 18 per cent in about 20 days and the fermented mash is squeezed to exude the liquid. The liquid is then pasteurized at 60°C/140°F and transferred to a brewing tank to mature. Sake-making starts in autumn and the wine is ready in 60 days. To best appreciate it, drink within a year of bottling.

Left: The three kinds of sake: junmai, hon-johzo and ginjo sake

1 Half-fill a small pan with water, bring it to the boil, then lower the heat to minimum.

2 Pour enough sake into a tokkuri (sake jug/pitcher) to bring it to about three-quarters full. Stand it in the water in the pan for about 5 minutes until the sake is warmed to your taste.

3 Check the temperature by lifting the jug and touching the bottom; it is normally indented in the centre. If it feels warm to the touch, it is ready.

Types of sake

The grading system of sake is very complicated but there are basically three kinds: ginjo, junmai and hon-johzo. Ginjo is made from rice refined by 60 per cent. The best, dai-ginjo (big ginjo), is made from rice refined by 50 per cent. Junmai is a pure rice sake while non-junmai sake contains some brewing alcohol and sugar. Hon-johzo is made from rice refined by 70 per cent with an added alcohol content. Ginjo is best drunk when cold, while junmai and hon-johzo are drunk cold or warmed.

There is another category called nama-zake (draught sake). Sake is heated twice during its manufacture but nama-zake is filtered rather than heated before bottling. It is particularly good for drinking chilled on hot summer days.

Most quality sakes are produced on a small scale, often by family run breweries, but have limited distributions even in Japan. Some of the larger sake makers export their quality brands but the majority of sake available overseas is standard factory-made. Some of these sakes are now produced outside Japan too, mainly in the United States, and include Ozeki, Shochikubai, Takara Masamune, Hakusan, Gekkeikan and Hakushika. They are widely available either in bottles or cartons at the food halls of good department stores.

Flavour and keeping qualities

Sake is a clear, fine, colourless wine with a fragrant aroma and subtle flavour. Unlike some wines, it keeps well but, once a bottle is opened, sake should be drunk as soon as possible. Store in a cool, dark place away from direct sunlight.

SHOCHU

Literally meaning fiery spirits, shochu is a distilled spirit made from rice and a mixture of various other grains or even, at times, sweet potatoes. It was initially considered a low-class beverage in Japan but recently shochu has become more fashionable, particularly among the young. The alcohol content is quite high, 20–25 per cent, and some varieties are as high

as 45 per cent, so it is normally drunk diluted with a little hot or cold water, depending on the season.

The most popular way to drink shochu in Japan is as *ume-jochu,* which is one part shochu diluted with four to five parts hot water. An umeboshi (dried salted Japanese apricot) is added to the glass before drinking. Shochu is also used for making umeshu (Japanese plum liqueur). Both shochu and umeshu are available from Japanese supermarkets.

Left: Shochu is customarily drunk diluted with hot water and accompanied by umeboshi, (dried salted Japanese apricots).

*Right: Super
Nikka 15
Year-Old
whisky*

WHISKY

The Japanese whisky industry started in the 1920s and the first bottle was produced by Suntory distillery at Yamazaki in Kyoto in 1929. Their main competitor, Nikka, produced their first one in 1934. The Japanese market is still dominated by these two distillers but the giant Suntory has a staggering 70 per cent share of all whisky sales including Scotch imports. The company was founded in 1899 producing what they called port wine, now renamed correctly as sweet wine. Their, as well as Japan's, first whisky, Suntory Shirofuda (white label), is still on the market today but the best selling blended whisky is by far the Suntory's Kakubin (square bottle). There are several other distillers such as Sanraku Ocean, Kirin Seagram and Godo Shusei, but their market shares are very small.

Together with Nikka's Super Nikka 15 Year-Old, Suntory's better varieties are available at Japanese supermarkets and at food halls of some upmarket department stores. Restaurants and bars in the West that cater for Japanese abroad also always carry these brands.

BEER

The Japanese beer industry started towards the end of the 19th century when the government-owned brewery, established by the American firm of Wiegrand and Copeland, was divided into three regional companies: Asahi in the west, Sapporo in the east and Kirin in the centre. It has now grown to over a £22 billion a year industry, and beer is the best-selling drink in Japan making up 55 per cent of the entire sales of alcoholic drinks. Beer production is still dominated by the three giant companies together with Suntory, which joined them in 1963. Although Kirin has long enjoyed a dominant market share of over 60 per cent, the recent fierce challenge from Asahi with its hit brand Asahi Super Dry pushed them into fighting for first place, and both now have a market share of around 40 per cent. Kirin have been exporting their lager beer to almost every country in the world for the past 20 years and now, with their latest success, Ichiban-shibori (first squeeze), they remain the top Japanese exporter. Many Japanese people drink lager as an aperitif and often change to sake during the meal.

Flavour of Japanese beer

The Japanese cherish nothing more than a glass of ice-cold lager on hot, humid summer days, and the vivid and crisp Japanese lager meets this thirst. Westerners may find Japanese lager a little hoppy. There are several types including canned draught beer, but Asahi Super Dry, Kirin Ichiban-shibori, Sapporo Black Label and Suntory Malt are the most popular brand names. These are normally available at Japanese restaurants and supermarkets, food halls of good department stores and some larger supermarkets. An even hoppier, low-malt beer has also been developed in Japan, but is not available abroad.

*Below: Kirin,
Sapporo and
Asahi beer*

LIQUEURS

The Japanese do not traditionally have a habit of drinking liqueur at the end of meal, however, drinking liqueurs diluted with soft drinks during the meal is increasingly popular, and the market is now on the increase. The two Japanese-invented ones, umeshu, Japanese apricot liqueur, and the newer Midori, a melon-scented liqueur, have become popular abroad and are available at some food halls of department stores.

Home-made umeshu
A great summer drink, pour over ice or dilute with ice-cold water.

MAKES ABOUT 4 LITRES/
7 PINTS/8½ US PINTS

INGREDIENTS
1kg/2¼lb unripe apricots
675–800g/1½–1¾lb crystallized sugar or 500g/1¼lb/scant 3 cups granulated sugar
1.75 litres/3 pints/7½ cups shochu

1 Remove the calyx from the apricots. Wipe each one with kitchen paper or dry dishtowel.

2 Put some of the apricots in a 4 litre/7 pint/8½ US pint screw-top jar, cover with a handful of sugar. Repeat the process until all the apricots and sugar are in the jar.

3 Pour the shochu over the apricots and sugar submerging the fruit. Seal the jar tightly and leave in a dark place, ideally for 1 year but for at least 3 months.

Umeshu

Also known as plum liqueur in the West, this is a white spirit scented with ume (Japanese apricot). Fresh, unripe apricots together with sugar are soaked in white spirit and left for three months. At one time almost every household used to make umeshu with shochu, since shochu was also traditionally made at home. This is less the case today and now there are quite a few drink makers including Choya and Ozeki and even other foodstuff manufacturers such as Kikkoman (shoyu) and Takara (mirin) producing bottled umeshu for export. It has become quite established in Europe, particularly so in Germany and France. Some bottles contain a few whole ume, which can be eaten as well.

Umeshu has a clear golden brown colour and densely sweet flavour with a hint of acidic taste and fruity aroma. It is traditionally a summer drink, poured over ice cubes or diluted with water, but it can also be drunk neat as a liqueur.

Midori

A product of Suntory, Midori is a melon-scented liqueur, invented in 1978. The liqueur base is a grain spirit and the rest of the ingredients are a closely guarded secret. It has a densely sweet, fruity flavour and rich melon aroma. Oddly, Midori is more popular abroad than in Japan, and is sold mostly to America, Australia and Britain. Its clear, elegant green colour and refreshing melon taste make an unusual addition to cocktails, which are its main use. It is also, however, sometimes used in cakes and jellies.

WINE

Japan started growing vines after World War II and now produce good quality grape wines, both red and white, in Kofu, the central mountain area of the mainland, and in Tokachi in Hokkaido, the northernmost island. The output is very small due to the extremely limited land availability. The popularity of wine has grown so enormously in recent times, with a 50 per cent increase each year during the 1990s, that Japanese wines, together with imports from all over the world, are just meeting the domestic demands. Consequently very little Japanese wine is exported abroad.

Below: Midori, melon-scented liqueur, left, and umeshu (plum liqueur), right.

JAPANESE COOKING

One of the great definers of culture is the food we eat, as well as the way we choose, combine, cook and present its ingredients. Japanese food displays all the great themes of the Japanese lifestyle: simplicity, elegance, attention to detail, an aesthetic sense, and a delight in miniatures.

SUSHI AND RICE

Rice is the very essence of Japanese cooking. Almost every

dish in Japanese cuisine is designed to accompany a bowl of

carefully prepared rice, not the other way round. This

chapter explains how to cook Japanese short grain rice to eat

by itself, and how to "vinegar" it for sushi. It also contains

some nutritious rice dishes, which are a meal in themselves.

MARINATED MACKEREL SUSHI

FRESH MACKEREL FILLETS ARE MARINATED, THEN PACKED INTO A MOULD WITH SUSHI RICE TO MAKE SABA-ZUSHI. START PREPARATIONS 8 HOURS IN ADVANCE TO ALLOW THE FISH TO ABSORB THE SALT.

MAKES ABOUT TWELVE

INGREDIENTS
  500g/1¼lb mackerel, filleted
  salt
  rice vinegar
  2cm/¾in fresh root ginger, peeled and
    finely grated, to garnish
  shoyu, to serve
For the *su-meshi* (vinegared rice)
  200g/7oz/1 cup Japanese short
    grain rice
  40ml/8 tsp rice vinegar
  20ml/4 tsp caster (superfine) sugar
  5ml/1 tsp salt

1 Place the fillets skin-side down in a flat dish, cover with a thick layer of salt, and leave them for 3–5 hours.

2 To make the *su-meshi*, put the rice in a large bowl and wash in plenty of water, until it runs clear. Tip into a sieve and leave to drain for 1 hour.

3 Put the rice into a small, deep pan with 15 per cent more water, i.e. 250ml/ 8fl oz/1⅛ cups water to 200g/7oz/1 cup rice. Cover and bring to the boil. This takes about 5 minutes. Reduce the heat and simmer for 12 minutes without lifting the lid. You should hear a faint crackling noise. The rice should now have absorbed the water. Remove from the heat and leave for 10 minutes.

4 Transfer the cooked rice to a wet Japanese rice tub or large bowl. In a small bowl, mix the vinegar, sugar and salt until well dissolved. Add to the rice, fluffing the rice with a wet spatula. Do not mash. If you have someone to help you, ask them to fan the rice to cool it quickly. This process makes the *su-meshi* glossy. Cover the bowl with wet dishtowels and leave to cool.

COOK'S TIP
All future uses, or variations of, *su-meshi* are based on the basic recipe provided above, hereafter referred to as 1 quantity of *su-meshi*.

5 Wipe the salt from the mackerel with kitchen paper. Remove all the remaining bones with tweezers. Lift the skin at the tail end of each fillet and peel towards the head end. Place the skinned fillets in a clean dish, and pour in enough rice vinegar to cover the fish completely. Leave for 20 minutes, then drain and wipe dry with kitchen paper.

6 Line a 25 × 7.5 × 4cm/10 × 3 × 1½in container with some clear film (plastic wrap), twice the size of the container. Lay the fillets in the container, skinned-side down, to cover the base. Cut the remaining mackerel to fill the gaps.

7 Put the *su-meshi* into the container, and press down firmly with dampened hands. Cover with the clear film and place a weight on top. Leave for at least 3 hours or overnight.

8 Remove the sushi from its container, then slice into 2cm/¾in pieces. After each slice, wipe the knife with kitchen paper dampened with rice vinegar.

9 Arrange on a plate and add a little grated ginger. Serve with shoyu.

HAND-MOULDED SUSHI

ORIGINALLY DEVELOPED IN TOKYO AS STREET FINGER FOOD, NIGIRI-ZUSHI IS PREPARED WITH THE FRESHEST OF FISH AND EATEN WITHIN A MATTER OF A FEW MINUTES OF MAKING.

SERVES FOUR

INGREDIENTS

  4 raw king prawns (jumbo shrimp),
    head and shell removed, tails intact
  4 scallops, white muscle only
  425g/15oz assorted fresh seafood,
    skinned, cleaned and filleted
  2 quantities *su-meshi*
  15ml/1 tbsp rice vinegar, for moulding
  45ml/3 tbsp wasabi paste from a
    tube, or the same amount of wasabi
    powder mixed with 15ml/1 tbsp water
  salt
  gari, to garnish
  shoyu, to serve

1 Insert a bamboo skewer or cocktail stick (toothpick) into each prawn lengthways. This stops the prawns curling up when cooked. Boil them in lightly salted water for 2 minutes, or until they turn pink. Drain and cool, then pull out the skewers. Cut open from the belly side but do not slice in two. With the point of a sharp knife, scoop up the black vein running down its length. Very gently pull it out, then discard. Open out flat and place on a tray.

2 Slice the scallops horizontally in half, but not quite through. Gently open each scallop at this "hinge" to make a butterfly shape. Place on the tray, cut-side down. Use a sharp knife to cut all the fish fillets into 7.5 x 4cm/3 x 1½in pieces, 5mm/¼in thick. Place all the raw fish and shellfish on the tray, cover with clear film (plastic wrap), then chill.

3 Place the *su-meshi* in a bowl. Have ready a small bowl filled with 150ml/ ¼ pint/⅔ cup water and the vinegar for moulding. This water is used for your hands while making *nigiri-zushi*. Take the tray of toppings from the refrigerator.

COOK'S TIP
Don't worry if your *su-meshi* block doesn't look very neat. Wet your hands with the hand water frequently, and keep the work surface tidy at all times.

4 Wet your hand with the vinegared water and scoop about 25ml/1½ tbsp *su-meshi* into your palm. Gently but firmly grip the *su-meshi* and make a rectangular block. Do not squash the rice, but ensure that the grains stick together. The size of the blocks must be smaller than the toppings.

5 Put the *su-meshi* block on a damp chopping board. Taking a piece of topping in your palm, rub a little wasabi paste in the middle of it. Put the *su-meshi* block on top of the fish slice and gently press it. Form your palm into a cup and shape the *nigiri-zushi* to a smooth-surfaced mound. Place it on a serving tray. Do not overwork, as the warmth of your hands can cause the toppings to lose their freshness.

6 Repeat this process until all of the rice and toppings are used. Serve immediately with a little shoyu dribbled on individual plates. To eat, pick up one *nigiri-zushi* and dip the tip into the shoyu. Eat a little gari between tasting different sushi to refresh your mouth.

JEWEL-BOX SUSHI

CHIRASHI IS THE MOST COMMON FORM OF SUSHI EATEN AT HOME IN JAPAN. A LACQUERED CONTAINER IS FILLED WITH SU-MESHI, AND VARIOUS COLOURFUL TOPPINGS ARE ARRANGED ON TOP.

SERVES FOUR

INGREDIENTS
  2 eggs, beaten
  vegetable oil, for frying
  50g/2oz mangetouts
    (snow peas), trimmed
  1 nori sheet
  15ml/1 tbsp shoyu
  15ml/1 tbsp wasabi paste from a
    tube, or the same amount of wasabi
    powder mixed with 10ml/2 tsp water
  1¼ quantity *su-meshi* made with
    40ml/8 tsp sugar
  salt
  30–60ml/2–4 tbsp ikura, to garnish
For the fish and shellfish toppings
  115g/4oz very fresh tuna steak,
    skin removed
  90g/3½oz fresh squid, body only,
    cleaned and boned
  4 raw king prawns (jumbo shrimp),
    heads and shells removed,
    tails intact
For the shiitake
  8 dried shiitake mushrooms, soaked
    in 350ml/12fl oz/1½ cups water for
    4 hours
  15ml/1 tbsp caster (superfine) sugar
  60ml/4 tbsp mirin
  45ml/3 tbsp shoyu

1 Slice the tuna across the grain into 7.5 × 4cm/3 × 1½in pieces, 5mm/¼in thick, using a very sharp knife. Slice the squid crossways into 5mm/¼in strips. Place both on a tray, cover with clear film (plastic wrap) and chill.

2 Remove and discard the stalks from the shiitake. Pour the soaking water into a pan, add the shiitake and bring to the boil. Skim the surface and reduce the heat. Cook for 20 minutes, then add the sugar. Reduce the heat further and add the mirin and shoyu. Simmer until almost all the liquid has evaporated. Drain and slice very thinly. Set aside.

3 Insert a bamboo skewer into each prawn lengthways. Boil in salted water for 2 minutes. Drain and leave to cool.

4 Remove the skewers from the prawns. Cut open from the belly side but do not slice in two. Remove the black vein. Open out flat and add to the tray.

5 Beat the eggs in a mixing bowl and add a pinch of salt. Heat a little oil in a frying pan until it smokes. Wipe away the excess oil with kitchen paper. Add enough beaten egg to thinly cover the bottom of the frying pan while tilting the pan. Cook on a medium low heat until the edge is dry and starting to curl. Lift the omelette and turn over. After 30 seconds, transfer to a chopping board. Use the remaining egg mixture to make several omelettes. Pile them up and roll them together into a tube. Slice very thinly to make strands.

6 Par-boil the mangetouts for 2 minutes in lightly salted water, then drain. Cut into 3mm/⅛in diagonal strips. Snip the nori into fine shreds using scissors. Mix with the shoyu and wasabi.

7 Divide half the *su-meshi* among four large rice bowls. Spread a quarter of the nori mixture over each bowl of *su-meshi*. Cover with the rest of the *su-meshi*. Flatten the surface with a wet spatula.

8 Sprinkle over egg strands to cover the surface completely. Arrange the tuna slices in a fan shape with a fan of shiitake on top. Place a prawn next to the tuna, and arrange the squid strips in a heap on the other side. Arrange the mangetouts and ikura decoratively on top.

HAND-ROLLED SUSHI

THIS IS A FUN WAY TO ENJOY SUSHI. CALLED TEMAKI-ZUSHI, *MEANING HAND-ROLLED, EACH GUEST ROLLS TOGETHER INDIVIDUAL FILLINGS OF FISH AND SHELLFISH, VEGETABLES AND* SU-MESHI.

SERVES FOUR TO SIX

INGREDIENTS

2 quantities *su-meshi*, made with
   40ml/8 tsp caster (superfine) sugar
225g/8oz extremely fresh tuna steak
130g/4½oz smoked salmon
17cm/6½in Japanese cucumber or
   salad cucumber
8 raw king prawns (jumbo shrimp)
   or large tiger prawns, peeled and
   heads removed
1 avocado
7.5ml/1½ tsp lemon juice
20 chives, trimmed and chopped into
   6cm/2½in lengths
1 packet mustard and cress, roots
   cut off
6–8 shiso leaves, cut in
   half lengthways
To serve
   12 nori sheets, cut into four
   mayonnaise
   shoyu
   45ml/3 tbsp wasabi paste from a
      tube, or the same amount of
      wasabi powder mixed with 15ml/
      1 tbsp water
   gari

1 Put the *su-meshi* into a large serving bowl and cover with a damp dishtowel.

2 Slice the tuna, with the grain, into 5mm/¼in slices then into 1 x 6cm/ ½ x 2½in strips. Cut the salmon and cucumber into strips the same size as the tuna.

3 Insert bamboo skewers into the prawns, then boil in lightly salted water for 2 minutes. Drain and leave to cool. Remove the skewers and cut in half lengthways. Remove the vein.

4 Halve the avocado and remove the stone (pit). Sprinkle with half the lemon juice and cut into 1cm/½in long strips. Sprinkle on the remaining lemon juice.

5 Arrange the fish, shellfish, avocado and vegetables on a plate. Place the nori sheets on a few plates and put the mayonnaise into a bowl. Put the shoyu in individual bowls, and the wasabi paste in a dish. Heap the gari in a small bowl. Half-fill a glass with water and place four to six rice paddles inside. Arrange everything on the table.

6 Each guest rolls their sushi as follows: take a sheet of nori on your palm, then scoop out 45ml/3 tbsp rice and spread it on the nori sheet. Spread some wasabi in the middle of the rice, then place a few strips of different fillings on top. Roll it up as a cone and dip the end into the shoyu. Have some gari between rolls to refresh your mouth.

NORI-ROLLED SUSHI

YOU WILL NEED A MAKISU (A SUSHI ROLLING MAT) TO MAKE THESE SUSHI, CALLED NORI MAKI. THERE ARE TWO TYPES: HOSO-MAKI (THIN-ROLLED SUSHI) AND FUTO-MAKI (THICK-ROLLED SUSHI).

SERVES SIX TO EIGHT

FUTO-MAKI (THICK-ROLLED SUSHI)
MAKES SIXTEEN PIECES

INGREDIENTS
  2 nori sheets
  1 quantity *su-meshi*
For the omelette
  2 eggs, beaten
  25ml/1½ tbsp second dashi stock,
    or the same amount of water and
    5ml/1 tsp dashi-no-moto
  10ml/2 tsp sake
  2.5ml/½ tsp salt
  vegetable oil, for frying
For the fillings
  4 dried shiitake mushrooms, soaked
    in a bowl of water overnight
  120ml/4fl oz/½ cup second dashi
    stock, or the same amount of water
    and 1½ tsp dashi-no-moto
  15ml/1 tbsp shoyu
  7.5ml/1½ tsp caster (superfine) sugar
  5ml/1 tsp mirin
  6 raw large prawns (shrimp), heads
    and shells removed, tails intact
  4 asparagus spears, boiled for
    1 minute in lightly salted
    water, cooled
  10 chives, about 23cm/9in long,
    ends trimmed

1 To make the omelette, mix the beaten eggs, dashi stock, sake and salt in a bowl. Heat a little oil in a frying pan on a medium-low heat. Pour in just enough egg mixture to thinly cover the base of the pan. As soon as the mixture sets, fold the omelette in half towards you and wipe the space left with a little oil.

2 With the first omelette still in the pan, repeat this process of frying and folding to make more omelettes. Each new one is laid on to the previous omelette, to form one multi-layered omelette. When all the mixture is used, slide the layered omelette on to a chopping board. Cool, then cut into 1cm/½in wide strips.

3 Put the shiitake, dashi stock, shoyu, sugar and mirin in a small pan. Bring to the boil then reduce the heat to low. Cook for 20 minutes until half of the liquid has evaporated. Drain, remove and discard the stalks, and slice the caps thinly. Squeeze out any excess liquid, then dry on kitchen paper.

4 Make three cuts in the belly of the prawns to stop them curling up, and boil in salted water for 1 minute, or until they turn bright pink. Drain and cool, then remove the vein.

5 Place a nori sheet at the front edge of the makisu. Scoop up half of the *su-meshi* and spread it on the nori as in *hoso-maki*. Leave a 1cm/½in margin at the side nearest you, and 2cm/¾in at the side furthest from you.

6 Make a shallow depression horizontally across the centre of the rice. Fill this with a row of omelette strips, then put half the asparagus and prawns on top. Place 5 chives alongside, and then put half the shiitake slices on to the chives.

7 Lift the makisu with your thumbs while pressing the fillings with your fingers and roll up gently.

8 When completed, gently roll the makisu on the chopping board to firm it up. Unwrap and set the *futo-maki* aside. Repeat the process to make another roll.

HOSO-MAKI (THIN-ROLLED SUSHI)
MAKES TWENTY FOUR PIECES

INGREDIENTS
  2 nori sheets, cut in half crossways
  1 quantity *su-meshi*
  45ml/3 tbsp wasabi paste from a
    tube, or the same amount of wasabi
    powder mixed with 10ml/2 tsp
    water, plus extra for serving
For the fillings
  90g/3½oz very fresh tuna steak
  10cm/4in cucumber or 17cm/6½in
    Japanese cucumber
  5ml/1 tsp roasted sesame seeds
  6cm/2½in takuan, cut into 1cm/½in
    thick long strips

1 For the fillings, cut the tuna with the grain into 1cm/½in wide strips. Cut the cucumber into 1cm/½in thick strips.

2 Place the makisu on the work surface, then place a nori sheet on it horizontally, rough-side up. Spread a quarter of the *su-meshi* over the nori to cover evenly, leaving a 1cm/½in margin on the side furthest from you. Press firmly to smooth the surface.

3 Spread a little wasabi paste across the the rice and arrange some of the tuna strips horizontally in a row across the middle. Cut off the excess.

4 Hold the makisu with both hands and carefully roll it up, wrapping the tuna in the middle, and rolling away from the side closest to you. Hold the rolled makisu with both hands and squeeze gently to firm the *nori-maki*.

5 Slowly unwrap the makisu, remove the rolled tuna *hoso-maki* and set aside. Make another tuna *hoso-maki* with the remaining ingredients.

6 Repeat the same process using only the cucumber strips with the green skin on. Sprinkle sesame seeds on the cucumber before rolling.

7 Repeat with the takuan strips, but omit the wasabi paste. Keep the sushi on a slightly damp chopping board, covered with clear film (plastic wrap) during preparation. When finished, you should have two *hoso-maki* of tuna, and one each of cucumber and takuan.

To serve the *nori-maki*

1 Cut each *futo-maki* roll into eight pieces, using a very sharp knife. Wipe the knife with a dishtowel dampened with rice vinegar after each cut. Cut each *hoso-maki* into six pieces in the same way.

2 Line up all the *maki* on a large tray. Serve with small dishes of wasabi, gari, and shoyu for dipping.

COOK'S TIP
Half-fill a small bowl with water and add 30ml/2 tbsp rice vinegar. Use this to wet your hands to prevent the rice sticking when rolling sushi.

COMPRESSED SUSHI WITH SMOKED SALMON

THIS SUSHI, KNOWN AS OSHI-ZUSHI, DATES BACK ALMOST A THOUSAND YEARS. THE EARLIEST FORMS OF SUSHI WERE MADE AS A MEANS OF PRESERVING FISH. THE COOKED RICE WAS USED AS A MEDIUM TO PRODUCE LACTIC ACID AND WAS DISCARDED AFTER ONE YEAR. ONLY THE MARINATED FISH WAS EATEN.

2 Wet a wooden Japanese sushi mould or line a 25 × 7.5 × 5cm/10 × 3 × 2in plastic container with a large sheet of clear film (cling wrap), allowing the edges to hang over.

3 Spread half the smoked salmon to evenly cover the bottom of the mould or container. Add a quarter of the cooked rice and firmly press down with your hands dampened with rice vinegar until it is 1cm/½in thick. Add the remainder of the salmon, and press the remaining rice on top.

4 Put the wet wooden lid on the mould, or cover the plastic container with the overhanging clear film. Place a weight, such as a heavy dinner plate, on top. Leave in a cool place overnight, or for at least 3 hours. If you keep it in the refrigerator, choose the least cool part.

5 Remove the compressed sushi from the mould or container and unwrap. Cut into 2cm/¾in slices and serve on a Japanese lacquered tray or a large plate. Quarter the lemon rings. Garnish with two slices of lemon on top of each piece and serve.

COOK'S TIPS
• You can also use smoked haddock instead of smoked salmon, if you like.
• If you don't have a mould or narrow container, use a container about 15cm/6in square. Cut the pressed sushi in half lengthways, then into 2cm/¾in slices. Cut the slices in half to make a nice canapé-type snack for a party.

MAKES ABOUT TWELVE

INGREDIENTS
175g/6oz smoked salmon, thickly sliced
15ml/1 tbsp sake
15ml/1 tbsp water
30ml/2 tbsp shoyu
1 quantity *su-meshi*
1 lemon, thinly sliced into 6 × 3mm/⅛in rings

1 Lay the smoked salmon on a chopping board and sprinkle with a mixture of the sake, water and shoyu. Leave to marinate for an hour, then wipe dry with kitchen paper.

SU-MESHI IN TOFU BAGS

ABURA-AGE (FRIED THIN TOFU) IS DIFFERENT TO OTHER TOFU PRODUCTS. IT CAN BE OPENED UP LIKE A BAG, AND IN THIS RECIPE IT'S SERVED WITH SOY SAUCE-BASED SEASONINGS AND FILLED WITH SU-MESHI.

SERVES FOUR

INGREDIENTS

8 fresh abura-age or 275g/10oz can ready-to-use abura-age (contains 16 halves)
900ml/1½ pints/3¾ cups second dashi stock, or the same amount of water and 2 tsp dashi-no-moto
90ml/6 tbsp caster (superfine) sugar
30ml/2 tbsp sake
70ml/4½ tbsp shoyu
generous 1 quantity *su-meshi*, made with 40ml/8 tsp sugar
30ml/2 tbsp toasted white sesame seeds
gari, to garnish

4 Mix the *su-meshi* and sesame seeds in a wet mixing bowl. Wet your hands and take a little *su-meshi*. Shape it into a rectangular block. Open one abura-age bag and insert the block. Press the edges together to close the bag.

5 Once all the bags have been filled, place them on a large serving plate or individual plates with the bottom of the bag on top. Garnish with gari.

COOK'S TIP
To open the abura-age without breaking them, place them on a chopping board and, with the palm of your hand, rub them gently on the board. Then pull apart little by little from the cut end and work towards the bottom. When fully open, put your finger inside to make sure the corners are opened completely.

1 Par-boil the fresh abura-age in rapidly boiling water for about 1 minute. Drain under running water and leave to cool. Squeeze the excess water out gently. Cut each sheet in half and carefully pull open the cut end to make bags. If you are using canned abura-age, drain the liquid.

2 Lay the abura-age bags in a large pan. Pour in the dashi stock to cover and bring to the boil. Reduce the heat and cover, then simmer for 20 minutes. Add the sugar in three batches during this time, shaking the pan to dissolve it. Simmer for a further 15 minutes.

3 Add the sake. Shake the pan again, and add the shoyu in three batches. Simmer until almost all the liquid has evaporated. Transfer the abura-age to a wide sieve and leave to drain.

RICE BALLS WITH FOUR FILLINGS

ONIGIRI, THE JAPANESE NAME FOR THIS DISH, MEANS HAND-MOULDED RICE. JAPANESE RICE IS IDEAL FOR MAKING RICE BALLS, WHICH ARE FILLED HERE WITH SALMON, MACKEREL, UMEBOSHI AND OLIVES. THE NORI COATING MAKES THEM EASY TO PICK UP WITH YOUR FINGERS.

SERVES FOUR

INGREDIENTS
  50g/2oz salmon fillet, skinned
  3 umeboshi, 50g/2oz in total weight
  45ml/3 tbsp sesame seeds
  2.5ml/½ tsp mirin
  50g/2oz smoked mackerel fillet
  2 nori sheets, each cut into
    8 strips
  6 pitted black olives, wiped and
    finely chopped
  fine salt
  Japanese pickles, to serve
For the rice
  450g/1lb/2¼ cups Japanese short
    grain rice
  550ml/18fl oz/2½ cups water

1 To cook the rice, wash it thoroughly with cold water. Drain and put into a heavy pan. Pour in the water and leave for 30 minutes. Put the lid on tightly and bring the pan to the boil. Reduce the heat and simmer for 12 minutes. When you hear a crackling noise remove from the heat and leave to stand, covered, for about 15 minutes.

2 Stir carefully with a dampened rice paddle or wooden spatula to aerate the rice. Leave to cool for 30 minutes while you prepare the fillings. Thoroughly salt the salmon fillet and leave for at least 30 minutes.

3 Stone (pit) the umeboshi. With the back of a fork, mash them slightly. Mix with 15ml/1 tbsp of the sesame seeds and the mirin to make a rough paste.

4 Wash the salt from the salmon. Grill (broil) the salmon and smoked mackerel under a high heat. Using a fork, remove the skin and divide the fish into loose, chunky flakes. Keep the salmon and mackerel pieces separate.

5 Toast the remaining sesame seeds in a dry frying pan over a low heat until they start to pop.

6 Check the temperature of the rice. It should be still quite warm but not hot. To start moulding, you need a teacup and a bowl of cold water to wet your hands. Put the teacup and tablespoons for measuring into the water. Put fine salt into a small dish. Wipe a chopping board with a very wet dishtowel. Wash your hands thoroughly with unperfumed soap and dry.

7 Remove the teacup from the bowl and shake off excess water. Scoop about 30ml/2 tbsp rice into the teacup. With your fingers, make a well in the centre of the rice and put in a quarter of the salmon flakes. Cover the salmon with another 15ml/1 tbsp rice. Press well.

8 Wet your hands and sprinkle them with a pinch of salt. Rub it all over your palms. Turn the rice in the teacup out into one hand and squeeze the rice shape with both hands to make a densely packed flat ball.

9 Wrap the rice ball with a nori strip. Put on to the chopping board. Make three more balls using the remaining salmon, then make four balls using the smoked mackerel and another four balls using the umeboshi paste.

10 Scoop about 45ml/3 tbsp rice into the teacup. Mix in a quarter of the chopped olives. Press the rice with your fingers. Wet your hands with water and rub with a pinch of salt and a quarter of the toasted sesame seeds. Turn the teacup on to one hand and shape the rice mixture into a ball as above. The sesame seeds should stick to the rice. This time, do not wrap with nori. Repeat, making three more balls.

11 Serve one of each kind of rice ball on individual plates with a small helping of Japanese pickles.

RED RICE WRAPPED IN OAK LEAVES

THIS STICKY RICE DISH, SEKIHAN, IS COOKED FOR SPECIAL OCCASIONS AND TAKES 8 HOURS TO PREPARE. EDIBLE KASHIWA (OAK) LEAVES ARE USED WHEN PREPARED FOR A BOY-CHILD'S FESTIVAL.

SERVES FOUR

INGREDIENTS
65g/2½oz/⅓ cup dried azuki beans
5ml/1 tsp salt
300g/11oz/1½ cups mochigome
50g/2oz/¼ cup Japanese short
  grain rice
12 kashiwa leaves (optional)
For the *goma-shio*
45ml/3 tbsp sesame seeds (black
  sesame, if available)
5ml/1 tsp ground sea salt

1 Put the azuki beans in a heavy pan and pour in 400ml/14fl oz/1⅔ cups plus 20ml/4 tsp water.

2 Bring to the boil, reduce the heat and simmer, covered, for 20–30 minutes, or until the beans look swollen but are still firm. Remove from the heat and drain. Reserve the liquid in a bowl and add the salt. Return the beans to the pan.

3 Wash the two rices together. Drain in a sieve and leave for 30 minutes.

4 Bring another 400ml/14fl oz/1⅔ cups plus 20ml/4 tsp water to the boil. Add to the beans and boil, then simmer for 30 minutes. The beans' skins should start to crack. Drain and add the liquid to the bowl with the reserved liquid. Cover the beans and leave to cool.

5 Add the rice to the bean liquid. Leave to soak for 4–5 hours. Drain the rice and reserve the liquid. Mix the beans into the rice.

6 Bring a steamer of water to the boil. Turn off the heat. Place a tall glass upside down in the centre of the steaming compartment. Pour the rice and beans into the steamer and gently pull the glass out. The hole in the middle will allow even distribution of the steam. Steam on high for 10 minutes.

7 Using your fingers, sprinkle the rice mixture with the reserved liquid from the bowl. Cover again and repeat the process twice more at 10 minute intervals, then leave to steam for 15 minutes more. Remove from the heat. Leave to stand for 10 minutes.

8 Make the *goma-shio*. Roast the sesame seeds and salt in a dry frying pan until the seeds start to pop. Leave to cool, then put in a small dish.

9 Wipe each kashiwa leaf with a wet dishtowel. Scoop 120ml/4fl oz/½ cup of the rice mixture into a wet tea cup and press with wet fingers. Turn the cup upside down and shape the moulded rice with your hands into a flat ball. Insert into a leaf folded in two. Repeat this process until all the leaves are used. Alternatively, transfer the red rice to a large bowl wiped with a wet towel.

10 Serve the red rice with a sprinkle of *goma-shio*. The kashiwa leaves (except for fresh ones) are edible.

FIVE INGREDIENTS RICE

THE JAPANESE LOVE RICE SO MUCH THEY INVENTED MANY WAYS TO ENJOY IT. HERE, CHICKEN AND VEGETABLES ARE COOKED WITH SHORT GRAIN RICE MAKING A HEALTHY LIGHT LUNCH DISH CALLED KAYAKU-GOHAN. SERVE WITH A SIMPLE, CLEAR SOUP AND TANGY PICKLES.

SERVES FOUR

INGREDIENTS

275g/10oz/1⅓ cups Japanese short
  grain rice
90g/3½oz carrot, peeled
2.5ml/½ tsp lemon juice
90g/3½oz gobo or canned
  bamboo shoots
225g/8oz oyster mushrooms
8 mitsuba sprigs, root part removed
350ml/12fl oz/1½ cups second dashi
  stock, or the same amount of water
  and 7.5ml/1½ tsp dashi-no-moto
150g/5oz chicken breast portion,
  skinned, boned and cut into 2cm/
  ¾in dice
30ml/2 tbsp shoyu
30ml/2 tbsp sake
25ml/1½ tbsp mirin
pinch of salt

1 Put the rice in a large bowl and wash well with cold water. Change the water until it becomes clear. Tip the rice into a sieve and leave to drain for 30 minutes.

2 Using a sharp knife, cut the carrot into 5mm/¼in rounds, then cut the discs into flowers.

COOK'S TIP
Although gobo or burdock is recognized as a poisonous plant in the West, the Japanese have long been eating it, but it must be cooked. It contains iron and other acidic elements that are harmful if eaten raw, but after soaking in alkaline water and cooking for a short time, gobo is no longer poisonous.

3 Fill a small bowl with cold water and add the lemon juice. Peel the gobo and then slice with a knife as if you were sharpening a pencil into the bowl. Leave for 15 minutes, then drain. If using canned bamboo shoots, slice into thin matchsticks.

4 Tear the oyster mushrooms into thin strips. Chop the mitsuba sprigs into 2cm/¾in long pieces. Put them in a sieve and pour over hot water from the kettle to wilt them. Allow to drain and then set aside.

5 Heat the dashi stock in a large pan and add the carrots and gobo or bamboo shoots. Bring to the boil and add the chicken. Remove any scum from the surface, and add the shoyu, sake, mirin and salt.

6 Add the rice and mushrooms and cover with a tight-fitting lid. Bring back to the boil, wait 5 minutes, then reduce the heat and simmer for 10 minutes. Remove from the heat without lifting the lid and leave to stand for 15 minutes. Add the mitsuba and serve.

Brown Rice <u>and</u> Mushrooms <u>in</u> Clear Soup

This is a good and quick way of using up leftover rice. In this hearty dish, known as Genmai Zousui, brown rice is used for its nutty flavour. Short grain Japanese or Italian brown rice, which can be found in health-food stores, are best for this recipe.

SERVES FOUR

INGREDIENTS
1 litre/1¾ pints/4 cups second dashi stock, or the same amount of water and 20ml/4 tsp dashi-no-moto
60ml/4 tbsp sake
5ml/1 tsp salt
60ml/4 tbsp shoyu
115g/4oz fresh shiitake mushrooms, thinly sliced
600g/1lb 5oz cooked brown rice (see Cook's Tip)
2 large (US extra large) eggs, beaten
30ml/2 tbsp chopped fresh chives
For the garnish
15ml/1 tbsp sesame seeds
shichimi togarashi (optional)

1 Mix the dashi stock, sake, salt and shoyu in a large pan. Bring to the boil, then add the sliced shiitake. Cook for 5 minutes over a medium heat.

2 Add the cooked brown rice to the pan and stir gently over a medium heat with a wooden spoon. Break up any large chunks, and thoroughly warm the rice through.

3 Pour the beaten eggs into the pan as if drawing a whirlpool. Lower the heat and cover. Do not stir.

4 Remove the pan from the heat after about 3 minutes, and allow to stand for 3 minutes more. The egg should be just cooked. Sprinkle the chopped chives into the pan.

5 Serve the dish in individual bowls. Garnish with sesame seeds and shichimi togarashi, if you like.

COOK'S TIP
To cook brown rice, wash and drain, then put 2 parts water to 1 part rice into a pan. Bring to the boil, cover, then simmer for 40 minutes, or until the water has been absorbed. Leave to stand, covered, for 5 minutes.

Rice <u>in</u> Green Tea <u>with</u> Salmon

A fast food, Ocha-zuke is a common Japanese snack to have after drinks and nibbles. In the Kyoto region, offering this dish to guests used to be a polite way of saying the party was over. The guests were expected to decline the offer and leave immediately!

SERVES FOUR

INGREDIENTS
150g/5oz salmon fillet
¼ nori sheet
250g/9oz/1¼ cups Japanese short grain rice cooked using 350ml/ 12fl oz/1½ cups water
15ml/1 tbsp sencha leaves
5ml/1 tsp wasabi paste from a tube, or 5ml/1 tsp wasabi powder mixed with 1.5ml/¼ tsp water (optional)
20ml/4 tsp shoyu
salt

1 Thoroughly salt the salmon fillet and leave for 30 minutes. If the salmon fillet is thicker than 2.5cm/1in, slice it in half and salt both halves.

2 Wipe the salt off the salmon with kitchen paper and grill (broil) the fish under a preheated grill (broiler) for about 5 minutes until cooked through. Remove the skin and any bones, then roughly flake the salmon with a fork.

3 Using scissors, cut the nori into short, narrow strips about 20 x 5mm/¾ x ¼in long, or leave as long narrow strips, if you prefer.

4 If the cooked rice is warm, put equal amounts into individual rice bowls or soup bowls. If the rice is cold, put in a sieve and pour hot water from a kettle over it to warm it up. Drain and pour into the bowls. Place the salmon pieces on top of the rice.

5 Put the sencha leaves in a teapot. Bring 600ml/1 pint/2½ cups water to the boil, remove from the heat and allow to cool slightly. Pour into the teapot and wait for 45 seconds. Strain the tea gently and evenly over the top of the rice and salmon. Add some nori and wasabi, if using, to the top of the rice, then trickle shoyu over and serve.

LUNCH-BOX RICE <u>WITH</u> THREE TOPPINGS

SAN-SHOKU BENTO IS A TYPICAL BENTO (LUNCH BOX) MENU FOR JAPANESE CHILDREN. COLOURFUL TOPPINGS AND A VARIETY OF TASTES HOLD THEIR ATTENTION SO THEY DON'T GET BORED.

MAKES FOUR LUNCH BOXES

INGREDIENTS
  275g/10oz/scant 1½ cups Japanese
    short grain rice cooked using 375ml/
    13fl oz/scant 1⅔ cups water, cooled
  45ml/3 tbsp sesame seeds, toasted
  salt
  3 mangetouts (snow peas), to garnish
For the *iri-tamago* (yellow topping)
  30ml/2 tbsp caster (superfine) sugar
  5ml/1 tsp salt
  3 large (US extra large) eggs, beaten
For the *denbu* (pink topping)
  115g/4oz cod fillet, skinned
    and boned
  20ml/4 tsp caster (superfine) sugar
  5ml/1 tsp salt
  5ml/1 tsp sake
  2 drops of red vegetable colouring,
    diluted with a few drops of water
For the *tori-soboro* (beige topping)
  200g/7oz minced (ground)
    raw chicken
  45ml/3 tbsp sake
  15ml/1 tbsp caster (superfine) sugar
  15ml/1 tbsp shoyu
  15ml/1 tbsp water

1 To make the *iri-tamago*, add the sugar and salt to the eggs in a pan. Cook over a medium heat, stirring with a whisk or fork as you would to scramble an egg. When it is almost set, remove from the heat and stir until the egg becomes fine and slightly dry.

2 To make the *denbu*, cook the cod fillet for 2 minutes in a large pan of boiling water. Drain and dry well with kitchen paper. Skin and remove all the fish bones.

3 Put the cod and sugar into a pan, add the salt and sake, and cook over a low heat for 1 minute, stirring with a fork to flake the cod. Reduce the heat to low and sprinkle on the colouring. Continue to stir for 15–20 minutes, or until the cod flakes become very fluffy and fibrous. Transfer the *denbu* to a plate.

4 To make the *tori-soboro*, put the minced chicken, sake, sugar, shoyu and water into a small pan. Cook over a medium heat for about 3 minutes, then reduce the heat to medium-low and stir with a fork or whisk until the liquid has almost evaporated.

5 Blanch the mangetouts for about 3 minutes in lightly salted boiling water, drain and carefully slice into fine 3mm/⅛in sticks.

6 Mix the rice with the sesame seeds in a bowl. With a wet spoon, divide the rice among four 17 × 12cm/6½ × 4½in lunch boxes. Flatten the surface using the back of a wooden spoon.

7 Spoon a quarter of the egg into each box to cover a third of the rice. Cover the next third with a quarter of the *denbu*, and the last section with a quarter of the chicken topping. Use the lid to divide the boxes, if you like. Garnish with the mangetout sticks.

CHICKEN AND EGG ON RICE

THIS DISH IS CALLED OYAKO DON WHICH MEANS A PARENT (THE CHICKEN) AND A CHILD (THE EGG). IT IS TRADITIONALLY COOKED IN A DON-BURI, WHICH IS A DEEP, ROUND CERAMIC BOWL WITH A LID, AND IS ESSENTIAL TABLEWARE IN JAPAN; RESTAURANTS OFTEN USE THEM IN LUNCHTIME MENUS.

SERVES FOUR

INGREDIENTS
    250g/9oz chicken thighs, skinned
    and boned
    4 mitsuba sprigs or a handful of
    mustard and cress
    300ml/½ pint/1¼ cups second dashi
    stock, or the same amount of water
    and 25ml/1½ tbsp dashi-no-moto
    30ml/2 tbsp caster (superfine) sugar
    60ml/4 tbsp mirin
    60ml/4 tbsp shoyu
    2 small onions, sliced
    thinly lengthways
    4 large (US extra large) eggs, beaten
    275g/10oz/scant 1½ cups Japanese
    short grain rice cooked with 375ml/
    13fl oz/scant 1⅔ cups water
    shichimi togarashi, to serve (optional)

1 Cut the chicken thighs into 2cm/¾in square bitesize chunks. Remove the root part from the mitsuba, and chop into 2.5cm/1in lengths.

2 Pour the dashi stock, sugar, mirin and shoyu into a clean frying pan with a lid and bring to the boil. Add the onion slices and lay the chicken pieces on top. Cook over a high heat for 5 minutes, shaking the pan frequently.

3 When the chicken is cooked, sprinkle with the mitsuba or mustard and cress, and pour the beaten eggs over to cover the chicken. Cover and wait for 30 seconds. Do not stir.

4 Remove from the heat and leave to stand for 1 minute. The egg should be just cooked but still soft, rather than set. Do not leave it so that the egg becomes a firm omelette.

5 Scoop the warm rice on to individual plates, then pour the soft eggs and chicken on to the rice. Serve immediately with a little shichimi-togarashi, if a spicy taste is desired.

COOK'S TIP
Ideally, this dish should be cooked in individual shallow pans with lids. A small omelette pan can work perfectly well.

SOUPS AND NOODLES

Soups, a showcase of the season in miniature, are usually

eaten with or at the end of the meal. Apart from ramen,

Japanese noodles are quite different to the Chinese, and the

soup stock is made with great care to set off their flavour.

Buckwheat noodles in particular have a very delicate aroma,

and are eaten with a simple dipping sauce.

MISO SOUP

ESSENTIAL TO ANY JAPANESE MEAL IS A BOWL OF RICE. NEXT IS MISO SOUP, SERVED IN A LACQUERED BOWL. OF THE MANY VARIATIONS, WAKAME TO TOFU NO MISO-SHIRU DEFINITELY COMES FIRST.

SERVES FOUR

INGREDIENTS

5g/⅛oz dried wakame
½ × 225–285g/8–10¼oz packet fresh
  soft tofu or long-life silken tofu
400ml/14fl oz/1⅔ cups second dashi
  stock or the same amount of water
  and 5ml/1 tsp dashi-no-moto
45ml/3 tbsp miso
2 spring onions (scallions),
  finely chopped
shichimi togarashi or sansho
  (optional), to serve

1 Soak the wakame in a large bowl of cold water for 15 minutes. Drain and chop into stamp-size pieces if using the long or broad type.

2 Cut the tofu into 1cm/½in strips, then cut horizontally through the strips. Cut the thin strips into squares.

3 Bring the dashi stock to the boil. Put the miso in a small cup and mix with 60ml/4 tbsp hot stock from the pan. Reduce the heat to low and pour two-thirds of the miso into the pan of stock.

4 Taste the soup and add more miso if required. Add the wakame and the tofu and increase the heat. Just before the soup comes to the boil again, add the spring onions and remove from the heat. Do not boil. Serve sprinkled with shichimi togarashi or sansho, if liked.

COOK'S TIPS

• To make first dashi stock, put a 10cm/ 4in square piece of dried konbu into a pan. Pour in 600ml/1 pint/2½ cups water and soak for an hour. Heat to near boiling point, then remove from the heat. Remove and reserve the konbu for the second dashi. Add 20g/¾oz kezuri-bushi to the pan and heat on low. Do not stir. Just before it reaches boiling point, turn off the heat. Allow the flakes to settle down to the bottom of the pan. Strain and reserve the kezuri-bushi flakes for the second dashi stock.

• To make second dashi stock, put the reserved konbu and kezuri-bushi from the first dashi into a pan with 600ml/ 1 pint/2½ cups water. Bring to the boil, then simmer for 15 minutes until the stock is reduced by a third. Add 15g/½oz kezuri-bushi to the pan. Immediately remove from the heat. Skim any scum from the surface. Leave to stand for 10 minutes, then strain.

CLEAR SOUP WITH SEAFOOD STICKS

THIS DELICATE SOUP, CALLED O-SUMASHI, WHICH IS OFTEN EATEN WITH SUSHI, IS VERY QUICK TO MAKE IF YOU PREPARE THE FIRST DASHI BEFOREHAND OR IF YOU USE FREEZE-DRIED DASHI-NO-MOTO.

SERVES FOUR

INGREDIENTS

4 mitsuba sprigs or 4 chives and a few sprigs of mustard and cress
4 seafood sticks
400ml/14fl oz/1⅔ cups first dashi stock, or the same amount of water and 5ml/1 tsp dashi-no-moto
15ml/1 tbsp shoyu
7.5ml/1½ tsp salt
grated rind of yuzu (optional), to garnish

1 Mitsuba leaves are normally sold with the stems and roots on to retain freshness. Cut off the root, then cut 5cm/2in from the top, retaining both the long straw-like stem and the leaf.

2 Blanch the stems in hot water from the kettle. If you use chives, choose them at least 10cm/4in in length and blanch them, too.

3 Take a seafood stick and carefully tie around the middle with a mitsuba stem or chive, holding it in place with a knot. Do not pull too tightly, as the bow will easily break. Repeat the process to make four tied seafood sticks.

4 Hold one seafood stick in your hand. With your finger, carefully loosen both ends to make it look like a tassel.

5 Place one seafood stick in each soup bowl, then put the four mitsuba leaves or mustard and cress on top.

6 Heat the stock in a pan and bring to the boil. Add shoyu and salt to taste. Pour the stock gently over the mitsuba and seafood stick. Sprinkle with grated yuzu rind, if using.

VARIATION
You can use small prawns (shrimp) instead of seafood sticks. Blanch 12 raw prawns in boiling water until they curl up and form a full circle. Drain. Tie mitsuba stems to make four bows. Arrange three prawns side by side in each bowl and put the mitsuba bows and leaves on top.

MISO SOUP WITH PORK AND VEGETABLES

THIS IS QUITE A RICH AND FILLING SOUP. ITS JAPANESE NAME, TANUKI JIRU, MEANS RACCOON SOUP FOR HUNTERS, BUT AS RACCOONS ARE NOT EATEN NOWADAYS, PORK IS NOW USED.

SERVES FOUR

INGREDIENTS
200g/7oz lean boneless pork
15cm/6in piece gobo or 1 parsnip
50g/2oz daikon
4 fresh shiitake mushrooms
½ konnyaku or ½ × 225–285g/
  8–10¼oz packet tofu
a little sesame oil, for stir-frying
600ml/1 pint/2½ cups second dashi
  stock, or the same amount of water
  and 10ml/2 tsp dashi-no-moto
70ml/4½ tbsp miso
2 spring onions (scallions), chopped
5ml/1 tsp sesame seeds

1 Press the meat down on a chopping board using the palm of your hand and slice horizontally into very thin long strips, then cut the strips crossways into stamp-size pieces. Set the pork aside.

2 Peel the gobo using a potato peeler, then cut diagonally into 1cm/½in thick slices. Quickly plunge the slices into a bowl of cold water to stop them discolouring. If you are using parsnip, peel, cut it in half lengthways, then cut it into 1cm/½in thick half-moon-shaped slices.

3 Peel and slice the daikon into 1.5cm/⅔in thick discs. Cut the discs into 1.5cm/⅔in cubes. Remove the shiitake stalks and cut the caps into quarters.

4 Place the konnyaku in a pan of boiling water and cook for 1 minute. Drain and cool. Cut in quarters lengthways, then crossways into 3mm/⅛in thick pieces.

5 Heat a little sesame oil in a heavy cast-iron or enamelled pan until purple smoke rises. Stir-fry the pork, then add the tofu, if using, the konnyaku and all the vegetables except for the spring onions. When the colour of the meat has changed, add the stock.

6 Bring to the boil over a medium heat, and skim off the foam until the soup looks fairly clear. Reduce the heat, cover, and simmer for 15 minutes.

7 Put the miso in a small bowl, and mix with 60ml/4 tbsp hot stock to make a smooth paste. Stir one-third of the miso into the soup. Taste and add more miso if required. Add the spring onion and remove from the heat. Serve very hot in individual soup bowls and sprinkle with sesame seeds.

NEW YEAR'S SOUP

THE ELABORATE NEW YEAR'S DAY CELEBRATION BRUNCH STARTS WITH A TINY GLASS OF SPICED WARM SAKE, O-TOSO. THEN, THIS NEW YEAR'S SOUP, O-ZONI, AND OTHER FESTIVE DISHES ARE SERVED.

SERVES FOUR

INGREDIENTS
4 dried shiitake mushrooms
300g/11oz chicken thighs, bones
removed and reserved
300g/11oz salmon fillet, skin on, scaled
30ml/2 tbsp sake
50g/2oz satoimo or
Jerusalem artichokes
50g/2oz daikon, peeled
50g/2oz carrots, peeled
4 spring onions (scallions), white part
only, trimmed
4 mitsuba sprigs, root part removed
1 yuzu or lime
4 large raw tiger prawns (shrimp),
peeled, but with tails left on
30ml/2 tbsp shoyu
8 canned gingko nuts (optional)
8 mochi slices
salt

1 First, make the soup stock. Soak the dried shiitake overnight in 1 litre/1¾ pints/4 cups cold water. Remove the softened shiitake and pour the water into a pan. Bring to the boil, add the chicken bones, then reduce the heat to medium. Skim frequently to remove scum. After 20 minutes, reduce the heat to low. Simmer for 30 minutes or until the liquid has reduced by a third. Strain the stock into another pan.

2 Chop the chicken and salmon into small bitesize cubes. Par-boil them both in boiling water with 15ml/1 tbsp sake for 1 minute. Drain and wash off the scum under cold water.

3 Scrub the satoimo or artichokes with a hard brush, and thickly peel. Put in a pan and add enough water to cover. Add a pinch of salt and bring to the boil. Reduce the heat to medium, cook for 15 minutes and drain. Rinse the satoimo (to remove the sticky juice) or artichokes under running water. Wipe gently with kitchen paper. Cut the satoimo or artichokes, daikon and carrots into 1cm/½in cubes.

4 Remove and discard the stalks from the soaked shiitake, and slice the caps thinly. Chop the white part of the spring onions into 2.5cm/1in lengths.

5 Put the mitsuba sprigs into a sieve and pour hot water over them. Divide the leaf and stalk parts. Take a stalk and fold it into two, then tie it in the middle to make a bow. Make four bows.

6 Cut the yuzu or lime into four 3mm/⅛in thick round slices. Hollow out the inside to make rings of peel.

7 Add the remaining sake to the soup stock and bring to the boil. Add the daikon, carrot and shiitake, then reduce the heat to medium and cook for 15 minutes.

8 Put the prawns, satoimo or artichokes, spring onions, chicken and salmon into the pan. Wait for 5 minutes, then add the shoyu. Reduce the heat to low and add the gingko nuts, if using.

9 Cut the mochi in half crossways. Toast under a moderate preheated grill (broiler). Turn every minute until both sides are golden and the pieces have started to swell like a balloon; this will take about 5 minutes.

10 Quickly place the toasted mochi in individual soup bowls and pour the hot soup over the top. Arrange a mitsuba leaf in the centre of each bowl, put a yuzu or lime ring on top, and lay a mitsuba bow across. Serve immediately.

SOBA NOODLES <u>IN</u> HOT SOUP <u>WITH</u> TEMPURA

WHEN YOU COOK JAPANESE NOODLE DISHES, EVERYONE SHOULD BE READY AT THE DINNER TABLE, BECAUSE COOKED NOODLES START TO SOFTEN AND LOSE THEIR TASTE AND TEXTURE QUITE QUICKLY.

SERVES FOUR

INGREDIENTS
  400g/14oz dried soba noodles
  1 spring onion (scallion), sliced
  shichimi togarashi (optional)
For the tempura
  16 medium raw tiger or king prawns
    (jumbo shrimp), heads and shell
    removed, tails intact
  400ml/14fl oz/1⅔ cups ice-cold water
  1 large (US extra large) egg, beaten
  200g/7oz/scant 2 cups plain
    (all-purpose) flour
  vegetable oil, for deep-frying
For the soup
  150ml/¼ pint/⅔ cup mirin
  150ml/¼ pint/⅔ cup shoyu
  900ml/1½ pints/3¾ cups water
  25g/1oz kezuri-bushi or 2 × 15g/
    ½oz packets
  15ml/1 tbsp caster (superfine) sugar
  5ml/1 tsp salt
  900ml/1½ pints/3¾ cups first dashi
    stock or the same amount of water
    and 12.5ml/2½ tsp dashi-no-moto

1 To make the soup, put the mirin in a large pan. Bring to the boil, then add the rest of the soup ingredients apart from the dashi stock. Bring back to the boil, then reduce the heat to low. Skim off the scum and cook for 2 minutes. Strain the soup and put back into a clean pan with the dashi stock.

2 Remove the vein from the prawns, then make 5 shallow cuts into each prawn's belly. Clip the tip of the tail with scissors and squeeze out any moisture from the tail.

3 To make the batter, pour the ice-cold water into a bowl and mix in the beaten egg. Sift in the flour and stir briefly; it should remain fairly lumpy.

4 Heat the oil in a wok or deep-fryer to 180°C/350°F. Hold the tail of a prawn, dunk it in the batter, then plunge it into the hot oil. Deep-fry 2 prawns at a time until crisp and golden. Drain on kitchen paper and keep warm.

5 Put the noodles in a large pan with at least 2 litres/3½ pints/9 cups rapidly boiling water, and stir frequently to stop them sticking.

6 When the water foams, pour in about 50ml/2fl oz/¼ cup cold water to lower the temperature. Repeat when the water foams once again. The noodles should be slightly softer than *al dente* pasta. Tip the noodles into a sieve and wash under cold water with your hands to rinse off any oil.

7 Heat the soup. Warm the noodles with hot water, and divide among individual serving bowls. Place the prawns attractively on the noodles and add the soup. Sprinkle with sliced spring onion and some shichimi togarashi, if you like. Serve immediately.

BUCKWHEAT NOODLES WITH DIPPING SAUCE

COLD SOBA NOODLES ARE OFTEN EATEN IN SUMMER AND SERVED ON A BAMBOO TRAY WITH A DIPPING SAUCE. THE JAPANESE LOVE THE TASTE OF THE NOODLES; THE SAUCE ENHANCES THEIR FLAVOUR.

SERVES FOUR

INGREDIENTS
4 spring onions (scallions),
   finely chopped
½ nori sheet, about 10cm/4in square
400g/14oz dried soba noodles
5ml/1 tsp wasabi paste from a tube,
   or 5ml/1 tsp wasabi powder mixed
   with 2.5ml/½ tsp water
For the dipping sauce
   30g/1¼oz kezuri-bushi
   200ml/7fl oz/scant 1 cup shoyu
   200ml/7fl oz/scant 1 cup mirin
   750ml/1¼ pints/3 cups water

1 To make the dipping sauce, mix all the ingredients in a small pan. Bring to the boil, and cook for 2 minutes. Reduce the heat to medium, and cook for a further 2 minutes. Strain through muslin (cheesecloth). Cool, then chill.

2 Soak the spring onions in ice-cold water in a bowl for 5 minutes. Drain and squeeze out the excess water.

3 Toast the nori over a medium flame until dry and crisp, then cut it into short strips, 3mm/⅛in wide, with scissors.

4 Heat 2 litres/3½ pints/9 cups water in a large pan. The water should not fill more than two-thirds of the pan's depth.

5 Bring to the boil, then add the soba. Distribute the noodles evenly in the pan, and stir to prevent them sticking. When the water is bubbling, pour in about 50ml/2fl oz/¼ cup cold water to lower the temperature.

6 Repeat this process and cook for the length of time stated on the packet, or about 5 minutes. To test if the noodles are ready, pick one out and cut it with your finger. It should be just tender to the touch.

7 Put a large sieve under cold running water. Pour the cooked soba into the sieve, and wash thoroughly with your hands. Rub the soba well to remove the starch; the soba should feel slightly elastic. Drain again.

8 Pour the cold dipping sauce into four cups. Put the wasabi and spring onions into individual dishes for each guest. Divide the soba among four plates or baskets. Sprinkle with nori strips and serve cold, with the sauce, wasabi and spring onions.

9 Instruct each guest to mix the wasabi and onions into the dipping sauce. To eat, hold the dipping-sauce cup in one hand. Pick up a mouthful of soba from the basket or plate using chopsticks and dip the end into the dipping sauce, then slurp the noodles in with your lips.

COOK'S TIP
Other condiment ideas include yuzu or lime rind, finely grated radish, thinly sliced garlic or grated fresh root ginger.

POT-COOKED UDON IN MISO SOUP

UDON IS A WHITE WHEAT NOODLE, MORE POPULAR IN THE SOUTH AND WEST OF JAPAN THAN THE NORTH. IT IS EATEN WITH VARIOUS HOT AND COLD SAUCES AND SOUPS. HERE, IN THIS DISH KNOWN AS MISO NIKOMI UDON, THE NOODLES ARE COOKED IN A CLAY POT WITH A RICH MISO SOUP.

SERVES FOUR

INGREDIENTS
  200g/7oz chicken breast portion,
    boned and skinned
  10ml/2 tsp sake
  2 abura-age
  900ml/1½ pints/3¾ cups second
    dashi stock, or the same amount
    of water and 7.5ml/1½ tsp
    dashi-no-moto
  6 large fresh shiitake mushrooms,
    stalks removed, quartered
  4 spring onions (scallions), trimmed
    and chopped into 3mm/⅛in lengths
  30ml/2 tbsp mirin
  about 90g/3½oz aka miso or
    hatcho miso
  300g/11oz dried udon noodles
  4 eggs
  shichimi togarashi (optional)

1 Cut the chicken into bitesize pieces. Sprinkle with sake and leave to marinate for 15 minutes.

2 Put the abura-age in a sieve and thoroughly rinse with hot water from the kettle to wash off the oil. Drain on kitchen paper and cut each abura-age into 4 squares.

3 To make the soup, heat the second dashi stock in a large pan. When it has come to the boil, add the chicken pieces, shiitake mushrooms and abura-age and cook for 5 minutes. Remove the pan from the heat and add the spring onions.

4 Put the mirin and miso paste into a small bowl. Scoop 30ml/2 tbsp soup from the pan and mix this in well.

5 To cook the udon, boil at least 2 litres/3½ pints/9 cups water in a large pan. The water should not come higher than two-thirds the depth of the pan. Cook the udon for 6 minutes and drain.

6 Put the udon in one large flameproof clay pot or casserole (or divide among four small pots). Mix the miso paste into the soup and check the taste. Add more miso if required. Ladle in enough soup to cover the udon, and arrange the soup ingredients on top of the udon.

7 Put the soup on a medium heat and break an egg on top. When the soup bubbles, wait for 1 minute, then cover and remove from the heat. Leave to stand for 2 minutes. Serve with shichimi togarashi, if you like.

UDON NOODLES WITH EGG BROTH AND GINGER

IN THIS DISH, CALLED ANKAKE UDON, THE SOUP FOR THE UDON IS THICKENED WITH CORNFLOUR AND RETAINS ITS HEAT FOR A LONG TIME. A PERFECT LUNCH FOR A FREEZING COLD DAY.

2 Heat at least 2 litres/3½ pints/9 cups water in a large pan, and cook the udon for 8 minutes or according to the packet instructions. Drain under cold running water and wash off the starch with your hands. Leave the udon in the sieve.

3 Pour the soup into a large pan and bring to the boil. Blend the cornflour with 60ml/4 tbsp water. Reduce the heat to medium and gradually add the cornflour mixture to the hot soup. Stir constantly. The soup will thicken after a few minutes. Reduce the heat to low.

4 Mix the egg, mustard and cress, and spring onions in a small bowl. Stir the soup once again to create a whirlpool. Pour the eggs slowly into the soup pan.

5 Reheat the udon with hot water from a kettle. Divide among four bowls and pour the soup over the top. Garnish with the ginger and serve hot.

COOK'S TIP
You can use ready-made noodle soup, available from Japanese food stores. Follow the instructions to dilute with water or use straight from the bottle.

SERVES FOUR

INGREDIENTS
  400g/14oz dried udon noodles
  30ml/2 tbsp cornflour (cornstarch)
  4 eggs, beaten
  50g/2oz mustard and cress
  2 spring onions (scallions),
   finely chopped
  2.5cm/1in fresh root ginger, peeled
   and finely grated, to garnish
For the soup
  1 litre/1¾ pints/4 cups water
  40g/1½oz kezuri-bushi
  25ml/1½ tbsp mirin
  25ml/1½ tbsp shoyu
  7.5ml/1½ tsp salt

1 To make the soup, place the water and the soup ingredients in a pan and bring to the boil on a medium heat. Remove from the heat when it starts boiling. Stand for 1 minute, then strain through muslin (cheesecloth). Check the taste and add more salt if required.

COLD SOMEN NOODLES

AT THE HEIGHT OF SUMMER, HIYA SOMEN — COLD SOMEN NOODLES SERVED IMMERSED IN COLD WATER WITH ICE CUBES AND ACCOMPANIED BY SAUCES AND RELISHES — ARE A REFRESHING MEAL.

SERVES FOUR

INGREDIENTS
300g/11oz dried somen noodles
For the dipping sauce
105ml/7 tbsp mirin
2.5ml/½ tsp salt
105ml/7 tbsp shoyu
20g/¾oz kezuri-bushi
400ml/14fl oz/1⅔ cups water
For the relishes
2 spring onions (scallions), trimmed
  and finely chopped
2.5cm/1in fresh root ginger, peeled
  and finely grated
2 shiso leaves, finely chopped
  (optional)
30ml/2 tbsp toasted sesame seeds
For the garnishes
10cm/4in cucumber (a small salad
  cucumber is the best)
5ml/1 tsp salt
ice cubes or a block of ice
ice-cold water
115g/4oz cooked, peeled small
  prawns (shrimp)
orchid flowers or nasturtium flowers
  and leaves

1 To make the dipping sauce, put the mirin in a medium pan and bring to the boil to evaporate the alcohol. Add the salt and shoyu and shake the pan gently to mix. Add the kezuri-bushi and mix with the liquid. Add the water and bring to the boil. Cook over vigorous heat for 3 minutes without stirring. Remove from the heat and strain through muslin or a jelly bag. Leave to cool, then chill in the refrigerator for at least an hour before serving.

2 Prepare the cucumber garnish. If the cucumber is bigger than 4cm/1½in in diameter, cut in half and scoop out the seeds, then slice thinly. For a smaller cucumber, first cut into 5cm/2in lengths, then use a vegetable peeler to remove the seeds and make a hole in the centre. Slice thinly. Sprinkle with the salt and leave in a sieve for 20 minutes, then rinse in cold water and drain.

3 Bring at least 1.5 litres/2½ pints/ 6¼ cups water to the boil in a large pan. Meanwhile, untie the bundle of somen. Have 75ml/2½fl oz/⅓ cup cold water to hand. Somen only take 2 minutes to cook. Put the somen in the rapidly boiling water. When it foams again, pour the glass of water in. When the water boils again, the somen are ready. Drain into a colander under cold running water, and rub the somen with your hands to remove the starch. Drain well.

4 Put some ice cubes or a block of ice in the centre of a chilled, large glass bowl, and add the somen. Gently pour on enough ice-cold water to cover the somen, then arrange cucumber slices, prawns and flowers on top.

5 Prepare all the relishes separately in small dishes or small sake cups.

6 Divide approximately one-third of the dipping sauce among four small cups. Put the remaining sauce in a jug (pitcher) or gravy boat.

7 Serve the noodles cold with the relishes. The guests are invited to put any combination of relishes into their dipping-sauce cup. Hold the cup over the somen bowl, pick up a mouthful of somen, then dip them into the sauce and eat. Add more dipping sauce from the jug and more relishes as required.

SAPPORO-STYLE RAMEN NOODLES <u>IN</u> SOUP

THIS IS A RICH AND TANGY SOUP FROM SAPPORO, THE CAPITAL OF HOKKAIDO, WHICH IS JAPAN'S MOST NORTHERLY ISLAND. RAW GRATED GARLIC AND CHILLI OIL ARE ADDED TO WARM THE BODY.

SERVES FOUR

INGREDIENTS
250g/9oz dried ramen noodles
For the soup stock
4 spring onions (scallions)
6cm/2½in fresh root ginger, quartered
raw bones from 2 chickens, washed
1 large onion, quartered
4 garlic cloves
1 large carrot, roughly chopped
1 egg shell
120ml/4fl oz/½ cup sake
90ml/6 tbsp miso (any colour)
30ml/2 tbsp shoyu
For the toppings
115g/4oz pork belly
5cm/2in carrot
12 mangetouts (snow peas)
8 baby corn
15ml/1 tbsp sesame oil
1 dried red chilli, seeded
and crushed
225g/8oz/1 cup beansprouts
2 spring onions (scallions), chopped
2 garlic cloves, finely grated
chilli oil
salt

1 To make the soup stock, bruise the spring onions and ginger by hitting with a rolling pin. Boil 1.5 litres/2½ pints/ 6¼ cups water in a heavy pan, add the bones, and cook until the meat changes colour. Discard the water and wash the bones under running water.

2 Wash the pan and boil 2 litres/3½ pints/ 9 cups water, then add the bones and other stock ingredients except for the miso and shoyu. Reduce the heat to low, and simmer for 2 hours, skimming any scum off. Strain into a bowl through a muslin- (cheesecloth-) lined sieve, this will take about 1–2 hours. Do not squeeze the muslin.

3 Cut the pork into 5mm/¼in slices. Peel and halve the carrot lengthways then cut into 3mm/⅛in thick, 5cm/2in long slices. Boil the carrot, mangetouts and corn for 3 minutes in water. Drain.

4 Heat the sesame oil in a wok and fry the pork slices and chilli. When the colour of the meat has changed, add the beansprouts. Reduce the heat to medium and add 1 litre/1¾ pints/4 cups soup stock. Cook for 5 minutes.

5 Scoop 60ml/4 tbsp soup stock from the wok and mix well with the miso and shoyu in a bowl. Stir back into the soup. Reduce the heat to low.

6 Bring 2 litres/3½ pints/9 cups water to the boil. Cook the noodles until just soft, following the instructions on the packet. Stir constantly. If the water bubbles up, pour in 50ml/2fl oz/¼ cup cold water. Drain well and divide among four bowls.

7 Pour the hot soup on to the noodles and heap the beansprouts and pork on top. Add the carrot, mangetouts and corn. Sprinkle with spring onions and serve with garlic and chilli oil.

TOKYO-STYLE RAMEN NOODLES IN SOUP

RAMEN IS A HYBRID CHINESE NOODLE DISH PRESENTED IN A JAPANESE WAY, AND THERE ARE MANY REGIONAL VARIATIONS FEATURING LOCAL SPECIALITIES. THIS IS A LEGENDARY TOKYO VERSION.

SERVES FOUR

INGREDIENTS
250g/9oz dried ramen noodles
For the soup stock
    4 spring onions (scallions)
    7.5cm/3in fresh root ginger, quartered
    raw bones from 2 chickens, washed
    1 large onion, quartered
    4 garlic cloves, peeled
    1 large carrot, roughly chopped
    1 egg shell
    120ml/4fl oz/½ cup sake
    about 60ml/4 tbsp shoyu
    2.5ml/½ tsp salt
For the *cha-shu* (pot-roast pork)
    500g/1¼lb pork shoulder, boned
    30ml/2 tbsp vegetable oil
    2 spring onions (scallions), chopped
    2.5cm/1in fresh root ginger, peeled
      and sliced
    15ml/1 tbsp sake
    45ml/3 tbsp shoyu
    15ml/1 tbsp caster (superfine) sugar
For the toppings
    2 hard-boiled (hard-cooked) eggs
    150g/5oz menma, soaked for
      30 minutes and drained
    ½ nori sheet, broken into pieces
    2 spring onions (scallions), chopped
    ground white pepper
    sesame oil or chilli oil

1 To make the soup stock, bruise the spring onions and ginger by hitting with the side of a large knife or a rolling pin. Pour 1.5 litres/2½ pints/6¼ cups water into a wok and bring to the boil. Add the chicken bones and boil until the colour of the meat changes. Discard the water and wash the bones under water.

2 Wash the wok, bring another 2 litres/3½ pints/9 cups water to the boil and add the bones and the other soup stock ingredients, except for the shoyu and salt. Reduce the heat to low, and simmer until the water has reduced by half, skimming off any scum. Strain into a bowl through a muslin- (cheesecloth-) lined sieve. This will take 1–2 hours.

3 Make the *cha-shu*. Roll the meat up tightly, 8cm/3½in in diameter, and tie it with kitchen string.

4 Wash the wok and dry over a high heat. Heat the oil to smoking point in the wok and add the chopped spring onions and ginger. Cook briefly, then add the meat. Turn often to brown the outside evenly.

5 Sprinkle with sake and add 400ml/14fl oz/1⅔ cups water, the shoyu and sugar. Boil, then reduce the heat to low and cover. Cook for 25–30 minutes, turning every 5 minutes. Remove from the heat.

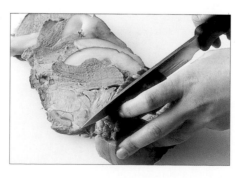

6 Slice the pork into 12 fine slices. Use any leftover pork for another recipe.

7 Shell and halve the boiled eggs, and sprinkle some salt on to the yolks.

8 Pour 1 litre/1¾ pints/4 cups soup stock from the bowl into a large pan. Boil and add the shoyu and salt. Check the seasoning; add more shoyu if required.

9 Wash the wok again and bring 2 litres/3½ pints/9 cups water to the boil. Cook the ramen noodles according to the packet instructions until just soft. Stir constantly to prevent sticking. If the water bubbles up, pour in 50ml/2fl oz/¼ cup cold water. Drain well and divide among four bowls.

10 Pour the soup over the noodles to cover. Arrange half a boiled egg, pork slices, menma and nori on top, and sprinkle with spring onions. Serve with pepper and sesame or chilli oil. Season to taste with a little salt, if you like.

VEGETABLES
AND SEAWEED

Creating a harmonious effect from seasonal harvests has been

a guiding spirit in Japanese cooking for centuries. Japanese

vegetable dishes are also nutritious and low in fat. In this

chapter there are inspiring combinations of vegetables,

mushrooms and seaweed that are typical of Japanese cooking.

SLOW-COOKED DAIKON

FRESHLY DUG DAIKON IS VERY JUICY, AND IT IS PRAISED AS THE KING OF WINTER VEGETABLES IN JAPAN. IN THIS DISH, KNOWN AS FURO FUKI DAIKON, THE DAIKON IS COOKED SLOWLY AND SERVED WITH TANGY MISO SAUCE. THE RICE ABSORBS THE BITTER JUICES, AND IS THEN DISCARDED.

SERVES FOUR

INGREDIENTS

1kg/2¼lb daikon, cut into 4 × 5cm/
  2in thick discs
15ml/1 tbsp rice (any kind except
  fragrant Thai or basmati)
100ml/3fl oz/scant ½ cup
  hatcho miso
60ml/4 tbsp caster (superfine) sugar
120ml/4fl oz/½ cup mirin
20cm/8in square dried konbu
rind of ¼ yuzu, shaved with a zester,
  to serve (optional)

1 Peel the skin from the daikon and shave the top and bottom edge of each section. Plunge into a bowl of cold water. Drain and place flat in a pan.

2 Pour in enough cold water to come 3cm/1¼in above the daikon. Add the rice and put on a high heat. When it comes to the boil, lower the heat and cook for a further 30 minutes.

3 Meanwhile, mix the miso and sugar in a pan and add the mirin, a tablespoonful at a time, to loosen the mixture. Over a medium heat, heat the miso mixture, stirring continuously. When the mixture thickens, turn the heat to very low. Cook, stirring, until the miso sauce is thick enough to stick to a spoon when you lift it from the pan. Remove from the heat and keep warm.

4 When the daikon is cooked (to test, insert a cocktail stick (toothpick): it should go in easily), gently scoop the daikon discs, one by one, on to a flat-bottomed sieve or a plate. Rinse each disc with water, to remove all the bitter juices. Discard the water and rice in the pan and wash the pan thoroughly.

5 Wipe the konbu with a wet cloth, and place in the bottom of the cleaned pan. Replace the daikon and pour in enough water to just cover. Over a very low heat, warm the daikon for 15 minutes to absorb the flavour of the konbu.

6 Place the daikon in individual bowls. Scoop out a little at the top, if you wish, then pour 15–20ml/3–4 tsp of the miso mixture on each piece and serve garnished with yuzu strips, if using. Serve with a spoon and eat it as you would a dessert.

LIGHTLY BOILED SPINACH WITH TOASTED SESAME SEEDS

O-HITASHI HAS BEEN SERVED AS A SIDE DISH ON JAPANESE DINING TABLES FOR CENTURIES. SEASONAL GREEN VEGETABLES ARE SIMPLY BLANCHED AND COOLED AND FORMED INTO LITTLE TOWERS. WITH A LITTLE HELP FROM SOY SAUCE AND SESAME SEEDS, THEY REVEAL THEIR TRUE FLAVOUR.

2 Drain immediately and place the spinach under running water. Squeeze out all the excess water by hand. Now what looked like a large amount of spinach has become a ball, roughly the size of an orange. Mix the shoyu and water, then pour on to the spinach. Mix well and leave to cool.

3 Meanwhile, put the sesame seeds in a dry frying pan and stir or toss until they start to pop. Remove from the heat and leave to cool.

4 Drain the spinach and squeeze out the excess sauce with your hands. Line up the spinach in the same direction on a chopping board, then form it into a log shape of about 4cm/1½in in diameter. Squeeze again to make it firm. With a sharp knife, cut it across into four cylinders.

5 Place the spinach cylinders on a large plate or individual dishes. Sprinkle with the toasted sesame seeds and a little salt, to taste, and serve.

SERVES FOUR

INGREDIENTS
  450g/1lb fresh spinach
  30ml/2 tbsp shoyu
  30ml/2 tbsp water
  15ml/1 tbsp sesame seeds
  salt

COOK'S TIP
Japanese spinach, the long-leaf type with the stalks and pink root intact, is best, but you can use ordinary young spinach leaves, or any soft and deep-green salad vegetables – such as watercress, rocket (arugula), lamb's lettuce – instead of the spinach, if you wish.

1 Blanch young spinach leaves in lightly salted boiling water for 15 seconds. For Japanese-type spinach, hold the leafy part and slip the stems into the pan. After 15 seconds, drop in the leaves and cook for 20 seconds.

DAIKON AND CARROT SALAD

THIS DISH, CALLED NAMASU IN JAPAN, IS ESSENTIAL FOR THE NEW YEAR'S CELEBRATION MEAL. THE BRIGHT COLOUR COMBINATION OF WHITE DAIKON AND RED CARROT IS PARTICULARLY FAVOURED BY MANY JAPANESE AS IT IS REGARDED AS A SYMBOL OF HAPPINESS. START PREPARATIONS FOR THIS RECIPE THE DAY BEFORE IT IS TO BE EATEN.

SERVES FOUR

INGREDIENTS
    20cm/8in daikon
    2 carrots
    5ml/1 tsp salt
    45ml/3 tbsp caster (superfine) sugar
    70ml/4½ tbsp rice vinegar
    15ml/1 tbsp sesame seeds

COOK'S TIP
This salad can be served with halved hard-boiled (hard-cooked) eggs, the yolk seasoned with a little mayonnaise and shoyu, and accompanied by sticks of cucumber rolled in smoked salmon. Offer a tiny cup of warm sake to drink with it.

1 Cut the daikon into three pieces, then thickly peel the skin. Peel the carrots and cut them into 5cm/2in pieces. Slice both vegetables very thinly lengthways then crossways to make very thin matchsticks. Alternatively, shred them with a grater or use a mandolin to achieve a similar effect.

2 Place the daikon and carrot in a mixing bowl. Sprinkle with the salt and mix well with your hands. Leave for about 30 minutes. Drain the vegetables in a sieve and gently squeeze out the excess liquid, then transfer them to another mixing bowl.

3 Mix the sugar and rice vinegar together in a bowl. Stir well until the sugar has completely dissolved. Pour over the daikon and carrot, and leave for at least a day, mixing at least two to three times.

4 To serve, mix the two vegetables evenly and heap in the middle of a small bowl or a plate. Sprinkle with sesame seeds and serve.

SPINACH WITH PEANUT SAUCE

TRADITIONAL JAPANESE COOKING RARELY USES FAT OR OIL, AND NUTS HAVE LONG BEEN AN IMPORTANT SOURCE OF ESSENTIAL NUTRITIONAL OILS IN THE JAPANESE DIET. IN THIS RECIPE, CALLED HORENSO PEANUTS AÉ, PEANUTS ARE TRANSFORMED INTO A CREAMY SAUCE AND MIXED WITH SPINACH.

SERVES FOUR

INGREDIENTS
    450g/1lb spinach
For the peanut sauce
    50g/2oz/⅓ cup unsalted
        shelled peanuts
    30ml/2 tbsp shoyu
    7.5ml/1½ tsp caster (superfine) sugar
    25ml/1½ tbsp second dashi stock,
        or the same amount of warm water
        with a pinch of dashi-no-moto

VARIATIONS
• You can use walnuts or sesame seeds to make different types of sauce.
• Young nettle leaves and coriander (cilantro), blanched and mixed with the peanut sauce, make an interesting "not quite Japanese" dish.

1 First, make the peanut sauce. Grind the shelled peanuts in a suribachi or a mortar and pestle. Alternatively, use an electric grinder.

2 Transfer the crushed nuts to a small mixing bowl and stir in the shoyu, sugar and dashi stock. When thoroughly mixed, the sauce will look like runny peanut butter.

3 Blanch the spinach for 30 seconds in rapidly boiling water until the leaves are wilted. Drain and cool under running water for 30 seconds.

4 Drain again and lightly squeeze out the excess water. Add the peanut sauce to the spinach in a bowl and mix gently but thoroughly. Serve on individual plates or small bowls.

BRAISED TURNIP WITH PRAWN AND MANGETOUT

TAKI-AWASE IS AN ELEGANT DISH IN WHICH THREE COLOURS — THE PINK OF THE PRAWNS, THE WHITE OF THE TURNIPS AND THE GREEN OF THE MANGETOUTS — RESEMBLE A LADY'S SPRING KIMONO.

SERVES FOUR

INGREDIENTS

8 small turnips, peeled
600ml/1 pint/2½ cups second dashi
  stock, or the same amount of water
  and 7.5ml/1½ tsp dashi-no-moto
10ml/2 tsp shoyu (use the Japanese
  pale awakuchi soy sauce
  if available)
60ml/4 tbsp mirin
30ml/2 tbsp sake
16 medium raw tiger prawns (jumbo
  shrimp), heads and shells removed
  with tails intact
dash of rice vinegar
90g/3½oz mangetouts (snow peas)
5ml/1 tsp cornflour (cornstarch)
salt

1 Par-boil the turnips in boiling water for 3 minutes. Drain, then place them side by side in a deep pan. Add the dashi stock and cover with a saucer to submerge the turnips. Bring to the boil, then add the shoyu, 5ml/1 tsp salt, the mirin and sake. Reduce the heat to very low, cover and simmer for 30 minutes.

2 Insert a cocktail stick (toothpick) into the back of each prawn, and gently scoop up the thin black vein running down its length. Very carefully pull the vein out, then discard.

3 Blanch the prawns in boiling water with the vinegar until the colour just changes. Drain. Cook the mangetouts in lightly salted water for 3 minutes. Drain well, then set aside.

4 Remove the saucer from the turnips and add the cooked prawns to the stock for about 4 minutes to warm through. Scoop out the turnips, drain and place in individual bowls. Transfer the prawns to a small plate.

5 Mix the cornflour with 15ml/1 tbsp water and add to the pan that held the turnips. Increase the heat a little bit and shake the pan gently until the liquid thickens slightly.

6 Place the mangetouts on the turnips and arrange the prawns on top, then pour about 30ml/2 tbsp of the hot liquid from the pan into each bowl. Serve immediately.

KABOCHA SQUASH <u>WITH</u> CHICKEN SAUCE

IN THIS DISH, KNOWN AS KABOCHA TORI-SOBORO KAKE, THE MILD SWEETNESS OF KABOCHA, SIMILAR TO THAT OF SWEET POTATO, GOES VERY WELL WITH THE RICH MEAT SAUCE.

<u>SERVES FOUR</u>

INGREDIENTS
    1 kabocha squash, about 500g/1¼ lb
    ½ yuzu or lime
    20g/¾ oz mangetouts (snow peas)
    salt
For the chicken sauce
    100ml/3fl oz/scant ½ cup water
    30ml/2 tbsp sake
    300g/11oz lean chicken,
      minced (ground)
    60ml/4 tbsp caster (superfine) sugar
    60ml/4 tbsp shoyu
    60ml/4 tbsp mirin

1 Halve the kabocha, then remove the seeds and fibre around the seeds. Halve again to make four wedges. Trim the stalky end of the kabocha wedge.

2 Remove strips of the peel on each of the wedges, cutting off strips length-ways of about 1–2.5cm/½–1in wide. The kabocha wedges will now have green (skin) and yellow (flesh) stripes. This will help preserve the kabocha's most tasty part just beneath the skin, and also allows it to be cooked until soft as well as being decorative.

3 Chop each wedge into large bitesize pieces. Place them side by side in a pan. Pour in enough water to cover, then sprinkle with some salt. Cover and cook for 5 minutes over a medium heat, then lower the heat and simmer for 15 minutes until tender. Test the kabocha by pricking with a skewer. When soft enough, remove from heat, cover and leave for 5 minutes.

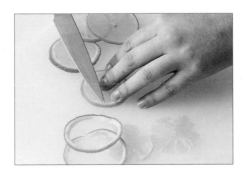

4 Slice the yuzu or lime into thin discs, then hollow out the inside of the skin to make rings of peel. Cover with a sheet of clear film (plastic wrap) until needed. Blanch the mangetouts in lightly salted water. Drain and set aside.

5 To make the chicken sauce, bring the water and sake to the boil in a pan. Add the minced chicken, and when the colour of the meat has changed, add the sugar, shoyu and mirin. Stir continuously with a hand whisk until the liquid has almost all evaporated.

6 Pile up the kabocha on a large plate, then pour the hot meat sauce on top. Add the mangetouts and serve, garnished with yuzu or lime rings.

COOK'S TIP
Use tofu for a vegetarian sauce. Wrap in kitchen paper and leave for 30 minutes. Mash with a fork, then add in step 5.

CARROT IN SWEET VINEGAR

IN THIS REFRESHING SIDE DISH, CALLED SAN BAI ZU, FINE CARROT STRIPS ARE MARINATED IN RICE VINEGAR, SHOYU AND MIRIN. IT MAKES A GOOD ACCOMPANIMENT FOR OILY FOODS SUCH AS TERIYAKI.

SERVES FOUR

INGREDIENTS
  2 large carrots, peeled
  5ml/1 tsp salt
  30ml/2 tbsp sesame seeds
For the sweet vinegar marinade
  75ml/5 tbsp rice vinegar
  30ml/2 tbsp shoyu (use the pale
    awakuchi soy sauce if available)
  45ml/3 tbsp mirin

COOK'S TIP
This marinade is called *san bai zu*, and is one of the essential basic sauces in Japanese cooking. Dilute the marinade with 15ml/1 tbsp second dashi stock, then add sesame seeds and a few dashes of sesame oil for a very tasty and healthy salad dressing.

1 Cut the carrots into thin matchsticks, 5cm/2in long. Put the carrots and salt into a mixing bowl, and mix well with your hands. After 25 minutes, rinse the wilted carrot in cold water, then drain.

2 In another bowl, mix together the marinade ingredients. Add the carrots, and leave to marinate for 3 hours.

3 Put a small pan on a high heat, add the sesame seeds and toss constantly until the seeds start to pop. Remove from the heat and cool.

4 Chop the sesame seeds with a large, sharp knife on a large chopping board. Place the carrots in a bowl, sprinkle with the sesame seeds and serve cold.

FRIED AUBERGINE WITH MISO SAUCE

IN NASU-MISO, STIR-FRIED AUBERGINE IS COATED IN A RICH MISO SAUCE. MAKE SURE THE OIL IS SMOKING HOT WHEN ADDING THE AUBERGINE PIECES, SO THAT THEY DO NOT ABSORB TOO MUCH OIL.

SERVES FOUR

INGREDIENTS
  2 large aubergines (eggplant)
  1–2 dried red chillies
  45ml/3 tbsp sake
  45ml/3 tbsp mirin
  45ml/3 tbsp caster (superfine) sugar
  30ml/2 tbsp shoyu
  45ml/3 tbsp red miso (use either the
    dark red aka miso or even darker
    hatcho miso)
  90ml/6 tbsp sesame oil
  salt

VARIATION
Sweet (bell) peppers could also be used for this dish instead of the aubergine. Take 1 red, 1 yellow and 2 green peppers. Remove the seeds and chop them into 1cm/½in strips, then follow the rest of the recipe.

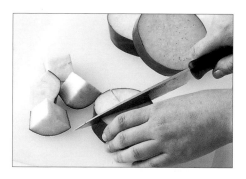

1 Cut the aubergines into bitesize pieces and place in a large colander, sprinkle with some salt and leave for 30 minutes to remove the bitter juices. Squeeze the aubergine pieces by hand. Remove the seeds from the chillies and chop the chillies into thin rings.

2 Mix the sake, mirin, sugar and shoyu in a cup. In a separate bowl, mix the red miso with 45ml/3 tbsp water to make a loose paste.

3 Heat the oil in a large pan and add the chilli. When you see pale smoke rising from the oil, add the aubergine, and, using cooking hashi, stir-fry for about 8 minutes, or until tender. Lower the heat to medium.

4 Add the sake mixture to the pan, and stir for 2–3 minutes. If the sauce starts to burn, lower the heat. Add the miso paste to the pan and cook, stirring, for another 2 minutes. Serve hot.

BROAD BEANS, DAIKON AND SALMON ROE

SORA-MAME NO AE-MONO IS A TYPICAL TSUMAMI BAR SNACK EATEN THROUGHOUT JAPAN. THIS UNUSUAL COMBINATION OF COLOURS, FLAVOURS AND TEXTURES MAKES IT IDEAL COMPANY FOR A REFRESHING GLASS OF COLD SAKE IN THE SUMMER MONTHS.

SERVES FOUR

INGREDIENTS
200g/7oz daikon, peeled
1 nori sheet
1kg/2¼lb broad (fava) beans in their pods, shelled
1.5ml/¼ tsp wasabi paste from tube or 2.5ml/½ tsp wasabi powder mixed with 1.5ml/¼ tsp water
20ml/4 tsp shoyu
60ml/4 tbsp ikura
salt

1 Grate the daikon finely with a daikon grater, or use a food processor to chop it into fine shreds. Place the daikon in a sieve and let the juices drain.

2 Tear the nori with your hands into flakes about 1cm/½in square.

3 In a small pan, cook the broad beans in plenty of rapidly boiling salted water for about 4 minutes. Drain and immediately cool under running water. Remove the skins.

4 Mix the wasabi paste with the shoyu in a small mixing bowl. Add the nori flakes, toasted if you wish, and skinned beans, and mix well.

5 Divide the beans among four individual small bowls, heap on the grated daikon, then spoon the ikura on top. Serve cold. Ask your guests to mix everything well just before eating.

COOK'S TIPS
• The Japanese don't eat the pods of broad beans. When the beans are in season, people buy huge quantities of them. Shelled, unskinned beans are cooked in salted water as salty as sea water, then drained and heaped into a large bowl. You pick one up and snap the top tip off the skins then squeeze the bright green contents into your mouth.
• Toasting the nori sheet gives it a crisp texture and enhances its flavour. Before tearing into small pieces, wave the edge of the nori over a medium gas flame very quickly a few times.

CABBAGE "NOODLE" PANCAKE

THE ORIGIN OF THIS PANCAKE IS SAID TO GO BACK TO THE DAYS OF RATIONING AFTER WORLD WAR II, WHEN FLOUR MADE UP FOR THE SHORTAGE OF RICE, AND CABBAGE WAS USED FOR BULK.

MAKES EIGHT

INGREDIENTS
    400g/14oz/3½ cups plain
        (all-purpose) flour
    200ml/7fl oz/scant 1 cup water
    2 large (US extra large) eggs, beaten
    pinch of salt
    4 spring onions (scallions),
        roughly chopped
    400g/14oz white cabbage, very
        finely sliced
    vegetable oil, for frying
    Japanese o-konomi yaki sauce or
        Worcestershire sauce
    English (hot) mustard
    mayonnaise
    kezuri-bushi
    ao nori
    beni-shoga
For the toppings
    225g/8oz pork chops, boned
    225g/8oz raw prawns (shrimp), heads
        and shells removed
    115g/4oz queen scallops

1 To prepare the pork topping, put the pork chops in the freezer for 1–2 hours, then wait until they're half defrosted. Slice the semi-frozen pork very thinly by pressing the meat on to the chopping board with your palm and cutting horizontally with a sharp knife. Set the slices aside.

2 To make the pancakes, put the flour into a large mixing bowl and mix well with the water. Add the beaten eggs and salt and blend together. Add the spring onions and one-third of the sliced cabbage, then mix well. Repeat until all of the cabbage is mixed in and evenly coated with the batter.

3 Put a heavy frying pan on high heat. When hot, oil the base with kitchen paper soaked in oil. Remove from the heat when the oil starts to smoke and wait for 10–15 seconds until the smoke dies down. Reduce the heat to medium and return the frying pan back to the heat.

4 With a ladle, pour some of the mixture into the centre of the pan. Make a circle of about 2.5cm/1in thick and 10cm/4in in diameter.

5 Sprinkle the surface of the pancake with one-eighth of the prawns and queen scallops. Lay some pork slices on top. Gently press the toppings down using a tablespoon.

6 When the edge of the pancake is cooked and the surface has started to dry, turn it over by sliding it to the far end of the pan, then sliding in two spatulas, turning it over towards you. Gently press the pancake to the base of the pan with a spatula, then stretch it out to 15cm/6in in diameter, and half the thickness.

7 After 2–3 minutes, turn over again. If the surface is still wet, turn over and cook for another few minutes. While the pancake is still in the frying pan, with the topping-side up, add the sauces and seasonings. First, spread on some o-konomi yaki sauce or Worcestershire sauce. Then add a little mustard and mayonnaise. Sprinkle with kezuri-bushi and ao nori.

8 Put the pancake on to a plate and keep warm while you make seven more pancakes in the same way. Serve hot with a sprinkle of beni-shoga on top.

COOK'S TIP
This recipe is ideal for cooking at the table on a hot-plate with guests. Eat the pancakes as you cook.

STEAMED AUBERGINE <u>WITH</u> SESAME SAUCE

THIS AUTUMN RECIPE, NASU RIKYU-NI, REPRESENTS A TYPICAL ZEN TEMPLE COOKING STYLE. FRESH SEASONAL VEGETABLES ARE CHOSEN AND COOKED WITH CARE. THIS DISH IS ALSO DELICIOUS COLD.

SERVES FOUR

INGREDIENTS
    2 large aubergines (eggplant)
    400ml/14fl oz/1⅔ cups second dashi
      stock, or the same amount of water
      with 5ml/1 tsp dashi-no-moto
    25ml/1½ tbsp caster (superfine)
      sugar
    15ml/1 tbsp shoyu
    15ml/1 tbsp sesame seeds, finely
      ground in a suribachi or mortar
      and pestle
    15ml/1 tbsp sake
    15ml/1 tbsp cornflour (cornstarch)
    salt
For the accompanying vegetables
    130g/4½oz shimeji mushrooms
    115g/4oz/¾ cup fine green beans
    100ml/3fl oz/scant ½ cup second
      dashi stock, or the same amount of
      water with 5ml/1 tsp dashi-no-moto
    25ml/1½ tbsp caster (superfine)
      sugar
    15ml/1 tbsp sake
    1.5ml/¼ tsp salt
    dash of shoyu

1 Peel the aubergines and cut in quarters lengthways. Prick all over with a skewer, then plunge into salted water for 30 minutes.

2 Drain and steam the aubergines in a steamer, or in a hot wok with a bamboo basket inside, for 20 minutes, or until soft. If the quarters are too long to fit in the steamer, cut in half.

3 Mix the dashi stock, sugar, shoyu and 1.5ml/¼ tsp salt together in a large pan. Gently transfer the aubergines to this pan, then cover and cook over a low heat for a further 15 minutes. Take a few tablespoonfuls of stock from the pan and mix with the ground sesame seeds. Add this mixture to the pan.

4 Thoroughly mix the sake with the cornflour, add to the pan with the aubergines and stock and shake the pan gently, but quickly. When the sauce becomes quite thick, remove the pan from the heat.

5 While the aubergines are cooking, prepare and cook the accompanying vegetables. Wash the mushrooms and cut off the hard base part. Separate the large block into smaller chunks with your fingers. Trim the green beans and cut in half.

6 Mix the stock with the sugar, sake, salt and shoyu in a shallow pan. Add the green beans and mushrooms and cook for 7 minutes until just tender. Serve the aubergines and their sauce in individual bowls with the accompanying vegetables over the top.

NEW POTATOES COOKED <u>IN</u> DASHI STOCK

NIKKOROGASHI *IS A SIMPLE YET SCRUMPTIOUS DISH, INVOLVING LITTLE MORE THAN NEW SEASON'S POTATOES AND ONION COOKED IN DASHI STOCK. AS THE STOCK EVAPORATES, THE ONION BECOMES MELTINGLY SOFT AND CARAMELIZED, MAKING A WONDERFUL SAUCE THAT COATS THE POTATOES.*

SERVES FOUR

INGREDIENTS
   15ml/1 tbsp toasted sesame oil
   1 small onion, thinly sliced
   1kg/2¼lb baby new potatoes,
      unpeeled
   200ml/7fl oz/scant 1 cup second
      dashi stock, or the same amount of
      water with 5ml/1 tsp dashi-no-moto
   45ml/3 tbsp shoyu

COOK'S TIP
Japanese chefs use toasted sesame oil for its distinctive strong aroma. If the smell is too strong, use a mixture of half sesame and half vegetable oil.

1 Heat the sesame oil in a wok or large pan. Add the onion slices and stir-fry for 30 seconds, then add the potatoes. Stir constantly, using cooking hashi for ease, until all the potatoes are well coated in sesame oil.

2 Pour on the dashi stock and shoyu and reduce the heat to the lowest setting. Cover and cook for 15 minutes, turning the potatoes every 5 minutes so that they are evenly cooked.

3 Uncover the wok or pan for a further 5 minutes to reduce the liquid. If there is already very little liquid remaining, remove the wok or pan from the heat, cover and leave to stand for 5 minutes. Check that the potatoes are cooked, then remove from the heat.

4 Transfer the potatoes and onions to a deep serving bowl. Pour the sauce over the top and serve immediately.

VEGETARIAN TEMPURA

IN THE HOT AND HUMID JAPANESE SUMMER, ZEN MONKS EAT DEEP-FRIED VEGETABLES, SHOJIN-AGÉ, TO GET OVER THE FATIGUE OF HARD TRAINING. ALTHOUGH TEMPURA PREPARATION NEEDS A LITTLE EFFORT, TAKE YOUR TIME AND ENJOY THE PROCESS AS AN ARTISTIC ACTIVITY, LIKE THE MONKS DO.

SERVES FOUR

INGREDIENTS
　15ml/1 tbsp lemon juice or
　　rice vinegar
　15cm/6in renkon
　½ sweet potato
　½ aubergine (eggplant)
　vegetable oil and sesame oil, for
　　frying (see Cook's Tips)
　4 shiso leaves
　1 green (bell) pepper, seeded and cut
　　lengthways into 2.5cm/1in wide strips
　⅛ kabocha squash, cut into 5mm/¼in
　　thick half-ring shapes
　4 green beans, trimmed
　4 fresh shiitake mushrooms
　4 okra, trimmed
　1 onion, sliced into 5mm/¼in rings
For the batter
　200ml/7fl oz/scant 1 cup ice-
　　cold water
　1 large (US extra large) egg, beaten
　90g/3½oz/generous ¾ cup sifted
　　plain (all-purpose) flour, plus extra
　　for dusting
　2–3 ice cubes
For the condiment
　450g/1lb daikon
　4cm/1½in piece fresh root ginger
For the dipping sauce
　400ml/14fl oz/1⅔ cups second dashi
　　stock, or the same amount of water
　　with 10ml/2 tsp dashi-no-moto
　100ml/3fl oz/scant ½ cup shoyu
　100ml/3fl oz/scant ½ cup mirin

1 To make the dipping sauce, mix all the ingredients in a pan. Bring to the boil, then remove from the heat. Set aside.

2 Fill a small bowl with cold water and add the lemon juice or rice vinegar. Peel the renkon, then slice it and the sweet potato into 5mm/¼in thick discs. Plunge the pieces into the bowl straightaway to prevent discolouring. Just before frying, drain and pat dry with kitchen paper.

3 Slice the aubergine horizontally into 5mm/¼in thick slices, then halve them lengthways. Soak in cold water until just before frying. Drain and pat dry.

4 To prepare the condiment, peel and grate the daikon and ginger separately, using a daikon-oroshi, or, alternatively, use a food processor. Lightly squeeze out excess liquid from both the daikon and ginger.

5 Line an egg cup with clear film (plastic wrap) and press about 2.5ml/½ tsp grated ginger into the bottom, then put in 30ml/2 tbsp grated daikon. Press again and turn upside-down on to a small plate. Make four of these tiny mounds.

6 To make the batter, pour the ice-cold water into a mixing bowl, add the beaten egg and mix well. Add the flour and very roughly fold in with a pair of chopsticks or a fork. Do not beat. The batter should still be quite lumpy. Add the ice cubes.

7 Pour in enough oil to come halfway up the depth of a wok or deep-fryer. Heat the oil until the temperature reaches about 150°C/300°F.

8 Deep-fry the shiso leaves. Hold the stalk of one leaf in your hand and stroke the leaf across the surface of the batter mix, coating only one side of the leaf. Gently slip it into the oil until it goes crisp and bright green. Leave to drain on kitchen paper. Deep-fry the renkon and sweet potato in the same way; first coating one side in batter then frying until golden.

9 Increase the temperature to 175°C/347°F. Lightly dust the rest of the vegetables with flour, dunk into the batter mix, then shake off the excess. Deep-fry them two to three pieces at a time until crisp. Leave to drain on kitchen paper.

10 Divide the warm dipping sauce among four small bowls. Place with the condiment. Arrange the tempura on a large plate. Serve immediately. Mix the condiment into the sauce, then dip in the tempura as you eat.

COOK'S TIPS
• If you like the strong flavour of sesame oil, mix it with 2 parts vegetable oil. For a lighter flavour, just add a few dashes of toasted sesame oil to the vegetable oil.
• To check the temperature of oil without a thermometer, drop a little batter into the hot oil. At 150°C/300°F it should sink down to the bottom and stay there for about 5 seconds before it floats to the surface. When the temperature reaches 175°C/347°F, a drop of batter sinks to the bottom, but immediately rises to the surface.

SLOW-COOKED SHIITAKE WITH SHOYU

SHIITAKE COOKED SLOWLY ARE SO RICH AND FILLING, THAT SOME PEOPLE CALL THEM "VEGETARIAN STEAK". THIS DISH, KNOWN AS FUKUMÉ-NI, CAN LAST A FEW WEEKS IN THE REFRIGERATOR, AND IS A USEFUL AND FLAVOURFUL ADDITION TO OTHER DISHES.

SERVES FOUR

INGREDIENTS
    20 dried shiitake mushrooms
    45ml/3 tbsp vegetable oil
    30ml/2 tbsp shoyu
    25ml/1½ tbsp caster (superfine)
      sugar
    15ml/1 tbsp toasted sesame oil

VARIATION

To make shiitake rice, cut the slow-cooked shiitake into thin strips. Mix with 600g/1lb 5oz/5¼ cups cooked rice and 15ml/1 tbsp finely chopped chives. Serve in individual rice bowls and sprinkle with toasted sesame seeds.

1 Start soaking the dried shiitake the day before. Put them in a large bowl almost full of water. Cover the shiitake with a plate or lid to stop them floating to the surface of the water. Leave to soak overnight.

2 Measure 120ml/4fl oz/½ cup liquid from the bowl. Drain the shiitake into a sieve. Remove and discard the stalks.

3 Heat the oil in a wok or a large pan. Stir-fry the shiitake over a high heat for 5 minutes, stirring continuously.

4 Reduce the heat to the lowest setting, then add the measured liquid, the shoyu and sugar. Cook until there is almost no moisture left, stirring frequently. Add the sesame oil and remove from the heat.

5 Leave to cool, then slice and arrange the shiitake on a large plate.

VEGETABLES AND SALMON IN A PARCEL

IN THIS RECIPE, THE VEGETABLES AND SALMON ARE WRAPPED AND STEAMED WITH SAKE IN THEIR OWN MOISTURE. WHEN MAKING SAKA-MUSHI, ARRANGING THE FISH AND ALL THE VEGETABLES CAN BE TRICKY, BUT WHEN YOU OPEN THE PARCEL, YOU'LL FIND A COLOURFUL AUTUMN GARDEN INSIDE.

3 Slice the carrot very thinly, then with a Japanese vegetable cutter or sharp knife, cut out 8–12 maple-leaf or flower shapes. Carefully slice the spring onions in half lengthways with a sharp knife. Trim the mangetouts.

4 Cut four sheets of foil, each about 29 × 21cm/11½ × 8½in wide. Place the long side of one sheet facing towards you. Arrange the salmon and shimeji mushrooms in the centre, then place a spring onion diagonally across them. Put 2 shiitake on top, 3–4 mangetouts in a fan shape and then sprinkle with a few carrot leaves.

SERVES FOUR

INGREDIENTS

600g/1lb 5oz salmon fillet, skinned
30ml/2 tbsp sake
15ml/1 tbsp shoyu, plus extra
  to serve (optional)
about 250g/9oz fresh shimeji
  mushrooms
8 fresh shiitake mushrooms
2.5cm/1in carrot
2 spring onions (scallions)
115g/4oz mangetouts (snow peas)
salt

1 Preheat the oven to 190°C/375°F/ Gas 5. Cut the salmon into bitesize pieces. Marinate in the sake and shoyu for about 15 minutes. Drain and reserve the marinade.

2 Clean the shimeji mushrooms and chop off the hard root. Remove and discard the stalks from the shiitake. Carve a shallow slit on the top of each shiitake with a sharp knife inserted at a slant. Repeat from the other side to cut out a notch about 4cm/1½in long, then rotate the shiitake 90° and carefully carve another notch to make a small white cross in the brown top.

5 Sprinkle the marinade and a good pinch of salt over the top. Fold the two longer sides of the foil together, then fold the shorter sides to seal. Repeat to make four parcels.

6 Place the parcels on a baking sheet and bake for 15–20 minutes in the middle of the preheated oven. When the foil has expanded into a balloon, the dish is ready to serve. Serve unopened with a little extra shoyu, if required.

DEEP-FRIED LAYERED SHIITAKE AND SCALLOPS

IN THIS DISH, YOU CAN TASTE THREE KINDS OF SOFTNESS: CHEWY SHIITAKE, MASHED NAGA-IMO WITH MISO, AND SUCCULENT SCALLOP. THE MIXTURE CREATES A MOMENT OF HEAVEN IN YOUR MOUTH. IF IT'S DIFFICULT TO EAT WITH CHOPSTICKS, FEEL FREE TO USE A KNIFE AND FORK!

SERVES FOUR

INGREDIENTS

4 scallops
8 large fresh shiitake mushrooms
225g/8oz naga-imo, unpeeled
20ml/4 tsp miso
50g/2oz/1 cup fresh breadcrumbs
cornflour (cornstarch), for dusting
vegetable oil, for deep-frying
2 eggs, beaten
salt
4 lemon wedges, to serve

1 Slice the scallops in two horizontally, then sprinkle with salt. Remove the stalks from the shiitake by cutting them off with a knife. Discard the stalks.

2 Cut shallow slits on the top of the shiitake to form a "hash" symbol or cut slits to form a white cross. Sprinkle with a little salt.

3 Heat a steamer and steam the naga-imo for 10–15 minutes, or until soft. Test with a skewer. Leave to cool.

4 Wait until the naga-imo is cool enough to handle. Skin, then mash the flesh in a bowl with a masher, getting rid of any lumps. Add the miso and mix well. Take the breadcrumbs into your hands and break them down finely. Mix half into the mashed naga-imo, keeping the rest on a small plate.

5 Fill the underneath of the shiitake caps with a scoop of mashed naga-imo. Smooth down with the flat edge of a knife and dust the mash with cornflour.

6 Add a little mash to a slice of scallop and place on top.

7 Spread another 5ml/1 tsp mashed naga-imo on to the scallop and shape to completely cover. Make sure all the ingredients are clinging together. Repeat to make eight little mounds.

8 Heat the oil to 150°C/300°F. Place the beaten eggs in a shallow container. Dust the shiitake and scallop mounds with cornflour, then dip into the egg. Handle with care as the mash and scallop are quite soft. Coat well with the remaining breadcrumbs and deep-fry in the oil until golden. Drain well on kitchen paper. Serve hot on individual plates with a wedge of lemon.

VARIATION
For a vegetarian option, use 16 shiitake mushrooms. Sandwich the naga-imo mash between two shiitake to make 8 bundles. Deep-fry in the same way as the scallop version.

COOK'S TIPS
• Fresh naga-imo produces a slimy liquid when it's cut. Try not to touch this as some people can react and develop a mild rash. When it's cooked, it is perfectly safe to touch.
• If you can't find naga-imo, use yam or 115g/4oz each of potatoes and peeled Jerusalem artichokes instead. Steam the potatoes and boil the artichokes until both are tender.

BACON-ROLLED ENOKITAKE MUSHROOMS

THE JAPANESE NAME FOR THIS DISH IS OBIMAKI ENOKI: AN OBI (BELT OR SASH) IS MADE FROM BACON AND WRAPPED AROUND ENOKITAKE MUSHROOMS BEFORE GRILLING THEM. THE STRONG, SMOKY FLAVOUR OF THE BACON ACCOMPANIES THE SUBTLE FLAVOUR OF ENOKI VERY WELL.

SERVES FOUR

INGREDIENTS

450g/1lb fresh enokitake mushrooms
6 rindless smoked streaky (fatty)
  bacon rashers (strips)
4 lemon wedges and ground white
  pepper, to serve

1 Cut off the root part of each enokitake cluster 2cm/¾in from the end. Do not separate the stems. Cut the rashers in half lengthways.

2 Divide the enokitake into 12 bunches. Take one bunch, then place the middle of the enokitake near the edge of 1 bacon rasher. You should be able to see 2.5–4cm/1–1½in of enokitake at each end of the bacon.

3 Carefully roll up the bunch of enokitake in the bacon. Tuck any straying short stems into the bacon and slide the bacon slightly upwards at each roll to cover about 4cm/1½in of the enokitake. Secure the end of the bacon roll with a cocktail stick (toothpick). Repeat using the remaining enokitake and bacon to make 11 more rolls.

4 Preheat the grill (broiler) to high. Place the enokitake rolls on an oiled wire rack. Grill (broil) both sides until the bacon is crisp and the enokitake start to burn. This takes about 10–13 minutes.

5 Remove the enokitake rolls and place on a board. Using a fork and knife, chop each roll in half in the middle of the bacon belt. Arrange the top part of the enokitake roll standing upright, the bottom part lying down next to it. Serve with a wedge of lemon and a small heap of ground white pepper.

VARIATIONS
A bunch of chives can be rolled and cooked in the same way. You can also use young garlic shoots when they are about 12cm/4½in long for this recipe.

HIJIKI SEAWEED <u>AND</u> CHICKEN

THE TASTE OF HIJIKI IS SOMEWHERE BETWEEN RICE AND VEGETABLE. IT GOES WELL WITH MEAT OR TOFU PRODUCTS, ESPECIALLY WHEN IT'S STIR-FRIED WITH A LITTLE OIL FIRST.

SERVES FOUR

INGREDIENTS
    90g/3½oz dried hijiki seaweed
    150g/5oz chicken breast portion
      with skin
    ½ small carrot, about 5cm/2in
    15ml/1 tbsp vegetable oil
    100ml/3fl oz/scant ½ cup second
      dashi stock, or the same amount of
      water plus 1.5ml/¼ tsp dashi-no-moto
    30ml/2 tbsp sake
    30ml/2 tbsp caster (superfine) sugar
    45ml/3 tbsp shoyu
    a pinch of shichimi togarashi or
      cayenne pepper

1 Soak the hijiki in cold water for about 30 minutes. When ready to cook, it is easily crushed between the fingers. Pour into a sieve and wash under running water. Drain.

2 Peel the skin from the chicken and par-boil the skin in rapidly boiling water for 1 minute, then drain. With a sharp knife, shave off all the yellow fat from the skin. Discard the clear membrane between the fat and the skin as well. Cut the skin into thin strips about 5mm/¼in wide and 2.5cm/1in long. Cut the meat into small, bitesize chunks.

3 Peel and chop the carrot into long, narrow matchsticks.

4 Heat the oil in a wok or frying pan and stir-fry the strips of chicken skin for 5 minutes, or until golden and curled up. Add the chicken meat and keep stirring until the colour changes.

5 Add the hijiki and carrot, then stir-fry for a further minute. Add the remaining ingredients. Lower the heat and cook for 5 minutes.

6 Remove the pan from the heat and leave to stand for about 10 minutes. Serve in small individual bowls. Sprinkle with shichimi togarashi, or cayenne pepper, if preferred.

COOK'S TIP
Chicken skin is unpopular today because of its high calorie content. However, in this dish the thick yellow fat is removed from the skin before cooking, thus greatly reducing the fat content.

WAKAME WITH PRAWNS AND CUCUMBER IN VINEGAR DRESSING

THIS SALAD-STYLE DISH, CALLED SUNO-MONO, USES WAKAME SEAWEED, WHICH IS NOT ONLY RICH IN MINERALS AND B COMPLEX VITAMINS AND VITAMIN C, BUT ALSO MAKES YOUR HAIR LOOK SHINY.

2 Peel the prawns, including the tails. Insert a cocktail stick (toothpick) into the back of each prawn and gently scoop up the thin black vein running down its length. Pull it out, then discard.

3 Boil the prawns in lightly salted water until they curl up completely to make full circles. Drain and cool.

4 Halve the cucumber lengthways. Peel away half of the green skin with a zester or vegetable peeler to create green and white stripes. Scoop out the centre with a tablespoon. Slice very thinly with a sharp knife or a mandolin. Sprinkle with 5ml/1 tsp salt, and leave for 15 minutes in a sieve.

5 Blanch the wakame very briefly in boiling water. Drain and cool under cold running water. Add to the cucumber in the sieve. Press the cucumber and wakame to remove the excess liquid. Repeat this two to three times.

6 Mix the dressing ingredients in a mixing bowl. Stir well until the sugar has dissolved. Add the wakame and cucumber to the dressing and mix.

7 Pile up in four small bowls. Lean the prawns against the heap. Garnish with ginger.

VARIATION
For a vegetarian version, omit the shellfish and add a handful of toasted pine nuts.

SERVES FOUR

INGREDIENTS
   10g/¼oz dried wakame
   12 medium raw tiger prawns
     (jumbo shrimp), heads removed
     but tails intact
   ½ cucumber
   salt
For the dressing
   60ml/4 tbsp rice vinegar
   15ml/1 tbsp shoyu
   7.5ml/1½ tsp caster (superfine) sugar
   2.5cm/1in fresh root ginger, peeled
     and cut into thin strips, to garnish

1 Soak the wakame in a pan or bowl of cold water for 15 minutes until fully open. The wakame expands by three to five times its original size. Drain.

ASSORTED SEAWEED SALAD

KAISOU SALADA IS A FINE EXAMPLE OF THE TRADITIONAL JAPANESE IDEA OF EATING: LOOK AFTER YOUR APPETITE AND YOUR HEALTH AT THE SAME TIME. SEAWEED IS A NUTRITIOUS, ALKALINE FOOD AND RICH IN FIBRE. MOREOVER, IT HAS VIRTUALLY NO CALORIES!

SERVES FOUR

INGREDIENTS
  5g/⅛oz each dried wakame, dried
    arame and dried hijiki seaweeds
  about 130g/4½oz enokitake
    mushrooms
  2 spring onions (scallions)
  a few ice cubes
  ½ cucumber, cut lengthways
  250g/9oz mixed salad leaves
For the marinade
  15ml/1 tbsp rice vinegar
  6.5ml/1¼ tsp salt
For the dressing
  60ml/4 tbsp rice vinegar
  7.5ml/1½ tsp toasted sesame oil
  15ml/1 tbsp shoyu
  15ml/1 tbsp second dashi stock, or
    the same amount of water with a
    pinch of dashi-no-moto
  2.5cm/1in piece fresh root ginger,
    finely grated

1 Soak the wakame for 10 minutes in one bowl of water and, in a separate bowl of water, soak the arame and hijiki for 30 minutes together.

2 Trim the hard end of the enokitake stalks, then cut the bunch in half and separate the stems.

3 Cut the spring onions into thin, 4cm/1½in long strips, then soak the strips in cold water with a few ice cubes to make them curl up. Drain. Slice the cucumber into thin, half-moon shapes.

4 Cook the wakame and enokitake in boiling water for 2 minutes, then add the arame and hijiki for a few seconds. Immediately remove from the heat. Drain and sprinkle over the vinegar and salt while still warm. Chill.

5 Mix the dressing ingredients in a bowl. Arrange the mixed salad leaves in a large bowl with the cucumber on top, then add the seaweed and enokitake mixture. Decorate with spring onion strips and serve with the dressing.

DAIKON LAYERED WITH SMOKED SALMON

THE ORIGINAL RECIPE CALLS FOR LAYERED, SALTED SLICED SALMON AND DAIKON, PICKLED IN A WOODEN BARREL FOR A LONG TIME. THIS MODERN VERSION IS LESS SALTY AND FAR EASIER TO MAKE.

SERVES FOUR

INGREDIENTS

10cm/4in daikon, about 6cm/2½in
  in diameter, peeled
10ml/2 tsp salt
5ml/1 tsp rice vinegar
5cm/2in square dashi-konbu,
  chopped into 1cm/½in strips
50g/2oz smoked salmon,
  thinly sliced
2.5ml/½ tsp white poppy seeds

COOK'S TIPS
• You can use a mandolin, a food cutter or a vegetable slicer to make paper-thin slices of daikon.
• If unsure, taste the daikon after salting and squeezing to check whether it needs to be rinsed. The degree of saltiness will depend on the original water content of the daikon.

1 Slice the daikon very thinly into rounds. Put in a shallow container, sprinkle with salt and vinegar, and add the snipped dashi-konbu. Mix and rub gently with the hands. Cover and leave in the refrigerator for 1 hour.

2 Drain in a sieve and squeeze out the excess liquid. If necessary, rinse with running water for 30 seconds, then drain and squeeze out again.

3 Cut the smoked salmon slices into 4cm/1½in squares. Take 1 slice of daikon, top with a salmon slice, then cover with another daikon slice. Repeat until all the salmon is used. Place in a shallow container, cover, then leave to pickle at room temperature for up to 1 day.

4 Arrange the daikon rounds on a serving plate and put a pinch of poppy seeds in the centre.

BROCCOLI AND CUCUMBER PICKLED IN MISO

BROCCOLI STEM IS USUALLY WASTED BECAUSE OF THE FIBROUS TEXTURE, BUT YOU WILL BE SURPRISED HOW TASTY IT IS WHEN MARINATED OR PICKLED. IN YASAI MISO ZUKE, MISO AND GARLIC GIVE A KICK TO ITS SUBTLE FLAVOUR. THIS MAKES A GOOD ACCOMPANIMENT TO DRINKS.

SERVES FOUR

INGREDIENTS

3 broccoli stems (use the florets in
  another dish, if you wish)
2 Japanese or salad cucumbers,
  ends trimmed
200ml/7fl oz/scant 1 cup miso
  (any kind)
15ml/1 tbsp sake
1 garlic clove, crushed

1 Peel the broccoli stems and quarter them lengthways.

2 With a vegetable peeler, peel the cucumber every 5mm/¼in to make green-and-white stripes. Cut in half lengthways. Scoop out the centre with a teaspoon. Cut into 7.5cm/3in lengths.

3 Mix the miso, sake and crushed garlic in a deep, plastic or metal container with a lid. Remove half the miso mix.

4 Lay some of the broccoli stems and cucumber flat in the container and push into the miso mix. Spread a little of the reserved miso over the top of the broccoli and cucumber as well.

5 Repeat this process to make a few layers of vegetables and miso, filling up the container. Cover with the lid and leave in the refrigerator for 1–5 days.

6 Take out the vegetables, wash off the miso under running water, then wipe with kitchen paper. Cut the broccoli stem pieces in half then slice into thin strips lengthways. Cut the cucumber into 5mm/¼in thick half-moon slices. Serve cold.

VARIATION
Carrot, turnip, kohlrabi, celery, radish or thinly sliced cabbage stems can be used in this way. The garlic can be replaced by ginger, chilli or lime rind.

BEANS, TOFU
AND EGGS

The virtues of tofu as a nutrient could fill a book,

and the uses of this wonder food are limitless. Its essential

blandness adapts to and absorbs a host of other flavours.

Beans and eggs are equally as versatile and are perfect for

making even the simplest of dishes healthy and filling.

SWEET AZUKI BEAN SOUP
WITH MOCHI RICE CAKE

AZUKI BEANS ARE COMMONLY USED IN TRADITIONAL JAPANESE DESSERTS. THIS SWEET SOUP FOR WINTER IS EATEN BETWEEN MEALS AS A SNACK, BUT NEVER AFTER THE MEAL AS IT IS QUITE FILLING.

SERVES FOUR

INGREDIENTS
  130g/4½oz/⅔ cup dried azuki beans
  pinch of baking powder
  130g/4½oz/scant ¾ cup caster
  (superfine) sugar
  1.5ml/¼ tsp salt
  4 mochi

1 Soak the azuki beans overnight in 1 litre/1¾ pints/4 cups water.

2 Pour the beans and the soaking water into a heavy large pan, then bring to the boil. Reduce the heat to medium-low and add the baking powder. Cover the pan and cook for about 30 minutes. Add a further 1 litre/1¾ pints/4 cups water, and bring back to the boil. Reduce the heat to low, and cook for a further 30 minutes.

3 To test that the beans are ready, pick out and press one bean between the fingers. It should crush without any effort. If it is still hard, cook for another 15–20 minutes, then check again.

4 Divide the sugar into two equal heaps. Add one heap to the pan containing the beans and stir gently. Cook for about 3 minutes, then add the rest and wait for another 3 minutes.

5 Add the salt and cook for another 3 minutes. The soup is now ready to eat. Reduce the heat and keep warm.

6 Cut the mochi in half. Grill (broil) under a moderate heat until light golden brown and puffy. Turn several times.

7 Put 2 pieces of mochi into small soup or Japanese wooden bowls and pour the soup around them. Serve hot, and eat with a ceramic or wooden spoon.

COOK'S TIP
This is an easy method for busy people to cook azuki. Soak the beans overnight. Next morning, empty the beans and liquid into a pan and bring to the boil. Transfer the beans and liquid to a vacuum flask. Seal and leave until the evening, ready for adding the sugar in step 4.

COOKED BLACK-EYED BEANS

TRADITIONALLY, THIS DISH WAS SERVED IN THE COLDEST TIME OF THE YEAR USING ONLY PRESERVED FOOD SUCH AS SALTED SALMON AND DRIED VEGETABLES. HERE, FRESH SALMON AND VEGETABLES ARE USED INSTEAD. IT KEEPS FOR 4–5 DAYS IN A COOL PLACE.

SERVES FOUR

INGREDIENTS

150g/5oz salmon fillet, boned
  and skinned
400g/14oz can black-eyed beans
  (peas) in brine
50g/2oz fresh shiitake mushrooms,
  stalks removed
50g/2oz carrot, peeled
50g/2oz daikon, peeled
5g/⅛oz dashi-konbu about 10cm/
  4in square
60ml/4 tbsp water
5ml/1 tsp caster (superfine) sugar
15ml/1 tbsp shoyu
7.5ml/1½ tsp mirin
salt
2.5cm/1in fresh root ginger, peeled
  and thinly sliced or grated,
  to garnish

1 Slice the salmon into 1cm/½in thick pieces. Thoroughly salt the fillet and leave for 1 hour, then wash away the salt and cut it into 1cm/½in cubes. Par-boil in rapidly boiling water in a small pan for 30 seconds, then drain. Gently wash under running water.

2 Slice the fresh ginger thinly lengthways, then stack the slices and cut into thin threads. Soak in cold water for 30 minutes, then drain well.

3 Drain the can of beans and tip the liquid into a medium pan. Set the beans and liquid aside.

4 Chop all the vegetables into 1cm/½in cubes. Wipe the dried konbu with a damp dishtowel or kitchen paper, then snip with scissors.

5 Add the salmon, vegetables and konbu to the bean liquid with the beans, water, sugar and 1.5ml/¼ tsp salt. Bring to the boil. Reduce the heat to low and cook for 6 minutes or until the carrot is cooked. Add the shoyu and cook for 4 minutes. Add the mirin, then remove the pan from the heat, mix well and check the seasoning. Leave for an hour. Serve garnished with the ginger.

PAN-FRIED TOFU <u>WITH</u> CARAMELIZED SAUCE

TOFU IN THE WEST IS OFTEN USED AS A MEAT SUBSTITUTE FOR VEGETARIANS, AS IT WAS BY CHINESE BUDDHIST MONKS WHO FIRST BROUGHT VEGETARIAN COOKING INTO JAPAN. THEY INVENTED MANY DELICIOUS AND FILLING PROTEIN DISHES FROM TOFU AND OTHER SOYA BEAN PRODUCTS. THIS DISH IS A MODERN ADDITION TO THAT TRADITION.

SERVES FOUR

INGREDIENTS
    2 × 285g/10¼oz packets tofu blocks
    4 garlic cloves
    10ml/2 tsp vegetable oil
    50g/2oz/¼ cup butter, cut into
      5 equal pieces
    watercress, to garnish
For the marinade
    4 spring onions (scallions)
    60ml/4 tbsp sake
    60ml/4 tbsp shoyu (tamari or sashimi
      soy sauce, if available)
    60ml/4 tbsp mirin

1 Unpack the tofu blocks and discard the liquid, then wrap in three layers of kitchen paper. Put a large plate or wooden chopping board on top as a weight and leave for 30 minutes to allow time for the excess liquid to be absorbed by the paper. This process makes the tofu firmer and, when cooked, it will crisp on the outside.

2 To make the marinade, chop the spring onions finely. Mix with the other marinade ingredients in a ceramic or aluminium tray with sides or a wide, shallow bowl. Leave for 15 minutes.

3 Slice the garlic very thinly to make garlic chips. Heat the vegetable oil in a frying pan and fry the garlic for a few moments until golden. Turn the chips frequently to prevent sticking and burning. Scoop them out on to kitchen paper. Reserve the oil in the pan.

4 Unwrap the tofu. Slice one block horizontally in half, then cut each half into four pieces. Repeat with the other tofu block. Soak in the marinade for about 15 minutes.

5 Take out the tofu and wipe off the excess marinade with kitchen paper. Reserve the marinade.

6 Reheat the oil in the frying pan and add one piece of butter. When the oil starts sizzling, reduce the heat to medium and add the pieces of tofu one by one. Cook in one layer, if possible.

7 Cover the pan and cook until the edge of the tofu is browned and quite firm, approximately 5–8 minutes on each side. (If the edges burn but the centre is pale, reduce the heat.)

8 Pour the marinade into the pan. Cook for 2 minutes, or until the spring onion is very soft. Remove the tofu and arrange four pieces on each serving plate. Pour the thickened marinade and spring onion mixture over the tofu and top with a piece of butter. Sprinkle with the garlic chips and garnish with watercress. Serve hot.

DEEP-FRIED TOFU BALLS

THERE ARE MANY VARIATIONS OF THESE DELICIOUS DEEP-FRIED TOFU BALLS CALLED HIRYOZU,
MEANING FLYING DRAGON'S HEAD. THIS IS ONE OF THE EASIEST TO MAKE.

MAKES SIXTEEN

INGREDIENTS
    2 × 285g/10¼oz packets tofu blocks
    20g/¾oz carrot, peeled
    40g/1½oz/1¼ cups green beans
    2 large (US extra large) eggs, beaten
    30ml/2 tbsp sake
    10ml/2 tsp mirin
    5ml/1 tsp salt
    10ml/2 tsp shoyu
    pinch of caster (superfine) sugar
    vegetable oil, for deep-frying
For the lime sauce
    45ml/3 tbsp shoyu
    juice of ½ lime
    5ml/1 tsp rice vinegar
For the garnish
    300g/11oz daikon, peeled
    2 dried red chillies, halved
      and seeded
    4 chives, finely snipped

1 Drain the tofu and wrap in a clean
dishtowel or some kitchen paper. Set
a chopping board, or large plate with a
weight, on top and leave for 2 hours, or
until the tofu loses most of its liquid and
its weight is halved.

2 Cut the daikon for the garnish into
about 4cm/1½in thick slices. Make
3–4 holes in each slice with a skewer
or chopstick and insert chilli pieces into
the holes. Leave for 15 minutes, then
grate the daikon and chilli finely.

3 To make the tofu balls, chop the
carrot finely. Trim and cut the beans
into 5mm/¼in lengths. Cook both
vegetables for 1 minute in boiling water.

4 In a food processor, mix the tofu,
eggs, sake, mirin, salt, shoyu and sugar
until smooth. Transfer to a bowl and mix
in the carrot and beans.

5 Fill a wok or pan with oil 4cm/1½in
deep, and heat to 185°C/365°F.

6 Soak a piece of kitchen paper with a
little vegetable oil, and wet your hands
with it. Scoop 40ml/2½ tbsp tofu mixture
in one hand and shape into a ball by
tossing the ball between your hands.

7 Carefully slide into the oil and deep-
fry until crisp and golden brown. Drain
on kitchen paper. Repeat with the
remaining mixture.

8 Arrange the tofu balls on a serving
plate and sprinkle with chives. Put
30ml/2 tbsp grated daikon in each of
four small bowls. Mix the lime sauce
ingredients in a serving bowl. Serve the
balls with the lime sauce to be mixed
with grated daikon by each guest.

DEEP-FRIED TOFU IN DASHI SOUP

A CREAMY TOFU BLOCK IS DEEP-FRIED IN A CRISP THIN BATTER, THEN SOAKED IN HOT BROTH. THIS TASTY AND FILLING DISH IS TYPICAL IN A SHOJIN RYORI (ZEN VEGETARIAN) MENU.

SERVES FOUR

INGREDIENTS
   2 × 295g/10¾oz packets long-life
      soft or silken tofu
   vegetable oil, for deep-frying
   30ml/2 tbsp plain (all-purpose) flour
For the sauce
   50ml/2fl oz/¼ cup shoyu
   50ml/2fl oz/¼ cup mirin
   pinch of salt
   300ml/½ pint/1¼ cups second dashi
      stock, or the same amount of water
      and 7.5ml/1½ tsp dashi-no-moto
For the garnish
   2.5cm/1in fresh root ginger, peeled
      and finely grated
   60ml/4 tbsp finely chopped chives

1 Drain the water from the tofu. Carefully open the packet and then wrap the tofu in 2–3 layers of kitchen paper. Set a chopping board, or large plate with a weight, on top to press the tofu, and leave for at least 30 minutes for the excess liquid to be absorbed by the kitchen paper.

2 To make the sauce, place the shoyu, mirin, salt and dashi stock in a small pan over a medium heat. Mix well, cook for 5 minutes, then set aside.

3 Squeeze the grated ginger and make into four small balls. Set aside.

4 Unwrap the tofu and pat dry with another sheet of kitchen paper. Slice one tofu block into four squares each about 2.5 × 6cm/1 × 2½in. Repeat with the other tofu block.

5 Heat the oil to about 190°C/375°F. Dust the tofu with the flour and slide into the oil. Deep-fry until golden brown. Drain well on kitchen paper.

6 Arrange two tofu pieces in each of four small bowls. Reheat the sauce and gently pour from the side of the bowl. Try not to splash over the tofu. Put a ginger ball on the tofu and sprinkle with chives. Serve hot.

STUFFED AND GRILLED THIN TOFU

AGE OR ABURA-AGE, FRIED THIN TOFU, CAN BE USED AS A BAG LIKE A MIDDLE EASTERN PITTA BREAD. HERE, A GENEROUS AMOUNT OF CHOPPED SPRING ONION AND OTHER AROMATIC INGREDIENTS FILL THE BAG. IN JAPAN, SPRING ONIONS ARE THOUGHT TO PREVENT COLDS IN THE WINTER, AND THIS DISH IS MADE DOUBLY EFFECTIVE BY ALSO INCLUDING GRATED GARLIC.

SERVES FOUR

INGREDIENTS
   1 packet abura-age (2 abura-age
      per packet)
For the filling
   4 spring onions (scallions), trimmed
      and very finely chopped
   about 15ml/1 tbsp shoyu
   1 garlic clove, grated
      or crushed
   30ml/2 tbsp lightly toasted
      sesame seeds

COOK'S TIP
If opening the abura-age is not easy, use a round-bladed knife and insert the blade gradually to open the bag out.

1 Put the abura-age in a sieve and pour hot water from a kettle over to wash off excess oil. Drain and gently dry on kitchen paper.

2 Put one abura-age on a chopping board and roll over several times with a rolling pin. Cut in half and carefully open at the cut part to make two bags. Repeat with the remaining piece.

3 Mix the spring onions, shoyu, garlic and sesame seeds in a small bowl. Check the seasoning and add more shoyu, if required.

4 Fill the four bags with the filling. Grill (broil) under a preheated grill (broiler) at high for 3–4 minutes on each side, or until crisp and lightly browned.

5 With a sharp knife, cut each abura-age bag into four triangles and arrange them on four small plates. Serve hot.

GRILLED VEGETABLE STICKS

FOR THIS TASTY KEBAB-STYLE DISH, MADE WITH TOFU, KONNYAKU AND AUBERGINE, YOU WILL NEED 40 BAMBOO SKEWERS, SOAKED IN WATER OVERNIGHT TO PREVENT THEM BURNING WHEN GRILLED.

SERVES FOUR

INGREDIENTS
1 × 285g/10¼oz packet tofu block
1 × 250g/9oz packet konnyaku
2 small aubergines (eggplant)
25ml/1½ tbsp toasted sesame oil
For the yellow and green sauces
45ml/3 tbsp shiro miso
15ml/1 tbsp caster (superfine) sugar
5 young spinach leaves
2.5ml/½ tsp sansho
salt
For the red sauce
15ml/1 tbsp aka miso
5ml/1 tsp caster (superfine) sugar
5ml/1 tsp mirin
To garnish
pinch of white poppy seeds
15ml/1 tbsp toasted sesame seeds

1 Drain the liquid from the tofu packet and wrap the tofu in three layers of kitchen paper. Set a chopping board on top to press out the remaining liquid. Leave for 30 minutes until the excess liquid has been absorbed by the kitchen paper. Cut into eight 7.5 × 2 × 1cm/ 3 × ¾ × ½in slices.

2 Drain the liquid from the konnyaku. Cut it in half and put in a small pan with enough water to cover. Bring to the boil and cook for about 5 minutes. Drain and cut it into eight 6 × 2 × 1cm/ 2½ × ¾ × ½in slices.

3 Cut the aubergines into two length-ways, then halve the thickness to make four flat slices. Soak in cold water for 15 minutes. Drain and pat dry.

4 To make the yellow sauce, mix the shiro miso and sugar in a pan, then cook over a low heat, stirring to dissolve the sugar. Remove from the heat. Place half the sauce in a small bowl.

5 Blanch the spinach leaves in rapidly boiling water with a pinch of salt for 30 seconds and drain, then cool under running water. Squeeze out the water and chop finely.

6 Transfer to a mortar and pound to a paste using a pestle. Mix the paste and sansho pepper into the bowl of yellow sauce to make the green sauce.

7 Put all the red sauce ingredients in a small pan and cook over a low heat, stirring constantly, until the sugar has dissolved. Remove from the heat.

8 Pierce the slices of tofu, konnyaku and aubergine with two bamboo skewers each. Heat the grill (broiler) to high. Brush the aubergine slices with sesame oil and grill (broil) for 7–8 minutes each side. Turn several times.

9 Grill the konnyaku and tofu slices for 3–5 minutes each side, or until lightly browned. Remove them from the heat but keep the grill hot.

10 Spread the red miso sauce on the aubergine slices. Spread one side of the tofu slices with green sauce and one side of the konnyaku with the yellow miso sauce from the pan. Grill the slices for 1–2 minutes. Sprinkle the aubergines with poppy seeds. Sprinkle the konnyaku with sesame seeds and serve all together.

SIMMERED TOFU WITH VEGETABLES

A TYPICAL JAPANESE DINNER AT HOME CONSISTS OF A SOUP, THREE DIFFERENT DISHES AND A BOWL OF RICE. ONE OF THE THREE DISHES IS ALWAYS A SIMMERED ONE LIKE THIS.

SERVES FOUR

INGREDIENTS
  4 dried shiitake mushrooms
  450g/1lb daikon
  2 atsu-age, about 200g/7oz each
  115g/4oz/¾ cup green beans,
    trimmed and cut in half
  5ml/1 tsp rice (any except for
    fragrant Thai or white basmati)
  115g/4oz carrot, peeled and cut into
    1cm/½in thick slices
  300g/11oz baby potatoes, unpeeled
  750ml/1¼ pints/3 cups second dashi
    stock, or the same amount of water
    and 7.5ml/1½ tsp dashi-no-moto
  30ml/2 tbsp caster (superfine) sugar
  75ml/5 tbsp shoyu
  45ml/3 tbsp sake
  15ml/1 tbsp mirin

1 Soak the dried shiitake in 250ml/ 8fl oz/1 cup water for 2 hours. Drain and discard the liquid. Remove and discard the stalks.

2 Peel the daikon and slice into 1cm/½in discs. Shave the edge of the daikon discs to ensure they are evenly cooked. Plunge into cold water.

3 Put the atsu-age in a sieve, and wash off the excess oil with hot water from the kettle. Drain and cut into pieces of about 2.5 × 5cm/1 × 2in.

4 Boil the green beans for 2 minutes and then drain them, cooling them under running water.

5 Cover the daikon with water in a pan and add the rice. Bring to the boil then reduce the heat to medium-low. Cook for 15 minutes, then drain. Discard the rice.

6 Put the atsu-age and the mushrooms, carrot and potatoes into the pan with the daikon. Add the dashi stock, bring to the boil, then reduce the heat to low. Regularly skim off any scum that comes to the surface. Add the sugar, shoyu and sake, gently shaking the pan to mix the ingredients thoroughly.

7 Cut greaseproof (wax) paper into a circle 1cm/½in smaller than the pan lid. Place the paper inside the pan to seal the ingredients. Cover with the lid and simmer for 30 minutes, or until the sauce has reduced by at least a half. Add the green beans for 2 minutes so that they just warm through.

8 Remove the paper and add the mirin. Taste the sauce and adjust with shoyu if required. Remove from the heat.

9 Arrange the ingredients attractively in groups on a large serving plate. Pour over a little sauce, and serve warm or cold.

ROLLED OMELETTE

EASIER TO MAKE THAN IT LOOKS, ALL THAT IS NEEDED TO MAKE THIS LIGHT AND SWEET OMELETTE IS A SUSHI ROLLING MAT, WRAPPED IN CLEAR FILM. USE A ROUND OR RECTANGULAR FRYING PAN.

4 Keeping the rolled omelette in the pan, push back to the farthest side from you. Oil the empty part of the pan again. Pour one-third of the egg mixture in at the empty side. Lift up the first roll with chopsticks, and let the egg mixture run underneath. When it looks half set, roll the omelette around the first roll to make a single roll with many layers.

5 Move the roll gently on to a sushi rolling mat covered with clear film (plastic wrap). Roll the omelette firmly into the roller mat. Leave to stand rolled up for 5 minutes. Repeat the whole process again to make another roll.

6 Grate the daikon with a daikon grater or a very fine grater. Alternatively, use a food processor. Squeeze out the juice with your hand.

7 Cut the rolled omelettes into 2.5cm/ 1in slices crossways.

SERVES FOUR

INGREDIENTS
    45ml/3 tbsp second dashi stock, or
    the same amount of water and a
    pinch of dashi-no-moto
    30ml/2 tbsp mirin
    15ml/1 tbsp caster (superfine) sugar
    5ml/1 tsp shoyu
    5ml/1 tsp salt
    6 large (US extra large) eggs, beaten
    vegetable oil
For the garnish
    2.5cm/1in daikon
    4 shiso leaves (optional)
    shoyu

2 Heat a omelette pan or a rectangular Japanese pan over a medium heat. Soak kitchen paper in a little oil and wipe the pan to grease it.

3 Pour in a quarter of the egg mixture. Tilt the pan to coat it evenly. When the omelette starts to set, roll it up towards you with chopsticks or a spatula.

1 Warm the dashi stock in a small pan. Mix in the mirin, sugar, shoyu and salt. Add to the beaten eggs and stir well.

8 Lay the shiso leaves, if using, on four small plates and place a few slices of the omelette on top. Put a small heap of grated daikon to one side and add a few drops of shoyu to the top.

SAVOURY EGG SOUP

THIS DELICIOUS CUSTARD-LIKE SOUP IS SOFTER AND RUNNIER THAN A WESTERN CUSTARD PUDDING.
IT CONTAINS TASTY SURPRISES, SUCH AS PINK PRAWNS AND JADE-GREEN GINGKO NUTS.

SERVES FOUR

INGREDIENTS
8 gingko nuts in shells (or canned)
4 medium raw tiger prawns (jumbo
  shrimp), peeled, heads and
  tails removed
5cm/2in carrot, thinly sliced
4 mitsuba sprigs or 8 chives
75g/3oz chicken breast portion, skinned
5ml/1 tsp sake
5ml/1 tsp shoyu
2 fresh shiitake mushrooms, thinly
  sliced, stalks discarded
salt
For the custard
3 large (US extra large) eggs, beaten
500ml/17fl oz/2⅓ cups first dashi
  stock, or the same amount of water
  and 2.5ml/½ tsp dashi-no-moto
15ml/1 tbsp sake
15ml/1 tbsp shoyu
2.5ml/½ tsp salt

1 Carefully crack the gingko nut shells with a nutcracker and boil the nuts for 5 minutes. Drain. Remove any skin.

2 Insert a cocktail stick (toothpick) into the back of each prawn and remove the vein. Blanch the prawns in hot water until they curl up. Drain and pat dry.

3 Cut the carrot slices into maple-leaf shapes with a sharp knife or a vegetable cutter. Blanch in salted water. Drain.

4 Cut off the mitsuba roots. Cut the stems 2.5cm/1in from the top and keep the leaves. Chop the stems in half and pour hot water over to wilt them. If using chives, chop into 7.5cm/3in lengths and wilt as the mitsuba stems. Put two mitsuba stems or two chives together and tie a knot in the middle.

5 Dice the chicken, then marinate in the sake and shoyu for 15 minutes.

6 To make the custard, put all the ingredients together in a bowl. Mix with chopsticks, and strain into a bowl.

7 Bring a steamer to the boil, then set the heat to very low.

8 Divide the chicken, shiitake, gingko nuts, prawns and carrots among four ramekins. Divide the egg mixture among the ramekins.

9 Put the mitsuba stems or chives on top, and the leaves if you like, and then cover each ramekin with a piece of foil. Carefully place them in the steamer. Steam on low for 15 minutes. Insert a cocktail stick into the egg: if the liquid stays clear, it's set. Serve hot.

VARIATIONS
• For a fish and shellfish variation, use scallops, crab meat, filleted lemon sole and asparagus tips.
• For a vegetarian version, try par-boiled turnips, oyster mushrooms, wakame seaweed and thinly sliced strips of spring onions (scallions).

FISH AND SHELLFISH

There are numerous delicious and healthy fish dishes in the

Japanese culinary tradition, including many using fish that is

so fresh it does not require cooking. Others employ a wide

variety of cooking methods, ranging from "cooking" the fresh

fish in vinegar, to flavouring it with seaweed, or lightly

deep-frying in tempura.

SASHIMI MORIAWASE

THE ARRANGEMENT OF A DISH OF SASHIMI IS AS IMPORTANT AS THE FRESHNESS OF THE FISH. CHOOSE TWO TO FIVE KINDS OF FISH FROM EACH GROUP AND ONLY USE THE FRESHEST CATCH OF THE DAY.

SERVES FOUR

INGREDIENTS

500g/1¼lb total of fish from the
   4 groups
Group A, skinned fillets (cut lengthways
if possible)
   Maguro akami: lean tuna
   Maguro toro: fatty tuna
   Sake: salmon
   Kajiki: swordfish
   Tai: sea bream or red snapper
   Suzuki: sea bass
   Hamachi: yellowtail
   Katsuo: skipjack tuna
Group B, skinned fillets
   Hirame: flounder or sole
   Karei: halibut or turbot
Group C
   Ika: squid body, cleaned, boned
      and skinned
   Tako: cooked octopus tentacles
   Hotate-gai: scallop (the coral, black
      stomach and frill removed)
Group D
   Aka-ebi: sweet prawns (shrimp),
      peeled, heads can be removed,
      tails intact
   Uni: sea urchin
   Ikura: salted salmon roe
To serve
   1 fresh daikon, peeled and cut into
      6cm/2½in lengths
   1 Japanese or salad cucumber
   4 shiso leaves
   2 limes, halved (optional)
   45ml/3 tbsp wasabi paste from a
      tube, or the same amount of wasabi
      powder mixed with 20ml/4 tsp water
   1 bottle tamari shoyu

1 Make the *tsuma* (the daikon strands). Slice the daikon pieces very thinly lengthways, then cut the slices into very thin strips lengthways. Rinse thoroughly under running water, drain and put in the refrigerator.

2 Prepare the cucumber. Trim and cut into 3cm/1¼in lengths, then cut each cucumber cylinder in half lengthways.

3 Place the cucumber on a chopping board, flat-side down. Make very fine cuts across each piece, leaving the slices joined together at one side. Then, gently squeeze the cucumber together between your fingers so that the slices fan out sideways. Set them aside and cover with clear film (plastic wrap).

4 Slice the fish. Group A needs *hira giri,* a thick cut: trim the fillet into a long rectangular shape. Skin-side up, cut into 1cm/½in thick slices with the grain.

5 Group B needs *usu zukuri,* very thin slices. Place the fillet horizontally to you on its skinned side. Hold the knife almost horizontally to the fillet, shave it very thinly across the grain.

6 Group C fish each require different cutting styles. Slice the cooked octopus diagonally into 5mm/¼in thick ovals. Slice the scallops in half horizontally. If they are thicker than 4cm/1½in, slice into three.

7 Cut open the squid body and turn to lie on its skinned side, horizontally to you. Score lines 5mm/¼in apart over the surface, then cut into 5mm/¼in strips. Group D is all ready to arrange.

8 Arrange the *sashimi* creatively. First, take a handful of daikon and heap up on to the serving plate a large mound or several small mounds. Then, base your design on the following basic rules:
Group A and C Put each slice of fish side by side like domino pieces. You can lay them on a shiso leaf.
Group B Use the thin, soft slices to make a rose shape, or overlap the slices slightly, so that the texture of the plate can be seen through them.
Group D Place the prawns by their tails, 2–3 at a time, in a bundle. If the sea urchins come tightly packed in a little box, try to get them out in one piece. The salmon roe can be heaped on thin cucumber slices or scooped into a lime case, made from a half lime, flesh removed. Fill the case with some daikon and place the roe on top.

9 Arrange the cucumber fans, heaped wasabi paste and shiso leaves to perfect your design. Serve immediately. Pour some shoyu into four dishes and mix in the wasabi. As the sauce is quite salty, only dip the edge of the *sashimi* into it.

SEARED SWORDFISH WITH CITRUS DRESSING

KAJIKI NO TATAKI SALAD IS A GOOD EXAMPLE OF HOW THE JAPANESE TRY OUT NEW DISHES FROM ALL OVER THE WORLD AND SOON START TO ARRANGE THEM IN A JAPANESE WAY. FRESH FISH IS SLICED THINLY AND SEARED OR MARINATED, THEN SERVED WITH SALAD LEAVES AND VEGETABLES.

SERVES FOUR

INGREDIENTS
    75g/3oz daikon, peeled
    50g/2oz carrot, peeled
    1 Japanese or salad cucumber
    10ml/2 tsp vegetable oil
    300g/11oz skinned fresh swordfish
        steak, cut against the grain
    2 cartons mustard and cress
    15ml/1 tbsp toasted
        sesame seeds
For the dressing
    105ml/7 tbsp shoyu
    105ml/7 tbsp second dashi stock,
        or the same amount of water and
        5ml/1 tsp dashi-no-moto
    30ml/2 tbsp toasted sesame oil
    juice of ½ lime
    rind of ½ lime, shredded into
        thin strips

1 Make the vegetable garnishes first. Use a very sharp knife, mandolin or vegetable slicer with a julienne blade to make very thin (about 4cm/1½in long) strands of daikon, carrot and cucumber. Soak the daikon and carrot in ice-cold water for 5 minutes, then drain well and keep in the refrigerator.

2 Mix together all the ingredients for the dressing and stir well, then chill.

3 Heat the oil in a small frying pan until smoking hot. Sear the fish for 30 seconds on all sides. Plunge it into cold water in a bowl to stop the cooking. Dry on kitchen paper and wipe off as much oil as possible.

4 Cut the swordfish steak in half lengthways before slicing it into 5mm/¼in thick pieces in the other direction, against the grain.

5 Arrange the fish slices into a ring on individual plates. Mix the vegetable strands, mustard and cress and sesame seeds. Fluff up with your hands, then shape them into a sphere. Gently place it in the centre of the plate, on the swordfish. Pour the dressing around the plate's edge and serve immediately.

COOK'S TIP
This dish is traditionally made with fillet cut with the grain. To prepare, cut it in half lengthways, then slice against the grain by holding a knife horizontally to the chopping board.

MARINATED SALMON <u>WITH</u> AVOCADO

USE ONLY THE FRESHEST OF SALMON FOR THIS DELICIOUS SALAD. THE MARINADE OF LEMON AND DASHI-KONBU "COOKS" THE SALMON, WHICH IS THEN SERVED WITH AVOCADO, TOASTED ALMONDS AND SALAD LEAVES AND ACCOMPANIED BY A MISO MAYONNAISE.

<u>SERVES FOUR</u>

INGREDIENTS

250g/9oz very fresh salmon tail, skinned and filleted
juice of 1 lemon
10cm/4in dashi-konbu, wiped with a damp cloth and cut into 4 strips
1 ripe avocado
4 shiso leaves, stalks removed and cut in half lengthways
about 115g/4oz mixed leaves such as lamb's lettuce, frisée or rocket (arugula)
45ml/3 tbsp flaked (sliced) almonds, toasted in a dry frying pan until just slightly browned

For the miso mayonnaise
90ml/6 tbsp good-quality mayonnaise
15ml/1 tbsp shiro miso
ground black pepper

1 Cut the first salmon fillet in half crossways at the tail end where the fillet is not wider than 4cm/1½in. Next, cut the wider part in half lengthways. This means the fillet from one side is cut into three. Cut the other fillet into three pieces, in the same way.

2 Pour the lemon juice and two of the dashi-konbu pieces into a wide shallow plastic container. Lay the salmon fillets in the base and sprinkle with the rest of the dashi-konbu. Marinate for about 15 minutes, then turn once and leave for a further 15 minutes. The salmon should change to a pink "cooked" colour. Remove the salmon from the marinade and wipe with kitchen paper.

3 Holding a very sharp knife at an angle, cut the salmon into 5mm/¼in thick slices against the grain.

4 Halve the avocado and sprinkle with a little of the remaining salmon marinade. Remove the avocado stone (pit) and skin, then carefully slice to the same thickness as the salmon.

5 Mix the miso mayonnaise ingredients in a small bowl. Spread about 5ml/1 tsp on to the back of each of the shiso leaves, then mix the remainder with 15ml/1 tbsp of the remaining marinade to loosen the mayonnaise.

6 Arrange the salad on four plates. Top with the avocado, salmon, shiso leaves and almonds, and drizzle over the remaining miso mayonnaise.

7 Alternatively, you can build a tower of avocado and salmon slices. For each serving, take an eighth of the avocado slices and place them in the centre of a plate, slightly overlapping. Add a shiso leaf, miso-side down. Then place the same number of salmon slices on top, again slightly overlapping. Repeat the process. Arrange the salad leaves and almonds, and spoon over the miso mayonnaise. Serve immediately.

SEAFOOD SALAD WITH FRUITY DRESSING

WHITE FISH IS BRIEFLY SEARED, THEN SERVED WITH PRAWNS AND SALAD TOSSED IN AN OIL-FREE
APRICOT AND APPLE DRESSING. THE FRUIT FLAVOURS MAKE A DELICATE ACCOMPANIMENT TO THE FISH.

SERVES FOUR

INGREDIENTS
  1 baby onion, sliced lengthways
  lemon juice
  400g/14oz very fresh sea bream or
    sea bass, filleted
  30ml/2 tbsp sake
  4 large king prawns (jumbo shrimp),
    heads and shells removed
  about 400g/14oz mixed salad leaves
For the fruity dressing
  2 ripe apricots, skinned and
    stoned (pitted)
  ¼ apple, peeled and cored
  60ml/4 tbsp second dashi stock or
    the same amount of water and
    5ml/1 tsp dashi-no-moto
  10ml/2 tsp shoyu
  salt and ground white pepper

1 Soak the onion slices in ice-cold water for 30 minutes. Drain well.

2 Bring a pan half-full of water to the boil. Add a dash of lemon juice and plunge the fish fillet into it. Remove after 30 seconds, and cool immediately under cold running water for 30 seconds to stop the cooking. Cut into 8mm/⅓in thick slices crossways.

3 Pour the sake into a small pan, bring to the boil, then add the prawns. Cook for 1 minute, or until their colour has completely changed to pink.

4 Cool immediately under cold running water for 30 seconds to again stop the cooking. Cut the prawns into 1cm/½in thick slices crossways.

5 Slice one apricot very thinly, then set aside. Purée the remaining dressing ingredients in a food processor. Add salt, if required, and pepper. Chill.

6 Lay a small amount of mixed leaves on four plates. Mix the fish, prawn, apricot and onion slices in a bowl. Add the remaining leaves, then pour on the dressing and toss well. Heap up on the plates and serve immediately.

COOK'S TIP
You can use a knife and fork to eat these salads, of course; however, marinated fish definitely tastes better with wooden rather than metal cutlery.

TURBOT SASHIMI SALAD WITH WASABI

EATING SASHIMI, OR RAW FISH, WITH TRADITIONAL SAUCES DISAPPEARED WHEN SHOYU BECAME
POPULAR IN THE 17TH CENTURY. THE USE OF SAUCES RETURNED WITH THE WESTERN-INSPIRED SALAD.

SERVES FOUR

INGREDIENTS
  ice cubes
  400g/14oz very fresh thick turbot,
    skinned and filleted
  300g/11oz mixed salad leaves
  8 radishes, thinly sliced
For the wasabi dressing
  25g/1oz rocket (arugula) leaves
  50g/2oz cucumber, chopped
  90ml/6 tbsp rice vinegar (use brown
    if available)
  75ml/5 tbsp olive oil
  5ml/1 tsp salt
  15ml/1 tbsp wasabi paste from a
    tube, or the same amount of
    wasabi powder mixed with 7.5ml/
    1½ tsp water

1 First make the dressing. Roughly tear the rocket leaves and process with the cucumber and rice vinegar in a food processor or blender. Pour into a small bowl and add the rest of the dressing ingredients, except for the wasabi. Check the seasoning and add more salt, if required. Chill until needed.

2 Chill the serving plates while you prepare the fish, if you like.

3 Prepare a bowl of cold water with a few ice cubes. Cut the turbot fillet in half lengthways, then cut into 5mm/¼in thick slices crossways. Plunge these into the ice-cold water as you slice. After 2 minutes or so, they will start to curl and become firm. Take out and drain on kitchen paper.

4 In a large bowl, mix the fish, salad leaves and radishes. Mix the wasabi into the dressing and toss well with the salad. Serve immediately.

LEMON SOLE <u>AND</u> FRESH OYSTER SALAD

OYSTERS, FLAVOURED WITH A RICE-VINEGAR DRESSING, TASTE WONDERFUL WITH LEMON SOLE SASHIMI. IN JAPAN, MENUS ARE BASED ON WHAT FISH WAS FRESHLY CAUGHT THAT DAY, NOT THE OTHER WAY AROUND. THIS DISH IS CALLED HIRAME KONBU JIME TO NAMA-GAKI NO SALADA.

SERVES FOUR

INGREDIENTS

1 very fresh lemon sole, skinned and
   filleted into 4 pieces
105ml/7 tbsp rice vinegar
dashi-konbu, in 4 pieces, big enough
   to cover the fillets
50g/2oz Japanese cucumber, ends
   trimmed, or ordinary salad
   cucumber with seeds removed
50g/2oz celery sticks, strings removed
450g/1lb large broad (fava)
   beans, podded
1 lime, ½ thinly sliced
60ml/4 tbsp walnut oil
seeds from ½ pomegranate
salt
For the oysters
15ml/1 tbsp rice vinegar
30ml/2 tbsp shoyu
15ml/1 tbsp sake
12 large fresh oysters, opened
25g/1oz daikon or radishes, peeled
   and very finely grated
8 chives

1 Sprinkle salt on the sole fillets. Cover and cool in the refrigerator for an hour.

2 Mix the rice vinegar and a similar amount of water in a bowl. Wash the fish fillets in the mixture, then drain well. Cut each fillet in half lengthways.

3 Lay 1 piece of dashi-konbu on a work surface. Place a pair of sole fillets, skinned-sides together, on to it, then lay another piece of konbu on top. Cover all the fillets like this and chill for 3 hours.

4 Halve the cucumber crossways and slice thinly lengthways. Then slice again diagonally into 2cm/¾in wide pieces. Do the same for the celery. Sprinkle the cucumber with salt and leave to soften for 30–60 minutes. Gently squeeze to remove the moisture. Rinse if it tastes too salty, but drain well.

5 Boil the broad beans in lightly salted water for 15 minutes, or until soft. Drain and cool under running water, then peel off the skins. Sprinkle with salt.

6 Mix the rice vinegar, shoyu and sake for the oysters in a small bowl.

7 Slice the sole very thinly with a sharp knife. Remove the slightly chewy dashi-konbu first, if you prefer.

8 Place some pieces of cucumber and celery in a small mound in the centre of four serving plates, then lay lime slices on top. Garnish with some chopped chives. Place the oysters to one side of the cucumber, topped with a few broad beans, then season with 5ml/1 tsp of the vinegar mix and 10ml/2 tsp grated daikon or radishes. Arrange the sole *sashimi* on the other side and drizzle walnut oil and a little lime juice on top. Add pomegranate seeds and serve.

SCALLOPS SASHIMI IN MUSTARD SAUCE

THE JAPANESE NAME, HOTATE KOBACHI, MEANS "SCALLOP IN A LITTLE DEEP BOWL". THIS IS A TYPICAL SERVING SIZE FOR LOTS OF JAPANESE DISHES AS A MEAL USUALLY CONSISTS OF AT LEAST THREE DISHES OR MORE. IN TRADITIONAL FORMAL DINING, KAISEKI, MORE THAN A DOZEN SMALL DISHES ARE SERVED ONE AFTER ANOTHER AND THIS ELEGANT DISH CAN BE ONE OF THEM.

2 Put the dried chrysanthemum or the flower petals in a sieve. Pour hot water from a kettle all over, and leave to drain for a while. When cool, gently squeeze the excess water out. Set aside and repeat with the watercress.

3 Mix together all the ingredients for the dressing in a bowl. Add the scallops 5 minutes before serving and mix well without breaking them. Add the flower petals and watercress, then transfer to four small bowls. Serve cold. Add a little more shoyu, if required.

SERVES FOUR

INGREDIENTS
8 scallops or 16 queen scallops, cleaned and coral removed
¼ dried sheet chrysanthemum petals (sold as kiku nori) or a handful of edible flower petals such as yellow nasturtium
4 bunches of watercress, leaves only
For the dressing
30ml/2 tbsp shoyu
5ml/1 tsp sake
10ml/2 tsp English (hot) mustard

1 Slice the scallops in three horizontally then cut in half crossways. If you use queen scallops, slice in two horizontally.

COOK'S TIPS
• Any white fish *sashimi* can be used in this dish.
• Substitute the watercress with the finely chopped green part of spring onions (scallions).
• Do not attempt to pick chrysanthemums from your garden, as the edible species are different to ornamental ones. Fresh edible chrysanthemums and other edible flowers are now increasingly available at specialist Japanese stores, or look for dried ones in Asian stores.

CUBED AND MARINATED RAW TUNA

THIS DISH IS CALLED MAGURO BUTSU. WHEN PREPARING BIG FISH LIKE TUNA OR SWORDFISH FOR SASHIMI, JAPANESE FISHMONGERS CUT THEM LENGTHWAYS TO MAKE A LONG RECTANGULAR SHAPE. AFTER THE PRIME PARTS ARE CUT OUT, THE TRIMMINGS ARE SOLD CHEAPLY. BUTSU IS A CHOPPED TRIMMING, AND IT HAS ALL THE QUALITY OF THE BEST TUNA SASHIMI.

SERVES FOUR

INGREDIENTS

  400g/14oz very fresh tuna, skinned
  1 carton mustard and cress (optional)
  20ml/4 tsp wasabi paste from a tube,
    or the same amount of wasabi
    powder mixed with 10ml/2 tsp water
  60ml/4 tbsp shoyu
  8 spring onions (scallions), green
    part only, finely chopped
  4 shiso leaves, cut into thin
    slivers lengthways

1 Cut the tuna into 2cm/¾in cubes. If using mustard and cress, tie into pretty bunches or arrange as a bed in four small serving bowls or plates.

2 Just 5–10 minutes before serving, blend the wasabi paste with the shoyu in a bowl, then add the tuna and spring onions. Mix well and leave to marinate for 5 minutes. Divide among the bowls and add a few slivers of shiso leaves on top. Serve immediately.

SPICY FRIED MACKEREL

THIS DISH GOES DOWN VERY WELL WITH CHILLED JAPANESE LAGER BEER. CALLED SABA TATSUTA AGGE, IT IS ALSO EXCELLENT COLD AND IS VERY GOOD SERVED WITH SALAD.

SERVES FOUR

INGREDIENTS

    675g/1½lb mackerel, filleted
    60ml/4 tbsp shoyu
    60ml/4 tbsp sake
    60ml/4 tbsp caster (superfine) sugar
    1 garlic clove, crushed
    2cm/¾in piece fresh root ginger,
      peeled and finely grated
    2–3 shiso leaves, chopped into thin
      strips (optional)
    cornflour (cornstarch), for dusting
    vegetable oil, for deep-frying
    1 lime, cut into thick wedges

VARIATION
Shiso leaves are only sold in Japanese food stores. If you can't find them, use 5–6 chopped basil leaves instead.

1 Using a pair of tweezers, remove any remaining bones from the mackerel. Cut the fillets in half lengthways, then slice diagonally crossways into bitesize pieces.

2 Mix the shoyu, sake, sugar, garlic, grated ginger and shiso in a mixing bowl to make the marinade. Add the mackerel pieces and leave to marinate for 20 minutes.

3 Drain and pat gently with kitchen paper. Dust the fillets with cornflour.

4 Heat plenty of oil in a wok or a deep-fryer. The temperature must be kept around 180°C/350°F. Deep-fry the fillets, a few pieces at a time, until the pieces turn a shiny brown colour. Drain on kitchen paper. Serve at once with wedges of lime.

DEEP-FRIED AND MARINATED SMALL FISH

THE INFLUENCE OF EARLY EUROPEANS, OR NANBAN, WHO FIRST BROUGHT DEEP-FRYING TO JAPAN A FEW HUNDRED YEARS AGO, IS STILL EVIDENT IN THIS DISH, KNOWN AS KOZAKANA NANBAN-ZUKE.

SERVES FOUR

INGREDIENTS
    450g/1lb sprats (US small whitebait)
    plain (all-purpose) flour, for dusting
    1 small carrot
    ⅓ cucumber
    2 spring onions (scallions)
    4cm/1½in piece fresh root
      ginger, peeled
    1 dried red chilli
    75ml/5 tbsp rice vinegar
    60ml/4 tbsp shoyu
    15ml/1 tbsp mirin
    30ml/2 tbsp sake
    vegetable oil, for deep-frying

1 Wipe the sprats dry with kitchen paper, then put them in a small plastic bag with a handful of flour. Seal and shake vigorously to coat the fish.

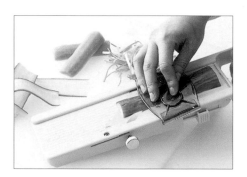

2 Cut the carrot and cucumber into thin strips by hand or using a mandolin or food processor. Cut the spring onions into three, then slice into thin, lengthways strips. Slice the ginger into thin, lengthways strips and rinse in cold water. Drain. Seed and chop the chilli into thin rings.

VARIATION
You can use small sardines, too. They have tougher bones and need to be deep-fried twice. Heat the oil and deep-fry until the outside of the fish is just crisp but still pale. Drain on kitchen paper and wait for 5 minutes. This process cooks the fish through before the coating starts to burn. Put them back into the oil again until deep golden brown.

3 In a mixing bowl, mix the rice vinegar, shoyu, mirin and sake together to make a marinade. Add the chilli and all the sliced vegetables. Stir well using a pair of chopsticks.

4 Pour plenty of oil into a deep pan and heat to 180°C/350°F. Deep-fry the fish five or six at a time until golden brown. Drain on layered kitchen paper, then plunge the hot fish into the marinade. Leave to marinate for at least an hour, stirring occasionally.

5 Serve the fish cold in a shallow bowl and put the marinated vegetables on top. This dish will keep for about a week in the refrigerator.

COOK'S TIP
The tiny sprats (US small whitebait) used here are eaten whole.

DEEP-FRIED PLAICE

IN THIS DISH, CALLED KAREI KARA-AGÉ, THE FLESH OF THE FISH AND ALSO THE SKELETON IS DEEP-FRIED TO SUCH CRISPNESS THAT YOU CAN EAT THE BONES, TAILS AND HEADS, IF YOU LIKE.

3 Pierce the daikon with a skewer or a chopstick in four places to make holes, then insert the chillies. After 15 minutes grate finely. Squeeze out the moisture by hand. Scoop a quarter of the grated daikon and chilli into an egg cup, then press with your fingers. Turn out the cup on to a plate. Make three more mounds.

4 Cut the fish fillets into four slices crossways and put into a plastic bag with the cornflour. Shake gently to coat. Heat the oil in a wok or pan to 175°C/347°F. Deep-fry the fillets, two to three at a time, until light golden brown.

5 Raise the temperature to 180°C/350°F. Dust the skeletons with cornflour and slide into the oil. Cook until golden, drain on a wire rack for 5 minutes, then fry again until very crisp. Drain again and sprinkle with some salt.

6 Mix the rice vinegar and shoyu and put in a bowl. Arrange the skeletons and fried fish on the plates. Put the daikon and chives to one side on each plate. Have small plates for the sauce. To eat, mix the condiment with the sauce and dip the fillets and bones into the sauce.

SERVES FOUR

INGREDIENTS
4 small plaice or flounder, about 500–675g/1¼–1½lb total weight, gutted, not trimmed
60ml/4 tbsp cornflour (cornstarch)
vegetable oil, for deep-frying
salt
For the condiment
130g/4½oz daikon, peeled
4 dried chillies, seeded
1 bunch of chives, finely chopped (to make 50ml/2fl oz/¼ cup)
For the sauce
20ml/4 tsp rice vinegar
20ml/4 tsp shoyu

1 Wash the fish under running water and put on a chopping board. Use a very sharp knife to make deep cuts around the gills and across the tail. Cut through the skin from the head down to the tail along the centre of the fish. Slide the knife under the cut near the head and gently cut the fillet from the bone. Fold the fillet with your hand as you cut as if peeling the fillet from the bone. Keep the knife horizontal to the fish.

2 Repeat for the other half, then turn the fish over and do the same to get four fillets from each fish. Place in a dish and sprinkle with a little salt on both sides. Keep the bony skeletons.

SIMMERED SQUID AND DAIKON

IKA TO DAIKON NI IS A CLASSIC DISH, THE SECRET OF WHICH USED TO BE HANDED DOWN FROM MOTHER TO DAUGHTER. NOWADAYS, YOU ARE MORE LIKELY TO TASTE THE REAL THING AT RESTAURANTS, BUT SOME GRANDMOTHERS STILL CELEBRATE FAMILY REUNIONS BY COOKING THIS HEARTY DISH.

SERVES FOUR

INGREDIENTS
    450g/1lb squid, cleaned, body and
      tentacles separated
    about 1kg/2¼lb daikon, peeled
    900ml/1½ pints/3¾ cups second
      dashi stock or the same amount of
      water and 5ml/1 tsp dashi-no-moto
    60ml/4 tbsp shoyu
    45ml/3 tbsp sake
    15ml/1 tbsp caster (superfine) sugar
    30ml/2 tbsp mirin
    grated rind of ½ yuzu or lime,
      to garnish

COOK'S TIP
When buying daikon look for one that is at least 7.5cm/3in in diameter, with a shiny, undamaged skin, and that sounds dense and heavy when you pat it.

1 Separate the two triangular flaps from the squid body. Cut the body into 1cm/½in thick rings. Cut the triangular flaps into 1cm/½in strips. Cut off and discard 2.5cm/1in from the thin end of the tentacles. Chop the tentacles into 4cm/1½in lengths.

2 Cut the daikon into 3cm/1¼in thick rounds and shave the edges of the sections with a sharp knife. Plunge the slices into cold water. Drain just before cooking.

3 Put the daikon and squid in a heavy pan and pour on the stock. Bring to the boil, and cook for 5 minutes, skimming constantly. Reduce the heat to low and add the shoyu, sake, sugar and mirin. Cover the surface with a circle of greaseproof (waxed) paper cut 2.5cm/1in smaller than the lid of the pan, and simmer for 45 minutes, shaking the pan occasionally. The liquid will reduce by almost a half.

4 Leave to stand for 5 minutes and serve hot in small bowls with a sprinkle of yuzu or lime rind.

SALMON TERIYAKI

SAKÉ TERIYAKI IS A WELL-KNOWN JAPANESE DISH, WHICH USES A SWEET AND SHINY SAUCE FOR MARINATING AS WELL AS FOR GLAZING THE INGREDIENTS.

SERVES FOUR

INGREDIENTS
    4 small salmon fillets with skin on,
      each weighing about 150g/5oz
    50g/2oz/¼ cup beansprouts, washed
    50g/2oz mangetouts (snow peas),
      ends trimmed
    20g/¾oz carrot, cut into thin strips
    salt
For the *teriyaki* sauce
    45ml/3 tbsp shoyu
    45ml/3 tbsp sake
    45ml/3 tbsp mirin
    15ml/1 tbsp plus 10ml/2 tsp caster
      (superfine) sugar

1 Mix all the ingredients for the *teriyaki* sauce except for the 10ml/2 tsp sugar, in a pan. Heat to dissolve the sugar. Remove and cool for an hour.

2 Place the salmon fillet in a shallow glass or china dish and pour over the *teriyaki* sauce. Leave to marinate for 30 minutes.

3 Meanwhile, boil the vegetables in lightly salted water. First add the beansprouts, then after 1 minute, the mangetouts. Leave for 1 minute again, and then add the thin carrot strips. Remove the pan from the heat after 1 minute, then drain the vegetables and keep warm.

4 Preheat the grill (broiler) to medium. Take the salmon fillet out of the sauce and pat dry with kitchen paper. Reserve the sauce. Lightly oil a grilling (broiling) tray. Grill (broil) the salmon for about 6 minutes, carefully turning once, until golden on both sides.

5 Pour the sauce into the pan. Add the remaining sugar and heat until dissolved. Remove from the heat. Brush the salmon with the sauce, then grill until the surface of the fish bubbles. Turn over and repeat on the other side.

6 Heap the vegetables on to serving plates. Place the salmon on top and spoon over the rest of the sauce.

CRAB MEAT IN VINEGAR

A refreshing summer tsumami (a dish that accompanies alcoholic drinks). For the dressing, use a Japanese or Greek cucumber, if possible — they are about one-third of the size of ordinary salad cucumbers and contain less water.

SERVES FOUR

INGREDIENTS
½ red (bell) pepper, seeded
pinch of salt
275g/10oz cooked white crab meat,
  or 2 × 165g/5½oz canned white
  crab meat, drained
about 300g/11oz Japanese or
  salad cucumber
For the vinegar mixture
15ml/1 tbsp rice vinegar
10ml/2 tsp caster (superfine) sugar
10ml/2 tsp awakuchi shoyu

1 Slice the red pepper into thin strips lengthways. Sprinkle with a little salt and leave for about 15 minutes. Rinse well and drain.

2 For the vinegar mixture, combine the rice vinegar, sugar and awakuchi shoyu in a small bowl.

3 Loosen the crab meat with cooking chopsticks and mix it with the sliced red pepper in a mixing bowl. Divide among four small bowls.

4 If you use salad cucumber, scoop out the seeds. Finely grate the cucumber with a fine-toothed grater or use a food processor. Drain in a fine-meshed sieve.

5 Mix the cucumber with the vinegar mixture, and pour a quarter on to the crab meat mixture in each bowl. Serve cold immediately, before the cucumber loses its colour.

VARIATIONS
• The vinegar mixture is best made using awakuchi shoyu, but ordinary shoyu can be used instead. It will make a darker dressing, however.
• This dressing can be made into a low-fat substitute for vinaigrette: reduce the sugar by half and add a few drops of oil.

ROLLED SARDINES WITH PLUM PASTE

JAPANESE COOKS SEEK TO TASTE AND EXPRESS THE SEASON IN THEIR COOKING, AND MENUS ALWAYS INCLUDE SOME SEASONAL INGREDIENTS. THIS DISH, IWASHI NO UMÉ MAKI YAKI, *IS ONE OF MANY RECIPES TO CELEBRATE THE ARRIVAL OF THE HARVEST, WHEN THE SARDINE SEASON PEAKS IN AUTUMN.*

SERVES FOUR

INGREDIENTS
   8 sardines, cleaned and filleted
   5ml/1 tsp salt
   4 umeboshi, about 30g/1¼oz total
     weight (choose the soft type)
   5ml/1 tsp sake
   5ml/1 tsp toasted sesame seeds
   16 shiso leaves, cut in
     half lengthways
   1 lime, thinly sliced, the centre
     hollowed out to make rings,
     to garnish

COOK'S TIP
Sardines deteriorate very quickly and must be bought and eaten on the same day. Be careful when buying: the eyes and gills should not be too pink. If the fish "melts" like cheese when grilled, don't bother to eat it.

1 Carefully cut the sardine fillets in half lengthways and place them side by side in a large, shallow container. Sprinkle with salt on both sides.

2 Remove the stones (pits) from the umeboshi and put the fruit in a small mixing bowl with the sake and toasted sesame seeds. With the back of a fork, mash the umeboshi, mixing well to form a smooth paste.

3 Wipe the sardine fillets with kitchen paper. With a butter knife, spread some umeboshi paste thinly on to one of the sardine fillets, then press some shiso leaves on top. Roll up the sardine starting from the tail and pierce with a wooden cocktail stick (toothpick). Repeat to make 16 rolled sardines.

4 Preheat the grill (broiler) to high. Lay a sheet of foil on a baking tray, and arrange the sardine rolls on this, spaced well apart to prevent sticking. Grill (broil) for 4–6 minutes on each side, or until golden brown, turning once.

5 Lay a few lime rings on four individual plates and arrange the rolled sardines alongside. Serve hot.

CLAMS AND SPRING ONIONS WITH MISO AND MUSTARD SAUCE

THE JAPANESE ARE REALLY FOND OF SHELLFISH, AND CLAMS ARE AMONG THE MOST POPULAR. IN SEASON, THEY BECOME SWEET AND JUICY, AND ARE EXCELLENT WITH THIS SWEET-AND-SOUR DRESSING.

SERVES FOUR

INGREDIENTS
   900g/2lb carpet shell clams or
      cockles, or 300g/11oz can baby
      clams in brine, or 130g/4½oz
      cooked and shelled cockles
   15ml/1 tbsp sake
   8 spring onions (scallions), green and
      white parts separated, then chopped
      in half
   10g/¼oz dried wakame
For the *nuta* dressing
   60ml/4 tbsp shiro miso
   20ml/4 tsp caster (superfine) sugar
   30ml/2 tbsp sake
   15ml/1 tbsp rice vinegar
   about 1.5ml/¼ tsp salt
   7.5ml/1½ tsp English (hot) mustard
   sprinkling of dashi-no-moto (if using
      canned shellfish)

1 If using fresh clams or cockles, wash the shells under running water. Discard any that remain open when tapped.

2 Pour 1cm/½in water into a small pan and add the clams or cockles. Sprinkle with the sake, cover, then bring to the boil. Cook over a vigorous heat for 5 minutes after the water reaches boiling point. Remove from the heat and leave to stand for 2 minutes. Discard any shells which remain closed.

3 Drain the shells and keep the liquid in a small bowl. Wait until the shells have cooled slightly, then remove the meat from most of the shells.

4 Cook the white part of the spring onions in a pan of rapidly boiling water, then add the remaining green parts after 2 minutes. Cook for 4 minutes altogether. Drain well.

5 Mix the shiro miso, sugar, sake, rice vinegar and salt for the *nuta* dressing, in a small pan. Stir in 45ml/3 tbsp of the reserved clam liquid, or the same amount of water and dashi-no-moto, if using canned shellfish.

6 Put the pan on a medium heat and stir constantly. When the sugar has dissolved, add the mustard. Check the seasoning and add a little more salt if desired. Remove from the heat and leave to cool.

7 Soak the wakame in a bowl of water for 10 minutes. Drain and squeeze out excess moisture by hand.

8 Mix together the clams or cockles, onions, wakame and dressing in a bowl. Heap up in a large bowl or divide among four small bowls and serve cold.

DEEP-FRIED SMALL PRAWNS AND CORN

THIS DISH IS CALLED KAKIAGÉ, *AN INEXPENSIVE AND INFORMAL STYLE OF TEMPURA. THIS IS ONLY ONE OF MANY VERSIONS AND IT IS A GOOD WAY OF USING UP SMALL QUANTITIES OF VEGETABLES.*

SERVES FOUR

INGREDIENTS
   200g/7oz small cooked, peeled
      prawns (shrimp)
   4–5 button (white) mushrooms
   4 spring onions (scallions)
   75g/3oz/½ cup canned, drained or
      frozen sweetcorn, thawed
   30ml/2 tbsp frozen peas, thawed
   vegetable oil, for deep-frying
   chives, to garnish
For the tempura batter
   300ml/½ pint/1¼ cups ice-cold water
   2 eggs, beaten
   150g/5oz/1¼ cups plain
      (all-purpose) flour
   1.5ml/¼ tsp baking powder
For the dipping sauce
   400ml/14fl oz/1⅔ cups second dashi
      stock, or the same amount of water
      and 5ml/1 tsp dashi-no-moto
   100ml/3fl oz/scant ½ cup shoyu
   100ml/3fl oz/scant ½ cup mirin
   15ml/1 tbsp chopped chives

1 Roughly chop half the prawns. Cut the mushrooms into small cubes. Slice the white part from the spring onions and chop this roughly.

2 To make the tempura batter, in a medium mixing bowl, mix the cold water and eggs. Add the flour and baking powder, and very roughly fold in with a pair of chopsticks or a fork. Do not beat. The batter should still be quite lumpy. Heat plenty of oil in a wok or a deep-fryer to 170°C/338°F.

3 Mix the prawns and vegetables into the batter. Pour a quarter of the batter into a small bowl, then drop gently into the oil. Using wooden spoons, carefully gather the scattered batter to form a fist-size ball. Deep-fry until golden. Drain on kitchen paper.

4 In a small pan, mix all the liquid dipping-sauce ingredients together and bring to the boil, then immediately turn off the heat. Sprinkle with chives.

5 Garnish the *kakiage* with chives, and serve with the dipping sauce.

FRIED PRAWN BALLS

WHEN THE MOON WAXES IN SEPTEMBER, THE JAPANESE CELEBRATE THE ARRIVAL OF AUTUMN BY MAKING AN OFFERING TO THE MOON, AND HAVE A FEAST. THE DISHES OFFERED, SUCH AS TINY RICE DUMPLINGS, SWEET CHESTNUTS AND THESE SHINJYO, SHOULD ALL BE ROUND IN SHAPE.

MAKES ABOUT FOURTEEN

INGREDIENTS
   150g/5oz raw prawns (shrimp),
      peeled
   75ml/5 tbsp second dashi stock
      or the same amount of water and
      2.5ml/½ tsp dashi-no-moto
   1 large (US extra large) egg white,
      well beaten
   30ml/2 tbsp sake
   15ml/1 tbsp cornflour (cornstarch)
   1.5ml/¼ tsp salt
   vegetable oil, for deep-frying
To serve
   25ml/1½ tbsp ground sea salt
   2.5ml/½ tsp sansho
   ½ lemon, cut into 4 wedges

1 Mix the prawns, dashi stock, beaten egg white, sake, cornflour and salt in a food processor or blender, and process until smooth. Scrape from the sides and transfer to a small mixing bowl.

2 In a wok or small pan, heat the vegetable oil to 175°C/347°F.

3 Take two dessertspoons and wet them with a little vegetable oil. Scoop about 30ml/2 tbsp prawn-ball paste into the spoons and form a small ball. Carefully plunge the ball into the hot oil and deep-fry until lightly browned. Drain on a wire rack. Repeat this process, one at a time, until all the prawn-ball paste is used.

4 Mix the salt and sansho on a small plate. Serve the fried prawn balls on a large serving platter or on four serving plates. Garnish with lemon wedges and serve hot with the sansho salt.

COOK'S TIP
Serve the salt and sansho in separate mounds on each plate, if you like.

TEPPAN YAKI

MANY JAPANESE HOMES HAVE A PORTABLE GAS COOKER, A TABLE GRIDDLE (TEPPAN), OR A TABLE EQUIPPED WITH A RECESSED COOKING SURFACE. THIS IS BECAUSE THE JAPANESE LOVE COOKING AS THEY EAT, AND EATING AS THEY COOK. IT'S FUN TO TRY.

SERVES FOUR

INGREDIENTS
275g/10oz monkfish tail
4 large scallops, cleaned and
  corals separated
250g/9oz squid body, cleaned
  and skinned
12 raw king or tiger prawns (jumbo
  shrimp), shells and heads removed,
  tails intact
115g/4oz/½ cup beansprouts, washed
1 red (bell) pepper, seeded and cut
  into 2.5cm/1in wide strips
8 fresh shiitake mushrooms,
  stalks removed
1 red onion, cut into 5mm/¼in
  thick rounds
1 courgette (zucchini), cut into
  1cm/½in thick rounds
3 garlic cloves, thinly sliced
  lengthways
vegetable oil, for frying
Sauce A, radish and chilli sauce
  8 radishes, finely grated
  1 dried chilli, seeded and crushed
  15ml/1 tbsp toasted sesame oil
  ½ onion, finely chopped
  90ml/6 tbsp shoyu
  30ml/2 tbsp caster (superfine) sugar
  45ml/3 tbsp toasted sesame seeds
  juice of ½ orange or 30ml/2 tbsp
    unsweetened orange juice
Sauce B, wasabi mayonnaise
  105ml/7 tbsp mayonnaise
  15ml/1 tbsp wasabi paste from a
    tube, or the same amount of
    wasabi powder mixed with 15ml/
    1 tbsp water
  5ml/1 tsp shoyu
Sauce C, lime and soy sauce
  juice of 1 lime
  grated rind of 1 lime
  20ml/4 tsp sake
  90ml/6 tbsp shoyu
  1 bunch chives, finely chopped

1 Sauce A Mix the grated radish with its juice and the chilli in a bowl. Heat the sesame oil in a frying pan and fry the onion until soft.

2 Pour in the shoyu and add the sugar and sesame seeds, removing the pan from the heat just as it starts to boil. Tip into the bowl and add the orange juice. Stir well and leave to cool.

3 Sauce B and C Mix the ingredients separately in small bowls, cover with clear film (plastic wrap) and set aside.

4 Cut the monkfish into large, bitesize, 5mm/¼in thick slices. Cut the scallops in half horizontally.

5 With a small sharp knife, make shallow criss-cross slits in the skinned side of the squid. Slice into 2.5 × 4cm/ 1 × 1½in pieces.

6 Place all the seafood on half of a serving platter, and arrange all the prepared vegetables (apart from the garlic) on the other half. Divide sauces A and C among eight small dishes; these are for dipping. Put the wasabi mayonnaise in a small bowl with a teaspoon. Prepare serving plates as well.

7 Heat the griddle on the table and oil it with a brush or kitchen paper. First, fry the garlic slices until crisp and golden. Remove the garlic chips to a small dish to mix with any sauces you like. Then fry the ingredients as you eat, dipping into the sauces or serving them with the wasabi mayonnaise. Oil the griddle from time to time.

TEMPURA SEAFOOD

THIS QUINTESSENTIALLY JAPANESE DISH ACTUALLY HAS ITS ORIGINS IN THE WEST, AS TEMPURA WAS INTRODUCED TO JAPAN BY PORTUGUESE TRADERS IN THE 17TH CENTURY.

SERVES FOUR

INGREDIENTS
    8 large raw prawns (shrimp), heads
        and shells removed, tails intact
    130g/4½oz squid body, cleaned
        and skinned
    115g/4oz whiting fillets
    4 fresh shiitake mushrooms,
        stalks removed
    8 okra
    ⅛ nori sheet, 5 × 4cm/2 × 1½in
    20g/¾oz dried harusame (a packet is
        a 150–250g/5–9oz mass)
    vegetable oil and sesame oil,
        for deep-frying
    plain (all-purpose) flour, for dusting
    salt
For the dipping sauce
    400ml/14fl oz/1⅔ cups second dashi
        stock, or the same amount of water
        mixed with 5ml/1 tsp dashi-no-moto
    200ml/7fl oz/scant 1 cup shoyu
    200ml/7fl oz/scant 1 cup mirin
For the condiment
    450g/1lb daikon, peeled
    4cm/1½in fresh root ginger, peeled
        and finely grated
For the tempura batter
    ice-cold water
    1 large (US extra large) egg, beaten
    200g/7oz/2 cups plain flour, sifted
    2–3 ice cubes

1 Remove the vein from the prawns, then make 4 × 3mm/⅛in deep cuts across the belly to stop the prawns curling up. Snip the tips of the tails and gently squeeze out any liquid. Pat dry.

2 Cut open the squid body. Lay flat, inside down, on a chopping board, and make shallow criss-cross slits on one side. Cut into 2.5 × 6cm/1 × 2½in rectangular strips. Cut the whiting fillets into similar-size strips.

3 Make two notched slits on the shiitake caps, in the form of a cross. Sprinkle your hands with some salt and rub over the okra, then wash the okra under running water to clean the surface.

4 Cut the nori into four long strips lengthways. Loosen the harusame noodles from the block and cut both ends with scissors to get a few strips. Make four bunches and tie them in the middle by wrapping with a nori strip. Wet the end to fix it.

5 Make the dipping sauce. In a pan, mix all the dipping-sauce ingredients and bring to the boil, then immediately remove from the heat. Set aside and keep warm.

6 Prepare the condiment. Grate the daikon very finely. Drain in a sieve, then squeeze out any excess water by hand. Lay clear film (plastic wrap) over an egg cup and press about 2.5ml/½ tsp grated ginger into the bottom. Add 30ml/2 tbsp grated daikon. Press and invert on to a small plate. Make three more.

7 Half-fill a pan or wok with 3 parts vegetable oil to 1 part sesame oil. Bring to 175°C/347°F over a medium heat.

8 Meanwhile, make the tempura batter. Add enough ice-cold water to the egg to make 150ml/¼ pint/⅔ cup, then pour into a large bowl. Add the flour and mix roughly with chopsticks. Do not beat; leave the batter lumpy. Add some ice cubes later to keep the temperature cool.

9 Dip the okra into the batter and deep-fry until golden. Drain on a rack. Batter the underside of the shiitake. Deep-fry.

10 Increase the heat a little, then fry the harusame by holding the nori tie with chopsticks and dipping them into the oil for a few seconds. The noodles instantly turn crisp and white. Drain on kitchen paper and sprinkle with salt.

11 Hold the tail of a prawn, dust with flour, then dip into the batter. Do not put batter on the tail. Slide the prawn into the hot oil very slowly. Deep-fry one to two prawns at a time until crisp.

12 Dust the whiting strips, dip into the batter, then deep-fry until golden. Wipe the squid strips well with kitchen paper, dust with flour, then dip in batter. Deep-fry until the batter is crisp.

13 Drain excess oil from the tempura on a wire rack for a few minutes, then arrange them on individual plates. Set the condiment alongside the tempura. Reheat the dipping sauce to warm through, then pour into four small bowls.

14 Serve. Ask your guests to mix the condiment into the dipping sauce and dunk the tempura as they eat.

MARINATED AND GRILLED SWORDFISH

IN MEDIEVAL TIMES, SAIKYO (THE WESTERN CAPITAL OF ANCIENT JAPAN) HAD A VERY SOPHISTICATED CULTURE. ARISTOCRATS COMPETED WITH EACH OTHER AS TO THEIR CHEF'S SKILLS, AND MANY OF THE CLASSIC RECIPES OF TODAY ARE FROM THIS PERIOD. KAJIKI SAIKYO YAKI IS ONE SUCH EXAMPLE.

SERVES FOUR

INGREDIENTS
  4 × 175g/6oz swordfish steaks
  2.5ml/½ tsp salt
  300g/11oz saikyo or shiro miso
  45ml/3 tbsp sake
For the asparagus
  25ml/1½ tbsp shoyu
  25ml/1½ tbsp sake
  8 asparagus spears, the hard ends
    discarded, each spear cut
    into three

1 Place the swordfish in a shallow container. Sprinkle with the salt on both sides and leave for 2 hours. Drain and wipe the fish with kitchen paper.

2 Mix the miso and sake, then spread half across the bottom of the cleaned container. Cover with a sheet of muslin (cheesecloth) the size of a dishtowel, folded in half, then open the fold. Place the swordfish, side by side, on top, and cover with the muslin. Spread the rest of the miso mixture on the muslin. Make sure the muslin is touching the fish. Marinate for 2 days in the coolest part of the refrigerator.

3 Preheat the grill (broiler) to medium. Oil the wire rack and grill (broil) the fish slowly for about 8 minutes on each side, turning every 2 minutes. If the steaks are thin, check every time you turn the fish to see if they are ready.

4 Mix the shoyu and sake in a bowl. Grill the asparagus for 2 minutes on each side, then dip into the bowl. Return to the grill for 2 minutes more on each side. Dip into the sauce again and set aside.

5 Serve the steak hot on four individual serving plates. Garnish with the drained, grilled asparagus.

PAPER-WRAPPED <u>AND</u> STEAMED RED SNAPPER

ORIGINALLY, THIS ELEGANT DISH FEATURED A WHOLE RED SNAPPER WRAPPED IN LAYERED JAPANESE HAND-MADE PAPER SOAKED IN SAKE AND TIED WITH RIBBONS. THIS VERSION IS A LITTLE EASIER.

4 At each end, fold the top corners down diagonally, then fold the bottom corners up to meet the opposite folded edge to make a triangle. Press flat with your palm. Repeat the process to make four parcels.

5 Cut 2.5cm/1in from the tip of the asparagus, and slice in half lengthways. Slice the asparagus stems and spring onions diagonally into thin ovals. Par-boil the tips for 1 minute in lightly salted water and drain. Set aside.

6 Open the parcels. Place the asparagus slices and the spring onions inside. Sprinkle with salt and place the fish on top. Add more salt and some sake, then sprinkle in the lime rind. Refold the parcels.

7 Pour hot water from a kettle into a deep roasting pan fitted with a wire rack to 1cm/½in below the rack. Place the parcels on the rack. Cook in the centre of the preheated oven for 20 minutes. Check by carefully unfolding a parcel from one triangular side. The fish should have changed from translucent to white.

8 Transfer the parcels on to individual plates. Unfold both triangular ends on the plate and lift open the middle a little. Insert a thin slice of lime and place two asparagus tips on top. Serve immediately, asking the guests to open their own parcels. Add a little shoyu, if you like.

SERVES FOUR

INGREDIENTS
  4 small red snapper fillets, no greater than 18 × 6cm/7 × 2½in, or whole snapper, 20cm/8in long, gutted but head, tail and fins intact
  8 asparagus spears, hard ends discarded
  4 spring onions (scallions)
  60ml/4 tbsp sake
  grated rind of ½ lime
  ½ lime, thinly sliced
  5ml/1 tsp shoyu (optional)
  salt

1 Sprinkle the red snapper fillets with salt on both sides and leave in the refrigerator for 20 minutes. Preheat the oven to 180°C/350°F/Gas 4.

2 To make the parcels, lay greaseproof (waxed) paper measuring 38 × 30cm/15 × 12in on a work surface. Use two pieces for extra thickness. Fold up one-third of the paper and turn back 1cm/½in from one end to make a flap.

3 Fold 1cm/½in in from the other end to make another flap. Fold the top edge down to fold over the first flap. Interlock the two flaps to form a long rectangle.

SEAFOOD, CHICKEN <u>AND</u> VEGETABLE HOTPOT

THIS DISH, CALLED YOSE NABE, IS COOKED AND EATEN AT THE TABLE, TRADITIONALLY USING A CLAY POT. YOU CAN USE A FLAMEPROOF CASSEROLE AND WILL NEED A PORTABLE TABLE-TOP STOVE.

SERVES FOUR

INGREDIENTS
   225g/8oz salmon, scaled and cut into
   5cm/2in thick steaks with bones
   225g/8oz white fish (sea bream, cod,
   plaice or haddock), cleaned and
   scaled then chopped into 4 chunks
   300g/11oz chicken thighs, cut into
   large bitesize chunks with bones
   4 hakusai leaves, base part trimmed
   115g/4oz spinach
   1 large carrot, cut into 5mm/¼in
   thick rounds or flower shapes
   8 fresh shiitake mushrooms, stalks
   removed, or 150g/5oz oyster
   mushrooms, base trimmed
   2 thin leeks, washed and cut
   diagonally into 5cm/2in lengths
   285g/10¼oz packet tofu block,
   drained and cut into 16 cubes
   salt
For the hot-pot liquid
   12 × 6cm/4½ × 2½in dashi-konbu
   1.2 litres/2 pints/5 cups water
   120ml/4fl oz/½ cup sake
For the condiments
   90g/3½oz daikon, peeled
   1 dried chilli, halved and seeded
   1 lemon, cut into 16 wedges
   4 spring onions (scallions), chopped
   2 × 5g/⅛oz packets kezuri-bushi
   1 bottle shoyu

1 Arrange the various prepared fish and chicken on a large serving platter.

2 Boil plenty of water in a large pan and cook the hakusai for 3 minutes. Drain in a sieve and leave to cool. Add a pinch of salt to the water and boil the spinach for 1 minute, then drain in a sieve under running water.

3 Squeeze the spinach and lay on a sushi rolling mat, then roll it up firmly. Leave to rest, then unwrap and take the cylinder out. Lay the hakusai leaves next to each other on the mat. Put the cylinder in the middle and roll again firmly. Leave for 5 minutes, then unroll and cut into 5cm/2in long cylinders.

4 Transfer the hakusai cylinders to the platter along with all the remaining vegetables and the tofu.

5 Lay the dashi-konbu on the bottom of the clay pot or flameproof casserole. Mix the water and sake in a small bowl.

6 Insert a metal skewer into the cut side of the daikon two to three times, and insert the chilli pieces. Leave for about 5 minutes, then grate finely. Drain in a fine-meshed sieve and squeeze the liquid out. Shape the pink daikon into a mound and put in a bowl. Put all the other condiments into small bowls.

7 Fill the pot or casserole with two-thirds of the water and sake mixture. Bring to the boil, then reduce the heat.

8 Put the carrot, shiitake, chicken and salmon into the pot. When the colour of the meat and fish changes, add the rest of the ingredients in batches.

9 Guests pour a little soy sauce into small bowls, and squeeze in a little lemon juice, then mix with a condiment. Pick up the food with chopsticks and dip into the sauce. Cook more ingredients as you go, adding more water and sake as the stock reduces.

FISH CAKES AND VEGETABLES

ODEN IS A SATISFYING AND EASY DISH TO MAKE AT HOME AS YOU CAN BUY ASSORTED READY-MADE FISH BALLS AND FISH CAKES FROM ASIAN FOOD STORES. YOU WILL ALSO NEED A LARGE CLAY POT OR A HEAVY FLAMEPROOF CASSEROLE AND A PORTABLE STOVE.

SERVES FOUR

INGREDIENTS
    30 × 7.5cm/12 × 3in dashi-konbu
    675g/1½lb daikon, peeled and cut
      into 4cm/1½in lengths
    12–20 ready-made fish balls and
      cakes (4 of each kind)
    1 konnyaku
    1 atsu-age
    8 small shiitake mushrooms,
      stalks removed
    4 medium potatoes, unpeeled,
      soaked in a bowl of water (to
      remove some of the starch)
    4 hard-boiled (hard-cooked) eggs,
      unshelled
    285g/10¼oz packet tofu block, cut
      into 8 cubes
    English (hot) mustard, to serve
For the soup stock
    1.5 litres/2½ pints/6¼ cups second
      dashi stock, or the same amount of
      water and 10ml/2 tsp dashi-no-moto
    75ml/5 tbsp sake
    15ml/1 tbsp salt
    40ml/8 tsp shoyu

1 Wrap the dashi-konbu in a wet, clean dishtowel for 5 minutes, or until soft enough to bend easily by hand without breaking. Snip it in half crossways, then cut each into four ribbons lengthways. Tie the centre of each "ribbon".

2 Slightly shave the edges of each of the daikon cylinders. Place all the fish balls and cakes, konnyaku and atsu-age in a large pan. Add enough hot water to cover all the ingredients, then drain.

3 Cut the konnyaku in quarters, then cut each quarter in half diagonally to make eight triangles. Cut large fish cakes in half. Put two shiitake mushrooms on to each of four bamboo skewers.

4 Mix all the ingredients for the soup stock, but only fill the pot or casserole by two-thirds. Add the daikon and potatoes and bring to the boil. Add the hard-boiled eggs. Reduce the heat to low and simmer for an hour, uncovered, skimming occasionally.

5 Increase the heat to medium and add the other ingredients. Cook, covered, for 30 minutes, then bring to the table cooker and keep warm on the lowest heat. Serve with mustard. Top up the pot with stock when it has reduced to half.

VARIATIONS
Deep-fry fish-ball mixtures in hot oil at 180°C/350°F until golden.
Fish Balls with Chives Process 150g/5oz chopped skinned cod fillet, 50g/2oz queen scallops, 1 egg white, 10ml/2 tsp grated ginger juice, 15ml/1 tbsp cornflour (cornstarch), 15ml/1 tbsp salt and 5ml/1 tsp sake in a food processor. Mix with 15ml/1 tbsp chopped chives.
Prawn Balls Combine 200g/7oz raw peeled small prawns (shrimp), 50g/2oz pork fat, 15ml/1 tbsp grated ginger juice, 1 egg white, 15ml/1 tbsp salt and 15ml/1 tbsp cornflour in a processor.
Squid and Ginger Balls Blend 200g/7oz chopped squid, 1 egg white, 15ml/1 tbsp cornflour, 10ml/2 tsp ginger juice and 15ml/1 tbsp salt in a food processor. Mix with 10ml/2 tsp chopped ginger.

POULTRY
AND MEAT

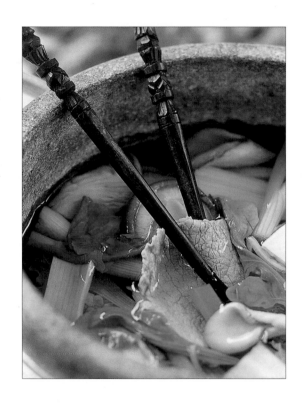

Most meat recipes in Japanese cooking use the meat as a rich

flavouring ingredient for vegetables and rice. Even in

sukiyaki, *the quintessential meat dish, plenty of vegetables*

of different textures and flavours accompany the meat.

Sauces and stocks are also used to enhance the meat's flavour.

GRILLED SKEWERED CHICKEN

THE JAPANESE ALWAYS ACCOMPANY DRINK WITH NIBBLES. THE NIBBLES ARE GENERALLY CALLED TSUMAMI, AND GRILLED SKEWERED CHICKEN DIPPED IN YAKITORI SAUCE IS ONE OF THE MOST POPULAR. THERE ARE THOUSANDS OF DEDICATED YAKITORI BARS IN JAPAN.

SERVES FOUR

INGREDIENTS
    8 chicken thighs with skin, boned
    8 large, thick spring onions
      (scallions), trimmed
For the *yakitori* sauce
    60ml/4 tbsp sake
    75ml/5 tbsp shoyu
    15ml/1 tbsp mirin
    15ml/1 tbsp caster (superfine) sugar
To serve
    shichimi togarashi, sansho or
      lemon wedges

1 First, make the *yakitori* sauce. Mix all the ingredients together in a small pan. Bring to the boil, then reduce the heat and simmer for 10 minutes, or until the sauce has thickened.

2 Cut the chicken into 2.5cm/1in cubes. Cut the spring onions into 2.5cm/1in long sticks.

3 To grill (broil), preheat the grill (broiler) to high. Oil the wire rack and spread out the chicken cubes on it. Grill both sides of the chicken until the juices drip, then dip the pieces in the sauce and put back on the rack. Grill for 30 seconds on each side, repeating the dipping process twice more.

4 Set aside and keep warm. Gently grill the spring onions until soft and slightly brown outside. Do not dip. Thread about four pieces of chicken and three spring onion pieces on to each of eight bamboo skewers.

5 Alternatively, to cook on a barbecue, soak eight bamboo skewers overnight in water. This prevents the skewers from burning. Prepare the barbecue. Thread the chicken and spring onion pieces on to skewers, as above. Place the sauce in a small bowl with a brush.

6 Cook the skewered chicken on the barbecue. Keep the skewer handles away from the fire, turning them frequently until the juices start to drip. Brush the chicken with sauce. Return to the coals and repeat this process twice more until the chicken is well cooked.

7 Arrange the skewers on a platter and serve sprinkled with shichimi togarashi or sansho, or accompanied by lemon wedges.

GRILLED CHICKEN BALLS COOKED ON BAMBOO SKEWERS

THESE TASTY CHICKEN BALLS, KNOWN AS TSUKUNE, ARE ANOTHER YAKITORI BAR REGULAR AS WELL AS A FAVOURITE FAMILY DISH, AS IT IS EASY FOR CHILDREN TO EAT DIRECTLY FROM THE SKEWER. YOU CAN MAKE THE BALLS IN ADVANCE UP TO THE END OF STEP 2, AND THEY FREEZE VERY WELL.

SERVES FOUR

INGREDIENTS
    300g/11oz skinless chicken,
        minced (ground)
    2 eggs
    2.5ml/½ tsp salt
    10ml/2 tsp plain (all-purpose) flour
    10ml/2 tsp cornflour (cornstarch)
    90ml/6 tbsp dried breadcrumbs
    2.5cm/1in piece fresh root
        ginger, grated
For the *"tare" yakitori* sauce
    60ml/4 tbsp sake
    75ml/5 tbsp shoyu
    15ml/1 tbsp mirin
    15ml/1 tbsp caster (superfine) sugar
    2.5ml/½ tsp cornflour (cornstarch)
        blended with 5ml/1 tsp water
To serve
    shichimi togarashi or
        sansho (optional)

1 Soak eight bamboo skewers overnight in water. Put all the ingredients for the chicken balls, except the ginger, in a food processor and blend well.

2 Wet your hands and scoop about a tablespoonful of the mixture into your palm. Shape it into a small ball about half the size of a golf ball. Make a further 30–32 balls in the same way.

3 Squeeze the juice from the grated ginger into a small mixing bowl. Discard the pulp.

4 Add the ginger juice to a small pan of boiling water. Add the chicken balls, and boil for about 7 minutes, or until the colour of the meat changes and the balls float to the surface. Scoop out using a slotted spoon and drain on a plate covered with kitchen paper.

5 In a small pan, mix all the ingredients for the *yakitori* sauce, except for the cornflour liquid. Bring to the boil, then reduce the heat and simmer for about 10 minutes, or until the sauce has slightly reduced. Add the cornflour liquid and stir until the sauce is thick. Transfer to a small bowl.

6 Thread 3–4 balls on to each skewer. Cook under a medium grill (broiler) or on a barbecue, keeping the skewer handles away from the fire. Turn them frequently for a few minutes, or until the balls start to brown. Brush with sauce and return to the heat. Repeat the process twice. Serve, sprinkled with shichimi togarashi or sansho, if you like.

CUBED CHICKEN AND VEGETABLES

A POPULAR JAPANESE COOKING STYLE SIMMERS VEGETABLES OF DIFFERENT TEXTURES WITH A SMALL AMOUNT OF MEAT TOGETHER IN DASHI STOCK. THIS CHICKEN VERSION IS KNOWN AS IRIDORI.

SERVES FOUR

INGREDIENTS
    2 chicken thighs, about 200g/7oz,
        boned, with skin remaining
    1 large carrot, trimmed
    1 konnyaku
    300g/11oz satoimo or small potatoes
    500g/1¼lb canned take-no-ko,
        drained
    30ml/2 tbsp vegetable oil
    300ml/½ pint/1¼ cups second dashi
        stock, or the same amount of water
        and 7.5ml/1½ tsp dashi-no-moto
    salt
For the simmering seasonings
    75ml/5 tbsp shoyu
    30ml/2 tbsp sake
    30ml/2 tbsp caster (superfine) sugar
    30ml/2 tbsp mirin

1 Cut the chicken into bitesize pieces. Chop the carrot into 2cm/¾in triangular chunks, the *ran-giri* shape. To do this, cut the carrot slightly diagonally and turn it 90° each time you cut.

2 Boil the konnyaku in rapidly boiling water for 1 minute and drain under running water. Cool, slice it crossways into 5mm/¼in thick rectangular strips. Cut a 4cm/1½in slit down the centre of a strip without cutting the ends. Carefully push the top of the strip through the slit to make a decorative tie. Repeat with all the konnyaku.

COOK'S TIP
When you cut satoimo, it produces a sticky juice. Rinsing with salt and water is the best way of washing it off.

3 Peel and halve the satoimo. Put the pieces in a colander and sprinkle with a generous amount of salt. Rub well and wash under running water. Drain. If using, peel and halve the new potatoes.

4 Halve the canned take-no-ko, then cut into the same shape as the carrot.

5 In a medium pan, heat the vegetable oil and stir-fry the chicken pieces until the surface of the meat turns white. Add the carrot, konnyaku ties, satoimo and take-no-ko. Stir well each time you add a new ingredient.

6 Add the dashi stock and bring to the boil. Cook on a high heat for 3 minutes then reduce to medium-low. Add the simmering seasonings, cover the pan then simmer for 15 minutes, until most of the liquid has evaporated, shaking the pan from time to time.

7 When the satoimo is soft, remove the pan from heat and transfer the chicken and vegetables to a large serving bowl. Serve immediately.

SIMMERED BEEF SLICES <u>AND</u> VEGETABLES

THIS TRADITIONAL DISH, NIKU JYAGA, IS A TYPICAL HOME-COOKED MEAL AND IS ONE OF THE TRADITIONAL DISHES REFERRED TO AS "MOTHER'S SPECIALITY". IT IS A GOOD STANDBY, AS IT IS EASY TO COOK, AND THERE IS NO NEED TO BUY EXPENSIVE CUTS OF BEEF.

SERVES FOUR

INGREDIENTS
  250g/9oz beef fillet (or any cut),
    very thinly sliced
  1 large onion
  15ml/1 tbsp vegetable oil
  450g/1lb small potatoes, halved then
    soaked in water
  1 carrot, cut into 5mm/¼in rounds
  45ml/3 tbsp frozen peas, defrosted
    and blanched for 1 minute
For the seasonings
  30ml/2 tbsp caster (superfine) sugar
  75ml/5 tbsp shoyu
  15ml/1 tbsp mirin
  15ml/1 tbsp sake

1 Cut the thinly sliced beef slices into 2cm/¾in wide strips, and slice the onion lengthways into 5mm/¼in pieces.

2 Heat the vegetable oil in a pan and lightly fry the beef and onion slices. When the colour of the meat changes, drain the potatoes and add to the pan.

3 Once the potatoes are coated with the oil in the pan, add the carrot. Pour in just enough water to cover, then bring to the boil, skimming a few times.

4 Boil vigorously for 2 minutes, then move the potatoes to the bottom of the pan and gather all the other ingredients to sit on top of the potatoes. Reduce the heat to medium-low and add all the seasonings. Simmer for 20 minutes, partially covered, or until most of the liquid has evaporated.

5 Check if the potatoes are cooked. Add the peas and cook to heat through, then remove the pan from the heat. Serve the beef and vegetables immediately in four small serving bowls.

SLICED SEARED BEEF

JAPANESE CHEFS USE A COOKING TECHNIQUE CALLED TATAKI TO COOK RARE STEAK. THEY NORMALLY USE A COAL FIRE AND SEAR A CHUNK OF BEEF ON LONG SKEWERS, THEN PLUNGE IT INTO COLD WATER TO STOP IT COOKING FURTHER. USE A WIRE MESH GRILL OVER THE HEAT SOURCE TO COOK THIS WAY.

SERVES FOUR

INGREDIENTS
  500g/1¼lb chunk of beef thigh
    (a long, thin chunk looks better
    than a thick, round chunk)
  generous pinch of salt
  10ml/2 tsp vegetable oil
For the marinade
  200ml/7fl oz/scant 1 cup rice
    vinegar
  70ml/4½ tbsp sake
  135ml/4½fl oz/scant ⅔ cup shoyu
  15ml/1 tbsp caster
    (superfine) sugar
  1 garlic clove, thinly sliced
  1 small onion, thinly sliced
  sansho
For the garnish
  6 shiso leaves and shiso flowers
    (if available)
  about 15cm/6in Japanese or ordinary
    salad cucumber
  ½ lemon, thinly sliced
  1 garlic clove, finely grated (optional)

1 Mix the marinade ingredients in a small pan and warm through until the sugar has dissolved. Remove from the heat and leave to cool.

COOK'S TIPS
• If you don't have a mesh grill or griddle, heat 15ml/1 tbsp vegetable oil in a hot frying pan to sear the beef. Wash all the oil from the meat and wipe off any excess with a kitchen paper.
• If preparing this dish ahead of time, spear the beef rolls with a cocktail stick (toothpick) to secure.

2 Generously sprinkle the beef with the salt and rub well into the meat. Leave for 2–3 minutes, then rub the oil in evenly with your fingers.

3 Fill a large mixing bowl with plenty of cold water. Put a mesh grill tray over the heat on the top of the stove, or heat a griddle to a high temperature. Sear the beef, turning frequently until about 5mm/¼in of the flesh in from the surface is cooked. Try not to burn grid marks on the meat. Immediately plunge the meat into the bowl of cold water for a few seconds to stop it from cooking further.

4 Wipe the meat with kitchen paper or a dishtowel and immerse fully in the marinade for 1 day.

5 Next day, prepare the garnish. Chop the shiso leaves in half lengthways, then cut into very thin strips crossways. Slice the cucumber diagonally into 5mm/¼in thick oval shapes, then cut each oval into 5mm/¼in matchsticks. Scoop out the watery seed part first if using an ordinary salad cucumber.

6 Remove the meat from the marinade. Strain the remaining marinade through a sieve, reserving both the liquid and the marinated onion and garlic.

7 Using a sharp knife, cut the beef thinly into slices of about 5mm/¼in thick.

8 Heap the cucumber sticks on a large serving plate and put the marinated onion and garlic on top. Arrange the beef slices as you would *sashimi*, leaning alongside or on the bed of cucumber and other vegetables. You can also either make a fan shape with the beef slices, or, if the slices are large enough, you could roll them.

9 Fluff the shiso strips and put on top of the beef. Decorate with some shiso flowers, if using. Lightly sprinkle with the lemon rings, and serve with the reserved marinade in individual bowls.

10 To eat, take a few beef slices on to individual plates. Roll a slice with your choice of garnish, then dip it into the marinade. Add a little grated garlic, if you like.

SUKIYAKI

YOU WILL NEED A SUKIYAKI PAN OR A SHALLOW CAST-IRON PAN, AND A PORTABLE TABLE STOVE TO COOK THIS TRADITIONAL DISH OF BEEF AND VEGETABLES.

SERVES FOUR

INGREDIENTS
   600g/1lb 5oz well-marbled beef
     sirloin, without bone, sliced into
     3mm/⅛in slices
   15ml/1 tbsp sake
   1 packet shirataki noodles, about
     200g/7oz, drained
   2 large onions, cut into 8 slices
     lengthways
   450g/1lb enokitake mushrooms,
     root part removed
   12 shiitake mushrooms,
     stalks removed
   10 spring onions (scallions), trimmed
     and quartered diagonally lengthways
   300g/11oz shungiku, cut in half
     lengthways, or watercress
   250–275g/9–10oz tofu, drained and
     cut into 8–12 large bitesize cubes
   4–8 very fresh eggs, at room
     temperature
   about 20g/¾oz beef fat
For the *wari-shita* sauce
   75ml/5 tbsp second dashi stock, or
     the same amount of water and
     5ml/1 tsp dashi-no-moto
   75ml/5 tbsp shoyu
   120ml/4fl oz/½ cup mirin
   15ml/1 tbsp sake
   15ml/1 tbsp caster (superfine) sugar

1 Arrange the beef slices on a large serving plate. Sprinkle with the sake and leave to settle.

2 Par-boil the shirataki in rapidly boiling water for 2 minutes, then drain. Wash under cold running water and cut into 5cm/2in lengths. Drain well.

3 Mix all the ingredients for the *wari-shita* sauce in a small pan and place over a medium heat until the sugar has dissolved. Pour into a jug (pitcher) or bowl.

4 On a tray, arrange all the vegetables, shirataki and tofu. Break one egg into each of four small serving bowls. Take everything to the table.

5 Start cooking when the guests are seated at the table. Heat the pan on a table cooker until very hot, then reduce the heat to medium, and add some beef fat. When it has melted, add the spring onions and onion slices, then increase the heat. Stir-fry for 2 minutes, or until the onions become soft. The guests should now start to beat the egg in their bowls.

6 Add a quarter of the *wari-shita* sauce to the pan. When it starts to bubble, add about a quarter of the vegetables, tofu and shirataki. Place them side by side but do not mix them. Keep some space clear for the beef.

7 Cook one beef slice per guest at a time. Put four slices in the space you kept in the pan. As they change colour, remove them immediately from the pan and dip them into the beaten egg. Eat straight away. Cook the vegetables and other ingredients in the same way; they might take 10–15 minutes to cook. Add the remaining ingredients as you eat. Add more *wari-shita* sauce when it is reduced in the pan. Add another egg to the dipping bowls if required.

PAPER-THIN SLICED BEEF COOKED IN STOCK

THE JAPANESE NAME FOR THIS DISH, SHABU SHABU, REFERS TO "WASHING" THE WAFER-THIN SLICES OF BEEF IN HOT STOCK. YOU WILL NEED A PORTABLE STOVE TO COOK THIS MEAL AT THE TABLE.

SERVES FOUR

INGREDIENTS
  600g/1lb 5oz boneless beef sirloin
  2 thin leeks, trimmed and cut into
    2 × 5cm/¾ × 2in strips
  4 spring onions (scallions), quartered
  8 shiitake mushrooms, less stalks
  175g/6oz oyster mushrooms, base
    part removed, torn into small pieces
  ½ hakusai, base part removed and
    cut into 5cm/2in squares
  300g/11oz shungiku, halved
  275g/10oz tofu, halved then cut in
    2cm/¾in thick slices crossways
  10 × 6cm/4 × 2½in dashi-konbu
    wiped with a damp cloth
For the *ponzu* (citrus sauce)
  juice of 1 lime made up to 120ml/
    4fl oz/½ cup with lemon juice
  50ml/2fl oz/¼ cup rice vinegar
  120ml/4fl oz/½ cup shoyu
  20ml/4 tsp mirin
  4 × 6cm/1½ × 2½in dashi-konbu
  5g/⅛oz kezuri-bushi
For the *goma-dare* (sesame sauce)
  75g/3oz white sesame seeds
  10ml/2 tsp caster (superfine) sugar
  45ml/3 tbsp shoyu
  15ml/1 tbsp sake
  15ml/1 tbsp mirin
  90ml/6 tbsp second dashi stock, or
    the same amount of water and
    5ml/1 tsp dashi-no-moto
For the condiments
  5–6cm/2–2½in daikon, peeled
  2 dried chillies, seeded and sliced
  20 chives, finely snipped

1 Mix all the *ponzu* ingredients in a glass jar and leave overnight. Strain and keep the liquid in the jar.

2 Make the *goma-dare*. Gently roast the sesame seeds in a dry frying pan on a low heat until the seeds pop. Grind the sesame seeds to form a smooth paste. Add the sugar and grind, then add the other ingredients, mixing well. Pour 30ml/2 tbsp into each of four small bowls, and put the rest in a jug (pitcher) or bowl.

3 Prepare the condiments. Pierce the cut ends of the daikon deeply four or five times with a skewer, then insert pieces of chilli. Leave for 20 minutes, then finely grate the daikon into a sieve. Divide the pink daikon among four small bowls. Put the chives in another bowl.

4 Cut the meat into 1–2mm/¹⁄₁₆in thick slices, and place on a large serving plate. Arrange the vegetables and tofu on another large plate.

5 Fill a flameproof casserole three-quarters full of water and add the dashi-konbu. Bring everything to the table and heat the casserole.

6 Pour 45ml/3 tbsp *ponzu* into the grated daikon in each bowl, and add the chives to the bowls of *goma-dare*.

7 When the water comes to the boil, remove the konbu and reduce the heat to medium-low. Add a handful of each ingredient except the beef to the casserole.

8 Each guest picks up a slice of beef using chopsticks and holds it in the stock for 3–10 seconds. Dip the beef into one of the sauces and eat. Remove the vegetables and other ingredients as they cook, and eat with the dipping sauces. Skim the surface occasionally.

PAN-FRIED PORK WITH GINGER SAUCE

REPUTEDLY CREATED BY A CANTEEN DINNER LADY AT A TOKYO UNIVERSITY DURING THE 1970s, THIS DISH, KNOWN AS BUTA-NIKU SHOGA YAKI, IS PARTICULARLY POPULAR WITH YOUNGSTERS.

<u>SERVES FOUR</u>

INGREDIENTS
450g/1lb pork chops, boned
   and trimmed
1 small onion, thinly sliced
   lengthways
50g/2oz/¼ cup beansprouts
50g/2oz mangetouts (snow peas),
   trimmed
15ml/1 tbsp vegetable oil
salt
For the marinade
15ml/1 tbsp shoyu
15ml/1 tbsp sake
15ml/1 tbsp mirin
4cm/1½in piece fresh root ginger,
   very finely grated,
   plus juice

1 Wrap the pork chops in clear film (plastic wrap) and freeze for 2 hours. Cut into 3mm/⅛in slices, then into 4cm/1½in wide strips.

2 To make the marinade, mix all the ingredients in a plastic container. Add the pork and marinate for 15 minutes.

3 Heat the oil in a heavy frying pan on a medium-high heat. Add the onion and fry for 3 minutes.

4 Take half of the pork slices out from the marinade and add to the frying pan. Transfer the meat to a plate when its colour changes; this will only take about 2–3 minutes. Repeat the process with the rest of the meat and reserve the marinade. Transfer all the cooked pork slices and onions to the plate.

5 Pour the reserved marinade into the pan and simmer until it has reduced by one-third. Add the beansprouts and mangetouts, then the pork and increase the heat to medium-high for 2 minutes.

6 Heap the beansprouts on individual serving plates and lean the meat, onions and mangetouts against them. Serve immediately.

DEEP-FRIED PORK FILLET

KNOWN AS TON-KATSU, SOME JAPANESE RESTAURANTS SERVE JUST THIS ONE INVIGORATING DISH. THE PORK IS ALWAYS GARNISHED WITH JUST A HEAP OF VERY FINELY SHREDDED WHITE CABBAGE.

<u>SERVES FOUR</u>

INGREDIENTS
1 white cabbage
4 pork loin chops or cutlets, boned
plain (all-purpose) flour, to dust
vegetable oil, for deep-frying
2 eggs, beaten
50g/2oz/1 cup dried
   white breadcrumbs
salt and ready-ground mixed pepper
prepared English (hot) mustard,
   to garnish
Japanese pickles, to serve
For the *ton-katsu* sauce
60ml/4 tbsp Worcestershire sauce
30ml/2 tbsp good-quality
   tomato ketchup
5ml/1 tsp shoyu

1 Quarter the cabbage and remove the central core. Slice the wedges very finely with a vegetable slicer or a sharp knife.

2 Make a few deep cuts horizontally across the fat of the meat. This prevents the meat curling up while cooking. Rub a little salt and pepper into the meat and dust with the flour, then shake off any excess.

3 Heat the oil in a deep-fryer or a large pan to 180°C/350°F.

4 Dip the meat in the beaten eggs, then coat with breadcrumbs. Deep-fry two pieces at a time for 8–10 minutes, or until golden brown. Drain on a wire rack or on kitchen paper. Repeat until all the pieces of pork are deep-fried.

5 Heap the cabbage on four individual serving plates. Cut the pork crossways into 2cm/¾in thick strips and arrange them to your liking on the cabbage.

6 To make the *ton-katsu* sauce, mix the Worcestershire sauce, ketchup and shoyu in a jug (pitcher) or gravy boat. Serve the pork and cabbage immediately, with the sauce, mustard and Japanese pickles. Pickles can also be served in separate dishes, if you like.

ROASTED AND MARINATED PORK

YUAN, A SAUCE MADE FROM SAKE, SHOYU, MIRIN AND CITRUS FRUIT, IS OFTEN USED TO MARINATE INGREDIENTS EITHER BEFORE OR AFTER COOKING. IN THIS RECIPE, THE SAUCE GIVES A DELICATE FLAVOUR TO PORK. IF POSSIBLE, LEAVE THE MEAT TO MARINATE OVERNIGHT.

SERVES FOUR

INGREDIENTS
  600g/1lb 5oz pork fillet
  1 garlic clove, crushed
  generous pinch of salt
  4 spring onions (scallions), trimmed,
    white part only
  10g/¼oz dried wakame, soaked in
    water for 20 minutes and drained
  10cm/4in celery stick, trimmed and
    cut in half crossways
  1 carton mustard and cress
For the *yuan* sauce
  105ml/7 tbsp shoyu
  45ml/3 tbsp sake
  60ml/4 tbsp mirin
  1 lime, sliced into thin rings

4 Cut the white part of the spring onions in half crossways, then in half lengthways. Remove the round cores, then lay the spring onion quarters flat on a chopping board. Slice them very thinly lengthways to make fine shreds.

5 Soak the shreds in a bowl of ice-cold water. Repeat with the remaining parts of the spring onions. When the shreds curl up, drain and gather them into a loose ball.

6 Cut the drained wakame into 2.5cm/1in squares or narrow strips. Slice the celery very thinly lengthways. Soak in cold water, then drain and gather together as before.

7 Remove the pork from the marinade and wipe with kitchen paper. Slice it very thinly. Strain the marinade and keep it in a gravy boat or jug (pitcher). Arrange the sliced pork on a large serving plate with the vegetables around it. Serve cold with the *yuan* sauce.

1 Preheat the oven to 200°C/400°F/Gas 6. Rub the pork with crushed garlic and salt, and leave for 15 minutes.

2 Roast the pork for 20 minutes, then turn the meat over and reduce the oven temperature to 180°C/350°F/Gas 4. Cook for a further 20 minutes, or until the pork is cooked and there are no pink juices.

3 Meanwhile, mix the *yuan* sauce ingredients in a container that is big enough to hold the pork. When the meat is cooked, immediately put it in the sauce, and leave it to marinate for at least 2 hours, or overnight.

POT-COOKED DUCK AND GREEN VEGETABLES

PREPARE THE INGREDIENTS FOR THIS DISH, KAMO NABE, BEFOREHAND, SO THAT THE COOKING CAN BE DONE AT THE TABLE. USE A HEAVY PAN OR FLAMEPROOF CASSEROLE WITH A PORTABLE STOVE.

SERVES FOUR

INGREDIENTS

4 duck breast fillets, about 800g/
 1¾lb total weight
8 large shiitake mushrooms, stalks
 removed, a cross cut into each cap
2 leeks, trimmed and cut diagonally
 into 6cm/2½in lengths
½ hakusai, stalk part removed and
 cut into 5cm/2in squares
500g/1¼lb shungiku or mizuna, root
 part removed, cut in half crossways
For the stock
 raw bones from 1 chicken, washed
 1 egg shell
 200g/7oz/scant 1 cup short grain
 rice, washed and drained
 120ml/4fl oz/½ cup sake
 about 10ml/2 tsp coarse sea salt
For the sauce
 75ml/5 tbsp shoyu
 30ml/2 tbsp sake
 juice of 1 lime
 8 white peppercorns, roughly crushed
For the soup
 130g/4½oz Chinese egg noodles,
 cooked and loosened
 1 egg, beaten
 1 bunch of chives
 freshly ground white pepper

1 To make the stock, put the chicken bones into a pan three-quarters full of water. Bring to the boil and drain when it reaches boiling point. Wash the pan and the bones again, then return to the pan with the same amount of water. Add the egg shell and then bring to the boil. Simmer, uncovered, for 1 hour, skimming frequently. Remove the bones and egg shell. Add the rice, sake and salt, then simmer for 30 minutes. Remove from the heat and set aside.

2 Heat a heavy frying pan until just smoking. Remove from the heat for 1 minute, then add the duck breasts, skin-side down. Return to a medium heat and sear for 3–4 minutes, or until crisp. Turn over and sear the other side for 1 minute. Remove from the heat.

3 When cool, wipe the duck fat with kitchen paper and cut the breast and skin into 5mm/¼in thick slices. Arrange on a large serving plate with all the prepared vegetables.

4 Heat through all the ingredients for the sauce in a small pan and transfer to a small jug (pitcher) or bowl.

5 Prepare four dipping bowls, four serving bowls and chopsticks. At the table, bring the pan of soup stock to the boil, then reduce to medium-low. Add half of the shiitake and leeks. Wait for 5 minutes and put in half of the stalk part of the hakusai. Add half of the duck and cook for 1–2 minutes for rare or 5–8 minutes for well-done meat.

6 Each person prepares some duck and vegetables in a serving bowl and drizzles over a little sauce. Add the soft hakusai leaves, shungiku and mizuna to the stock as you eat, adjusting the heat as you go. When the stock is less than a quarter of the pot's volume, top up with 3 parts water to 1 part sake.

7 When the duck has been eaten, bring the reduced stock to the boil. Skim the oil from the surface, and reduce the heat to medium. Add the noodles, cook for 1–2 minutes and check the seasoning. Add more salt if required. Pour in the beaten egg and swirl in the stock. Cover, turn off the heat, then leave to stand for 1 minute. Decorate with the chopped chives and serve with ground pepper.

SUMO WRESTLER'S HOTPOT

THIS FILLING HOT-POT, CALLED CHANKO NABE, IS PROBABLY RESPONSIBLE FOR THE VAST SIZE OF SUMO WRESTLERS, AS IT IS THEIR FIRST MEAL OF THE DAY AFTER 4–6 HOURS OF MORNING EXERCISE. YOU NEED A JAPANESE CLAY POT OR HEAVY PAN AND A PORTABLE TABLE STOVE OR A PLATE WARMER.

SERVES FOUR TO SIX

INGREDIENTS
    2 abura-age
    1 bunch of shungiku or pak choi (bok
        choy), 200g/7oz, root part trimmed
    1 large leek, trimmed
    1 daikon, thickly peeled
    ½ hakusai
    1 dashi-konbu, 4 × 10cm/1½ × 4in
    350g/12oz chicken, boned and cut
        into large bitesize pieces
    12 shiitake mushrooms, stalks
        removed, a cross cut into each cap
    285g/10¼oz packet tofu block,
        drained and cut into 8 cubes
For the fish balls
    6 sardines, about 350g/12oz,
        cleaned and filleted
    2.5cm/1in fresh root ginger, chopped
    1 large (US extra large) egg
    25ml/1½ tbsp miso (any except
        hatcho or aka)
    20 chives, roughly chopped
    30ml/2 tbsp plain (all-purpose) flour
For the soup stock
    550ml/18fl oz/2½ cups sake
    550ml/18fl oz/2½ cups water
    60ml/4 tbsp shoyu
For the citrus pepper (optional)
    grated rind of 1 lime
    10–12 white peppercorns

1 Make the fish balls by chopping all the ingredients on a chopping board, or use a mortar and pestle to grind them. Alternatively, use a food processor. Pulse briefly so the texture is rough, not fine. Transfer to a container, cover with clear film (plastic wrap) until needed.

2 Blanch the abura-age in rapidly boiling water for 30 seconds. Drain under cold running water and squeeze out the water by hand. Cut each abura-age in half lengthways, and then quarter crossways to make eight rectangles. Cut each rectangle in half diagonally to make two triangles. You should have 32 triangles.

3 Cut the shungiku or pak-choi into 6cm/2½in lengths. Cut the leek diagonally in 2.5cm/1in thick oval shapes. Cut the daikon into 5mm/¼in rounds. Cut the hakusai leaves into strips crossways, keeping the leaves and stalks separate.

4 Grind the citrus pepper ingredients, if using, in a mortar using a pestle and set aside in a small bowl.

COOK'S TIP
At the end of the meal there is a tasty, rich soup left in the pot. Add 200g/7oz cooked udon noodles into the remaining soup and bring to the boil again. After 2 minutes, serve the noodles in bowls with plenty of soup and chopped chives on top.

5 Lay the dashi-konbu on the base of the pan. Pour in the ingredients for the soup stock to fill half the pan, and bring to the boil on a high heat.

6 To cook the fish balls, reduce the heat to medium. Scoop up the fish-ball paste with a spoon and shape roughly like a rugby ball using a palette knife (metal spatula). Drop into the boiling stock. Repeat until all the paste is used. Skim the surface of the stock frequently. Cook for 3 minutes.

7 Carefully add the chicken pieces, daikon rounds, the stalks of the hakusai, the shiitake and leek, then the tofu and abura-age. Simmer for about 12 minutes, or until the chicken is cooked. Add the soft parts of the hakusai and the shungiku and wait for 3 minutes. Remove from the heat.

8 Put the pan on the portable stove on the table, set at the lowest heat, or on a plate warmer. Serve small amounts of the ingredients in individual bowls. Guests help themselves from the pot. Sprinkle on citrus pepper, if you like.

DESSERTS
AND CAKES

Glutinous rice, azuki beans, squash, sweet potatoes and sugar

are, surprisingly, the most commonly used ingredients in Japanese

desserts; no dairy foods are used at all. It is not customary in

Japan to have a dessert after a meal, so the dishes here are

normally eaten as an accompaniment to Japanese tea.

GREEN TEA ICE CREAM

In the past, the Japanese did not follow a meal with dessert, apart from some fruit. This custom is slowly changing and now many Japanese restaurants offer light desserts such as sorbet or ice cream. Here, ice cream is flavoured with matcha — the finest green powdered tea used in the tea ceremony. It gives the ice cream a sophisticated twist.

SERVES FOUR

INGREDIENTS
    500ml/17fl oz carton good-quality
        vanilla ice cream
    15ml/1 tbsp matcha
    15ml/1 tbsp lukewarm water from
        the kettle
    seeds from ¼ pomegranate (optional)

COOK'S TIPS
Sweet azuki beans and French sweet chestnut purée can be used to make other Japanese-style ice creams. Use 30ml/2 tbsp soft cooked sweet azuki beans or 20ml/4 tsp chestnut purée per 100ml/3fl oz/scant ½ cup good-quality vanilla ice cream.

1 Soften the ice cream by transferring it to the refrigerator for 20–30 minutes. Do not allow it to melt.

2 Mix the matcha powder and lukewarm water in a cup and stir well to make a smooth paste.

3 Put half the ice cream into a mixing bowl. Add the matcha liquid and mix thoroughly with a rubber spatula, then add the rest of the ice cream. You can stop mixing at the stage when the ice cream looks a marbled dark green and white, or continue mixing until the ice cream is a uniform pale green. Put the bowl into the freezer.

4 After 1 hour, the ice cream is ready to serve. Scoop into individual glass cups, and top with a few pomegranate seeds to decorate, if you like.

KABOCHA SQUASH CAKE

YOKAN (CAKE) IS A VERY SWEET DESSERT OFTEN MADE WITH AZUKI BEANS, TO BE EATEN AT TEA TIME WITH GREEN TEA. THE BITTERNESS OF THE GREEN TEA BALANCES THE SWEETNESS OF THE YOKAN. IN THIS VERSION, KABOCHA SQUASH IS USED INSTEAD OF AZUKI AND THE CAKE IS SERVED WITH FRUITS.

SERVES FOUR

INGREDIENTS
 1 × 350g/12oz kabocha squash
 30ml/2 tbsp plain
  (all-purpose) flour
 15ml/1 tbsp cornflour (cornstarch)
 10ml/2 tsp caster (superfine) sugar
 1.5ml/¼ tsp salt
 1.5ml/¼ tsp ground cinnamon
 25ml/1½ tbsp water
 2 egg yolks, beaten
To serve
 ½ nashi
 ½ kaki (optional)

2 Steam the kabocha in a covered steamer for about 15 minutes over a medium heat. Check if a chopstick can be pushed into the centre easily. Remove and leave, covered, for 5 minutes.

3 Remove the skin from the kabocha. Mash the flesh and push it through a sieve using a wooden spoon, or use a food processor. Transfer the flesh to a mixing bowl, add the rest of the cake ingredients, and mix well.

4 Roll out the makisu sushi mat as you would if making a sushi roll. Wet some muslin or a dishtowel slightly with water and lay it on the mat. Spread the kabocha mixture evenly. Hold the nearest end and tightly roll up the makisu to the other end. Close both outer ends by rolling up or folding the muslin over.

5 Put the rolled kabocha in the makisu back into the steamer for 5 minutes. Remove from the heat and leave to set for 5 minutes.

6 Peel, trim and slice the nashi and kaki, if using, very thinly lengthways.

7 Open the makisu when the roll has cooled down. Cut the cake into 2.5cm/1in thick slices and serve cold on four small plates with the thinly sliced nashi and kaki, if using.

1 Cut off the hard part from the top and bottom of the kabocha, then cut it into three to four wedges. Scoop out the seeds with a spoon. Cut into chunks.

STEAMED CAKE WITH SWEET POTATOES

THIS SOFT STEAMED CAKE, KNOWN AS MUSHI-KASUTERA, IS NOT TOO SWEET, AND CAN BE EATEN LIKE BREAD. THE SECRET IS A LITTLE MISO, WHICH ADDS A SUBTLE SALTINESS TO THE CAKE.

SERVES FOUR

INGREDIENTS
    200g/7oz/scant 2 cups plain (all-
      purpose) flour
    140g/4¾oz/scant ¾ cup caster
      (superfine) sugar
    45ml/3 tbsp sweetened
      condensed milk
    4 eggs, beaten
    40g/1½oz shiro miso
    150g/5oz sweet potatoes
    10ml/2 tsp cream of tartar
    2.5ml/½ tsp bicarbonate of soda
      (baking soda)
    30ml/2 tbsp melted butter

1 Sift the flour and the sugar together into a large mixing bowl. In a separate bowl, beat the condensed milk, eggs and shiro miso together to make a smooth cream. Add to the flour and mix well. Cover the bowl with clear film (plastic wrap) and leave to rest for 1 hour.

2 Trim the hard end of the sweet potatoes and thinly peel, then cut into 2cm/¾in dice. Cover with water. Drain just before using. Preheat the steamer, and line with muslin (cheesecloth).

3 Mix the cream of tartar and bicarbonate of soda with 15ml/1 tbsp water. Add to the cake mixture with the melted butter and two-thirds of the diced sweet potato. Pour the cake mixture into the steamer, then push the rest of the sweet potato on to the surface of the cake.

4 Steam the cake for 30 minutes, or until risen to a dome shape. Remove from the heat and cool a little. Serve warm or cold, cut into wedges.

STICKY RICE CAKE WRAPPED IN SWEET AZUKI BEAN PASTE

THIS TEA-TIME SNACK, OHAGI, IS AN ABSOLUTE FAVOURITE AMONG ALL AGES IN JAPAN. IT IS ALSO MADE ON OCCASIONS SUCH AS BIRTHDAYS AND FESTIVALS. DECORATE WITH CAMELLIA LEAVES.

MAKES TWELVE

INGREDIENTS
    150g/5oz glutinous rice
    50g/2oz Japanese short grain rice
    410g/14¼oz can azuki beans
      (canned in water, with sugar
      and salt)
    90g/3½oz/6½ tbsp caster
      (superfine) sugar
    pinch of salt

1 Put the two kinds of rice into a sieve, wash well under running water, then drain. Leave for 1 hour to dry.

2 Tip the rice into a heavy cast-iron pan or flameproof casserole with a lid, and add 200ml/7fl oz/scant 1 cup water.

3 Cover and bring to the boil, then reduce the heat to low and simmer for 15 minutes, or until a slight crackling noise is heard from the pan. Remove from the heat and leave to stand for 5 minutes. Remove the lid, cover with a dishtowel and leave to cool.

4 Pour the contents of the azuki bean can into a pan and cook over a medium heat. Add the sugar a third at a time, mixing well after each addition. Reduce the heat to low and mash the beans using a potato masher. Add the salt and remove from the heat. The consistency should be of mashed potatoes. Heat it over a low heat to remove any excess liquid. Leave to cool.

5 Wet your hands. Shape the sticky rice into 12 golf-ball-size balls.

6 Dampen some muslin and place on the work surface. Scoop 30ml/2 tbsp of azuki bean paste and spread in the centre of the muslin about 5mm/¼in thick. Put a rice ball in the middle, then wrap the ball up in the paste using the muslin. Open the cloth and gently remove the ball. Repeat the process until all the rice balls are used up. Serve at room temperature.

SWEET AZUKI BEAN PASTE JELLY

IN THIS SUMMERY DESSERT A DARK RED KANTEN AND SWEET BEAN CUBE IS CAPTURED IN A CLEAR KANTEN JELLY, AND LOOKS LIKE A SMALL STONE TRAPPED IN A BLOCK OF MOUNTAIN ICE.

SERVES TWELVE

INGREDIENTS
    200g/7oz can azuki beans
    40g/1½oz/3 tbsp caster
      (superfine) sugar
For the kanten jelly
    2 × 5g/⅛oz sachets powdered kanten
    100g/3¾oz/½ cup caster sugar
    rind of ¼ orange in one piece

1 Drain the beans, then tip into a pan over a medium heat. When steam begins to rise, reduce the heat to low.

2 Add the sugar one-third at a time, stirring constantly until the sugar has dissolved and the moisture evaporated. Remove from the heat.

3 Pour 450ml/¾ pint/scant 2 cups water into a pan, and mix with one kanten sachet. Stir until dissolved, then add 40g/1½oz of the sugar and the orange rind. Bring to the boil and cook for about 2 minutes, stirring constantly until the sugar has all dissolved. Remove from the heat and discard the orange rind.

4 Transfer 250ml/8fl oz/1 cup of the hot liquid into a 15 × 10cm/6 × 4in container so that it fills only 1cm/½in. Leave at room temperature to set.

5 Add the bean paste to the kanten liquid in the pan, and mix well. Move the pan on to a wet dishtowel and keep stirring for 8 minutes.

6 Pour the bean and kanten liquid into an 18 × 7.5 × 2cm/7 × 3 × ¾in container and leave to set for 1 hour at room temperature, then 1 hour in the refrigerator. Turn upside down on to a chopping board covered with kitchen paper. Leave for 1 minute, then cut into 12 rectangular pieces.

7 Line 12 ramekins with clear film (plastic wrap). With a fork, cut the set kanten block into 12 squares. Put one square in each ramekin, then place a bean and kanten cube on top of each.

8 Pour 450ml/¾ pint/scant 2 cups water into a pan and mix with the remaining kanten sachet. Bring to the boil, add the remaining sugar, then stir constantly until dissolved. Boil for a further 2 minutes, and remove from the heat. Place the pan on a wet dishtowel to cool quickly and stir for 5 minutes, or until the liquid starts to thicken.

9 Ladle the liquid into the ramekins to cover the cubes. Twist the clear film at the top. Leave to set in the refrigerator for at least 1 hour. Carefully remove the ramekins and clear film and serve cold on serving plates.

SWEET PANCAKE

IN JAPAN, THE SWEET BEAN PASTE IS TRADITIONALLY SANDWICHED BETWEEN TWO PANCAKES TO RESEMBLE A LITTLE GONG, HENCE ITS NAME DORA YAKI; "DORA" MEANING A GONG. ALTERNATIVELY, THE PANCAKES CAN BE FOLDED TO MAKE A HALF GONG.

MAKES 6–8 DORA YAKI PANCAKES

INGREDIENTS
  65g/2½oz/5 tbsp caster
    (superfine) sugar
  3 large (US extra large) eggs, beaten
  15ml/1 tbsp maple syrup or
    golden (light corn) syrup
  185g/6½oz/1⅔ cups plain (all-
    purpose) flour, sifted
  5ml/1 tsp bicarbonate of soda
    (baking soda)
  150ml/¼ pint/⅔ cup water
  vegetable oil, for frying
For the sweet bean paste
  250g/9oz canned azuki beans
  40g/1½oz/3 tbsp caster sugar
  pinch of salt

1 To make the sweet bean paste, put the canned azuki beans and their liquid into a pan, then heat over a medium heat. Add the sugar gradually and stir the pan vigorously. Cook over a low heat until the liquid has almost evaporated and the beans have become mushy. Add the salt and remove from the heat. Stir for 1 minute, then leave to cool.

2 Mix the sugar, eggs and syrup in a mixing bowl. Blend well until the sugar has dissolved, then add the flour to make a smooth batter. Cover and leave for 20 minutes.

3 Mix together the bicarbonate of soda and water in a cup and then mix into the batter.

4 Heat a little oil in a small frying pan until very hot. Remove from the heat and wipe with kitchen paper. Return to a medium heat and ladle some batter into the centre. Make a small pancake about 13cm/5in in diameter and 5mm/¼in thick.

5 Cook for about 2–3 minutes on each side until both sides are golden brown. Reduce the heat if the outside burns before the inside is cooked. Make a further 11–15 pancakes.

COOK'S TIP
You can make a half "gong" by folding a pancake in the middle and filling the inside with a little of the bean paste.

6 Take one pancake and spread about 30ml/2 tbsp of the sweet bean paste in the middle leaving about 2.5cm/1in around the edge. Cover with another pancake. Place on a tray and repeat until all the pancakes are used. Serve the filled pancakes warm or cold.

GLOSSARY

Abura-age Fried thin rectangular blocks of tofu. Available frozen and fresh.

Aka miso A medium-strength flavoured dark red soybean paste.

Ao nori Green seaweed flakes.

Arame A brown variety of seaweed.

Atsu-age Thick, deep-fried tofu. These are usually bought in pieces; 1 atsu-age = 1 piece.

Awakuchi shoyu Pale soy sauce.

Azuki beans Small, brownish red beans that are often used in sweet recipes.

Beni-shoga Salt-pickled finely shredded root ginger.

Cha-shu Pot-roast pork.

Daikon A long, white vegetable of the radish family.

Daikon-oroshi A fine-toothed grater especially intended for daikon.

Dashi-konbu Dried kelp seaweed.

Dashi-no-moto Freeze-dried stock granules for making a quick dashi stock with water.

Dashi stock A stock for soups and hotpots using kezuri-bushi and konbu. It is possible to make your own dashi stock but stock granules (dashi-no-moto) are also available.

Eda-mame Fresh young beans.

Enokitake Small delicately flavoured mushrooms with slender stalks.

Gammodoki Deep-fried tofu balls with vegetables

Gari Thinly sliced and pickled ginger.

Ginnan Gingko nuts.

Gobo (burdock root) A long, stick-like root vegetable.

Hakusai (Chinese cabbage) A vegetable with white stem and green leaves.

Harusame Thin cellophane noodles made from azuki beans or starchy roots.

Hatcho miso Dark brown soybean paste.

Hashi Chopsticks.

Hijiki Twiggy, black marine algae (seaweed) available dried.

Ikura Salted orange-red salmon roe.

Kabocha A squash with dark green skin and yellow flesh and a nutty flavour.

Kaki Japanese persimmon, also known as Sharon fruit.

Kanten (agar-agar) A gelling agent made from seaweed.

Kashiwa Salted Japanese oak leaves.

Katsuo-bushi Whole cooked and dried block of katsuo (skipjack tuna), ready for shaving.

Kezuri-bushi Ready shaved, dried katsuo (skipjack tuna) flakes for use in dashi fish stock.

Kiku nori Dried crysanthemum petals in a sheet.

Kinako Yellow soya bean flour.

Konbu Giant kelp seaweed, sold dried as dashi-konbu.

Konnyaku A dense, gelatinous cake made from the konnyaku, a yam-like plant.

Koya-dofu Frozen tofu.

Makisu Sushi rolling mat.

Matcha Powdered green tea.

Menma Pickled bamboo shoots.

Mirin Sweet rice wine used for cooking, rather than drinking.

Miso Mixture of fermented soybeans and grains that mature into a paste of different strengths.

Mitsuba Aromatic herb used mostly for soups. Member of the parsley family.

Mizuna Japanese greens.

Mochi Rice cakes made from mochigome rice.

Mochigome Glutinous rice.

Naga-imo (or yama-imo) A mountain potato similar to a yam.

Nashi Japanese pear.

Natto Fermented soya beans.

Nori Dried, paper-thin seaweed product.

Pak choi (bok choy) Loose-leafed brassica with white stems.

Ramen Thin egg noodles.

Renkon A white-fleshed root from the lotus plant.

Saikyo miso Pale yellow soybean paste, lightly flavoured.

Sake A traditional rice wine for drinking and cooking.

Sansho Ground Japanese pepper with a minty aroma.

Sashimi Raw fish and shellfish sliced thinly and arranged decoratively.

Satoimo Oval-shaped potato, covered in a hairy skin.

Second dashi stock Stock made from reserved liquid from first dashi stock.

Sencha Green tea made from the young leaves.

Shichimi togarashi (seven-spice powder) Containing chilli, sesame, poppy, hemp, shiso, sansho and nori.

Shiitaki A variety of fungus with a brown cap and white stem.

Shimeji Meaty-textured mushroom, similar to oyster mushrooms.

Shiratake Noodles made from konnyaku.

Shiro miso Pale yellow soybean paste, lightly flavoured.

Shiso Basil-flavoured leaves used as a herb garnish.

Shoga Fresh ginger.

Shoyu Ordinary Japanese soy sauce.

Shungiku Edible leaves from the vegetable chrysanthemum (not the garden plant).

Soba Dried buckwheat noodles.

Soba tsuyu Instant soya soup base.

Somen Very fine wheat noodles.

Sora mame Broad (fava) beans.

Sukiyaki Wafer-thin meat and vegetables cooked in a sauce.

Su-meshi Vinegared rice, the essential basis for all sushi.

Suribachi and **surikogi** A ceramic bowl with grooves inside and a pestle made of pepper wood.
Sushi Small rolls of *su-meshi* and flavourings topped with thin slices of raw fish.
Takanotsume Fresh red chilli.
Takenoko Fresh, young bamboo shoots.

Takuan Pickled and dyed daikon.
Tamari shoyu Naturally fermented dark soy sauce.
Tempura A lumpy batter made with ice-cold water for deep-frying fish and sliced vegetables.
Tofu A nutritious, coagulated soya bean protein.
Tsukemono Pickled vegetables, such as takuan, to serve with rice
Tsuma Daikon cut very thinly into strands, for decorative purposes.
Tsumami Dishes to accompany drinks.
Udon Thick wheat noodles.
Umeboshi Salted pickled ume, a fruit similar to apricot.
Usukuchi shoyu Reduced salt soy sauce.
Usu zukuri Very thin slices of fish.
Wakame A curly seaweed, available in a dried form.

Wasabi A Japanese pungent root similar to horseradish, available as a paste or in powder form.
Yakitori Skewered grilled chicken.
Yuzu (citron) A citrus fruit the size of a clementine. Lime can be sustituted.

ACKNOWLEDGEMENTS

Authors' acknowledgements
Emi Kazuko: I am indebted to many of my Japanese friends, who readily responded to my many questions with their expert knowledge gained through cooking for their respective families for over 30 years. I am particularly grateful to my bosom friend Katsuko Hirose, without whose support, especially in research, I could not have written this book. I also thank Yasuko Fukuoka, who wrote the recipe section of this book so well; a wonderful result for her first professional work in English.

Yasuko Fukuoka: Love and thanks for help, encouragement and patience to: Nayo and Hiroji Fukuoka; Susan Fleming; Atsuko Console and her friends; Yoko Ono and my mentor, Kazuko-san, but most of all to Paul Ellis, who had to try all the recipes day after day for months then had to feed me for many days while I was writing.

Picture acknowledgements
AKG London p16l; Bridgeman Art Library Irises at Horikin, No.56 in the series "100 Views of Edo", (Meisho Edo hyakkei) pub. 1857, (colour woodblock print) by Ando or Utagawa Hiroshige (1797–1858) Fitzwilliam Museum, Uni. of Cambridge, UK p6br, Portrait of Izumi Tadahira (d. 1189) with a poem, from "Famous Generals of Japan", *c.* 1858 (colour woodblock print) by Yoshitora (fl.1850–80) School of Oriental & African Studies Library, Uni. of London p8tr, Otsu, illustration from "Fifty Three Stations of the Tokaido Road", pub. by Takenouchi Magohachi, *c.* 1831–4 (coloured woodblock) by Ando or Utagawa Hiroshige (1797–1858) Victoria & Albert Museum, London, UK p9, Satsuma oviform vase decorated with woman playing the samisen, 19th century (porcelain), Private Collection/Bonhams p13b, The Teahouse at Mariko, from the series "53 Stations on the Eastern Coast Road", 1833 (woodblock print) by Ando or Utagawa Hiroshige (1797–1858) Fitzwilliam Museum, Uni. of Cambridge, UK p16b, New Year's Festival, (woodcut) by Utagawa Hiroshige (1797–1864) Victoria & Albert Museum, London, UK p19, A Carp Swimming among Waterweeds, *c.*1832 (ink) by Katsushika II Taito (Hokusen) (fl.1820–50) Chester Beatty Library, Dublin p20b, Decorated Boats at the Sanno Festival at Tsushima, Owari Province from "Famous Places of the Sixty Provinces", 1853 (colour woodblock print by Ando or Utagawa Hiroshige (1797–1858) Blackburn Museum and Art Gallery, Lancashire, UK p21; Cephas Picture Library p10, p11 t & b, p15t & b, p23t, p24b, p25t & b, p26t; Japanese Information and Cultural Centre, Embassy of Japan, London p6tl, p22tr, p23b, p24t, p26b; Mary Evans Picture Library p13t, p14t & b, p20t; The Art Archive p8bl, p12, p17, p18; and Dr. Steven Turnbull p22bl.

SHOPPING INFORMATION

United Kingdom
Arigato
48–50 Brewer Street
London
W1R 3HN
Tel: 020 7287 1722

Atariya Foods
595 High Road
West Finchley
London
N12 0DY
Tel: 020 8446 6669

Atariya Foods
(West Acton Branch)
7 Station Parade
Noel Road
London
W3 0DF
Tel: 020 8896 1552

Intel
126 Malden Road
New Malden
Surrey
KT3 6DD
Tel: 020 8942 9552

Miura Japanese Foods
44 Coombe Road
Norbiton, Nr Kingston
KT2 7AF
Tel: 020 8549 8076

Miura Japanese Foods
(Croydon Branch)
5 Limpsfield Road
Sanderstead
Surrey
CR2 9LA
Tel: 020 8651 4498

Natural House
Japan Centre,
212 Piccadilly
W1V 9RV
Tel: 020 7434 4218

Ninjin Food Shop
244 Great Portland Street
London
W1
Tel: 020 7388 4657

Oriental City
399 Edgware Road
Colindale
London
NW9 0JJ
Tel: 020 8200 0009

T.K. Trading
Japanese foods
Unit 6/7 The Chase Centre
Chase Road
North Acton
W10 6QD
Tel: 020 8453 1001

Above: Two young Japanese girls enjoy baked satsuma-imo (sweet potatoes).

United States of America
Abestkitchen
424 West Exchange Street
Akron, OH 44302
Tel: (330) 535-2811
e-mail: sales@abestkitchen.com

Akasaka Japanese Restaurant
and Supplies
37152 6 Mile Road
Newburgh Livonia
Detroit, MI 48152
Tel: (734) 462-2630

Anzen Importers
736 NE Martin Luther King Blvd.
Portland, OR 97232
Tel: (503) 233-5111

Asian Market
3335 Federal Blvd.
Denver, CO
Tel: (303) 937-1431

Bowery Kitchen
460 West 16th Street
New York, NY 10011
Tel: (212) 376-4982
Fax: (212) 843-0351

Cherry Blossom Gardens
Route 1, Box 301-B
New Prague, MN 56071
Tel: (877) 226-4387

Daido Market
522 Mamaroneck Avenue
White Plains, NY 10605
Tel: (914) 683-6735

Left: A typically bustling Tokyo shopping arcade.

Katagiri
224 East 59th Street
New York, NY 10022
Tel: (212) 755-3566
Fax: (212) 752-4197

Kondo Grocery
314 East 78th Street
New York, NY 10021
Tel: (212) 794-7065

Midori Mart
2104 Chestnut Street
Philadelphia, PA 19103
Tel: (215) 569-3381
Fax: (215) 569-3308

Naniwa Food
6730 Curran Street
McLean, VA 22101
Tel: (703) 893-7209
Fax: (703) 893-6281

Pacific Mercantile Co.
1925 Lawrence Street
Denver, CO
Tel: (303) 295-0293

Rafal's Spice Co.
2521 Russell
Detroit, MI 48207
Tel: (313) 259-6373
Fax: (313) 259-6220

Sunri Market
111 North Lincoln
Montery Park
Pasadena, CA
Tel: (626) 573-3860

Tanto
839 White Plains Road
Scarsdale, NY 10583
Tel: (914) 725-9100

Toyo Foods
625 Port Washington Blvd.
Port Washington,
NY 11050
Tel: (516) 944-6464

Yagura
24 East 41st Street
New York, NY 10017
Tel: (212) 679-3777

Yama Seafood
911 West Las Tunas
San Gabriel
Pasadena, CA
Tel: (626) 281-8045

Yamada Seika
Confections
1955 Sutter Street
San Francisco, CA
Tel: (415) 922-3848

Above: Japanese temple

Australia
Asian Supermarket Pty Ltd
116 Charters Towers Rd
Townsville QLD 4810
Tel: (07) 4772 3997
Fax: (07) 4771 3919

Daimaru
211 Latrobe Street
Melbourne VIC 3000
Tel: (03) 9660 6666
Fax: (03) 9660 6601

David Jones
86–108 Castlereagh Street,
Sydney NSW 2000
Tel: (02) 9266 5544
Fax: (02) 9266 6531

Exotic Asian Groceries Q Supercentre
Cnr Markeri & Bermuda Streets
Mermaid Waters QLD 4218
Tel: (07) 5572 8188

Hoya's Mixed Business
365 Anzac Parade,
Kingsford NSW 2032
Tel: (02) 9313 8074

Kam Fu Food Manufacturers
3b 1/7 Unwins Bridge Road,
St Peters NSW 2044
Tel: (02) 9519 9680

Left: Nebuta festival held in northern Japan each August. "Spirits" ward off sleepiness at the start of the harvest.

INDEX